Shostakovich in Context

Edited by
Rosamund Bartlett

OXFORD
UNIVERSITY PRESS

OXFORD

UNIVERSITY PRESS

Great Clarendon Street, Oxford OX2 6DP

Oxford University Press is a department of the University of Oxford.
It furthers the University's objective of excellence in research, scholarship,
and education by publishing worldwide in

Oxford New York

Athens Auckland Bangkok Bogotá Buenos Aires Cape Town
Chennai Dar es Salaam Delhi Florence Hong Kong Istanbul Karachi
Kolkata Kuala Lumpur Madrid Melbourne Mexico City Mumbai Nairobi
Paris São Paulo Shanghai Singapore Taipei Tokyo Toronto Warsaw

with associated companies in Berlin Ibadan

Oxford is a registered trade mark of Oxford University Press
in the UK and in certain other countries

Published in the United States
by Oxford University Press Inc., New York

British Library Cataloguing in Publication Data

Data available

Library of Congress Cataloging in Publication Data

Shostakovich in context / edited by Rosamund Bartlett.
p. cm.
Includes bibliographical references and index.
1. Shostakovich, Dmitri Dmitrievich, 1906–1975—Criticism and interpretation.
I. Bartlett, Rosamund.
ML410.S53 S47 2000   780'.92—dc21   99–047564

ISBN 0–19–816666–4

3 5 7 9 10 8 6 4 2

Typeset by Joshua Associates Ltd., Oxford
Printed in Great Britain
on acid-free paper by
Biddles Ltd, Guildford and King's Lynn

ACKNOWLEDGEMENTS

I would like to acknowledge the many people who have contributed in varying ways to the publication of this book. Gratitude should firstly be expressed to Valentin Berlinsky, Dmitry Shebalin, Mikhail Kopelman, and Andrey Abramenkov, the members of the Borodin Quartet of 1994, who expressed a hope that their performance of Shostakovich's string quartets in Ann Arbor would be marked by Shostakovich-related activities in some form. Secondly, I wish to recognize the vision and boldness shown by Ken Fischer and Michael Kondziolka at the University Musical Society in Ann Arbor, with whom it was a privilege and a pleasure to collaborate.

The conference 'Shostakovich: The Man and His Age', as well as the various exhibitions, film showings, and the teaching of an undergraduate course on Shostakovich, would not have taken place without the fervent support of Jane Burbank, then Director at the Center for Russian and East European Studies at the University of Michigan, where I was a faculty associate. To Marysia Ostafin, associate director of CREES, I owe a particular debt of thanks for her supreme organizational skills, artistic flair, and good humour. Erika Wolf, Marga Miller, Gillian Kahn, and Karen Rosenflanz are among other CREES associates who contributed freely of their time and energy. To Irina Antonovna Shostakovich, who gave her blessing to the conference and the subsequent publication of this volume, and for her gracious gift of copies of the Glikman correspondence to American university libraries, warm thanks are due.

The conference was partially funded by the National Endowment for the Humanities, the Michigan Humanities Council, and University of Michigan Office of the Vice-President for Research, and their support is gratefully acknowledged. Thanks are due to Malcolm Hamrick Brown who generously lent help and expertise in the initial stages of publishing this volume, and also to Maryann Szporluk and Liza Wilson. Anthony Phillips made very fine initial translations of the articles by Svetlana Savenko, Lyudmila Mikheyeva-Sollertinskaya, Olga Komok, Lyudmila Kovnatskaya, and Manashir Yakubov, the revisions to which, and the translations of the articles by Barsova and Kravetz, completed by myself, I take full responsibility for in the event of inaccuracies.

The articles (in some cases earlier versions) of Inna Barsova, Rosamund Bartlett, Laurel Fay, Olga Komok, Lyudmila Kovnatskaya, Nelly Kravetz, Lyudmila Mikheyeva-Sollertinskaya, and Svetlana Savenko have been published in Russian in L. G. Kovnatskaya (ed.), *D. D. Shostakovich: Sbornik statei k 90-letiyu so dnya rozhdeniya* (St Petersburg, 1996). Grateful acknowledgement is made to 'Kompozitor' publishers for permission to reproduce the articles by Olga Komok, Lyudmila Kovnatskaya, and Lyudmila Mikheyeva-Sollertinskaya in this volume. Finally I should like to thank Bruce Phillips at Oxford University Press for his help in overseeing this book's progress towards publication, and want to express my deepest gratitude to Laurel Fay, David Fanning, and Lyudmila Kovnatskaya, without whom I would have been certainly lost.

CONTENTS

Contents

LIST OF ILLUSTRATIONS

(*between pp. 112 and 113*)

The photographs appear by courtesy of Manashir Yakubov.

ABBREVIATIONS

ASM	[Assotsiatsiya Sovremennoi Muzyki] Association of Contemporary Music
LASM	[Leningradskaya Assotsiatsiya Sovremennoi Muzyki] Leningrad Association of Contemporary Music
RAPM	[Russkaya Assotsiatsiya Proletarskikh Muzykantov] Russian Association of Proletarian Musicians
RGALI	[Russkii Gosudarstvennyi Arkhiv Literatury i Iskusstva] Russian State Archive of Literature and Art
RMMK	[Russkii Muzei Muzykal'noi Kul'tury] Russian Museum of Musical Culture
RMS	Russian Musical Society [in Russian RMO—Russkoe Muzykal'noe Obshchestvo]
RNB	[Russkaya Natsional'naya Biblioteka] Russian National Library
TRAM	[Teatr rabochei molodezhi] Theatre of Working Youth
TsGALI	[Tsentral'nyi Gosudarstvennyi Arkhiv Literatury i Iskusstva—now known as RGALI] Central State Archive of Literature and Art
TsGA (SPb)	[Tsentral'nyi Gosudarstvennyi Arkhiv (Sankt-Peterburg)] Central State Archive (St Petersburg)

NOTE ON TRANSLITERATION

A simplified form of transliteration has been used throughout this book, although the more familiar spelling of personal names (e.g. 'Tchaikovsky' instead of 'Chaikovsky') has been preserved, and 'Kruchonykh' has been preferred to the more accurate 'Kruchenykh'.

LIST OF CONTRIBUTORS

INNA BARSOVA is Professor of Music at the Moscow Conservatoire. She is author of *The Symphonies of Mahler* (1975) and *A History of Score Notation* (Moscow, 1988), as well as many articles on Shostakovich, Mosolov, and other aspects of Soviet music.

ROSAMUND BARTLETT is currently Leverhulme Research Fellow in Russian Cultural History at Birkbeck College, University of London, and Fellow at the European Humanities Research Centre, University of Oxford. She is the author of *Wagner and Russia* (Cambridge, 1995), and co-author of *Literary Russia: A Guide* (London, 1997).

CARYL EMERSON is the Watson Armour III University Professor of Slavic languages and literatures at Princeton University. She is the author of works on Russian philosopher and literary scholar Mikhail Bakhtin, on nineteenth-century Russian literature (Pushkin, Dostoevsky, Tolstoy), and on Russian music, especially Musorgsky.

DAVID FANNING is Senior Lecturer in Music at the University of Manchester. Also active as pianist, broadcaster, and critic, he is the author of *The Breath of the Symphonist: Shostakovich's Tenth* (London, 1988) and *Carl Nielsen: Symphony no. 5* (Cambridge, 1997), and editor of *Shostakovich Studies* (Cambridge, 1995).

LAUREL E. FAY is author of the major new biography of Shostakovich published by Oxford University Press.

DAVID HAAS is Associate Professor of Music History at the University of Georgia. He is the author of *Leningrad's Modernists: Studies in Music and Musical Thought, 1917–1932* (New York, 1998). He is currently translating Boris Asafiev's *Book about Russian Opera*, to be entitled: *Symphonic Etudes*.

OLGA KOMOK graduated from the St Petersburg Conservatoire in 1998. She is a professional harpsichordist, and, as a post-graduate student at the St Petersburg Conservatoire, is researching English baroque music.

LYUDMILA KOVNATSKAYA is Senior Research Fellow at the Institute of the History of the Fine Arts, St Petersburg, and Professor of Music at the St Petersburg Conservatoire. She is author of *Benjamin Britten* (Moscow, 1974), and *English Music in the Twentieth Century* (Moscow, 1986), as well as many articles on the music of British composers of various periods and Shostakovich.

NELLY KRAVETZ completed her postgraduate studies at the Institute of the Arts in Moscow, and is currently Lecturer in Music at Tel Aviv University. She is the author of several articles on Prokofiev and Shostakovich.

LYUDMILA MIKHEYEVA-SOLLERTINSKAYA is a member of the Union of Composers in St Petersburg, and author of several biographical works about Shostakovich.

SVETLANA SAVENKO is a Senior Research Fellow at the Institute of the Arts in Moscow and is a specialist in twentieth-century music, particularly Stravinsky. Author of many works on Russian and Soviet composers, her most recent article is 'Stravinsky and Shostakovich' which appeared in *Muzykal'naya akademiya* in 1997.

RICHARD TARUSKIN is Class of 1955 Professor of Music at the University of California at Berkeley. His most recent books are *Stravinsky and the Russian Traditions* (Berkeley and Los Angeles, 1996) and *Defining Russia Musically* (Princeton, 1997).

MANASHIR YAKUBOV is head of the Shostakovich Family Archive in Moscow. He has written over a thousand articles and twenty books on musical form and melody, on ethnomusicology and the instruments of Daghestan, and on Russian music of the nineteenth and twentieth centuries. He has written extensively on Shostakovich, several of whose works he published for the first time, and he is author of prefaces to the twenty-five-volume complete edition of the composer's collected works.

INTRODUCTION

The publication of this volume, which presents recent research into Shostakovich's life and work by British, American, Russian, and Israeli scholars, is occasioned by the ever-growing interest in Dmitry Shostakovich, whose significance in and for the history of twentieth-century music is, as Richard Taruskin has commented, 'immense, possibly unparalleled and above all, continuing'. The authors of the thirteen articles are professional musicologists, Russian literature specialists, biographers, and cultural historians, whose diverse fields of expertise are reflected in the multidisciplinary nature of the materials collected here. The majority of the articles in the volume first originated as papers given at a conference on Shostakovich held at the University of Michigan in 1994. They are partnered by translations of four articles by Russian scholars written for a Shostakovich conference held in St Petersburg also in 1994 (whose published proceedings included four articles from the Michigan conference). 'Shostakovich: The Man and his Age, 1906–75', the University of Michigan conference, was organized to coincide with the week-long residency in Ann Arbor of the Borodin String Quartet.

The collapse of Soviet power in 1991 inaugurated a new era in Shostakovich scholarship heralded by the publication of two important books, one in Russian and one in English. These were the collected letters of Shostakovich to his friend Isaak Glikman, *Pis'ma k drugu* (1993), and Elizabeth Wilson's collection of contemporaries' memoirs of the composer, *Shostakovich: A Life Remembered* (1994). The recent appearance, after a relative dearth of activity, of serious Russian publications such as the collection of articles on Shostakovich edited by Lyudmila Kovnatskaya, *Dmitry Shostakovich: Sbornik statei k 90–letiyuy so dnya rozhdeniya* (1996), and a substantial issue of Russia's premier music journal *Muzykal'naya akademiya* (1997), solely dedicated to Shostakovich, is also a sign that old ideological shackles are now finally being cast off in the composer's native land. This is an era in which speculation can now begin to be replaced by objective enquiry based on evidence, that cannot so easily be compromised by agendas, political or otherwise. This was the *raison d'être* of the conference in 1994, which took place appropriately within the context of the performance of Shostakovich's music. Day-time discussions of the composer and his works were complemented, on five consecutive nights, with performances of the fifteen string quartets by an ensemble uniquely qualified to give definitive performances of these works. At that point just short of their fiftieth anniversary, the Borodin Quartet's founding members, cellist Valentin Berlinsky and violist Dmitry Shebalin, had played extensively to Shostakovich during his lifetime.

Unlike the string quartets themselves, which reflect Shostakovich's artistic development in the latter period of his life, between 1938 and 1974, the articles collected here span the composer's entire career, beginning in the 1920s with Laurel Fay's account of the young Shostakovich's fraught relations with the doyen of Soviet music, Boris Asafiev, and ending with a history of Shostakovich's plans to write an opera on Chekhov's 'The Black Monk', which he embarked upon in the last months of his life in 1975. There is an article here for every decade of Shostakovich's adult life, in each case showing the composer in a different context, but in a way which often sheds light on other contributions or echoes them. The goal of the present volume is, in fact, to present Shostakovich and his legacy in a variety of different contexts, in an attempt to continue the process of allowing it to acquire many-sided meanings, and to stress the legitimacy of each of those meanings. The interdisciplinary nature of the collection will also serve, it is hoped, to open up discussion about Shostakovich still further, and thus move away from prior tendencies to focus on the purely extrinsic qualities of the composer's musical *œuvre*, which has so often been interpreted in terms of autobiography. That discussion is regrettably still often limited to the ideological context is evidenced by the profusion of articles and passionate internet debates (although in the latter case, 'debate' is perhaps too polite a word: slanging match would be more appropriate) which continue to explore this angle, and usually on the level of the binary opposition of whether Shostakovich was or was not a secret dissident. Peter Porter's article 'Marx on a Stave', published in the *Guardian* on 13 February 1998 to coincide with the inauguration of the London Symphony Orchestra's Shostakovich series under Rostropovich at London's Barbican Arts Centre is a case in point. Admittedly not aided by the unfortunate heading 'Was Dimitri Shostakovich just a hack in the USSR, or a genius of musical irony, criticising Stalin with his bitterly triumphalist scores?', it comes to the following conclusion: 'Shostakovich's music is his own and is always sui generis. We should try to hear it as dispassionately as we do Palestrina's from counterreformation Rome, or Wagner's from Bismarckian Germany.' Yet this comes at the end of a discussion of precisely the political context of Shostakovich's music. The desire to listen to music without bringing to it purely introversive preconceptions is wholly admirable, of course, but is it ever possible? When is there not a context? And which context ever remains the same? As Richard Taruskin notes in the keynote article to this volume, the 'terrain of subtexts and multivalent meaning' has been 'the interpretive space in which, for at least half a century, the vast majority of Shostakovich readings have taken place'. His task is to show, however, how attempts to fix the meaning of music and locate its true message are doomed from the start, since they invariably diminish rather than expand our understanding. In Shostakovich's case, this results in the lamentable situation where Soviet methods are countered by similarly reductive approaches. Too often forgotten is the role that the listener plays in the interpretational process. As Taruskin comments, 'What made Shostakovich's music the secret diary of a nation was not only what he put into it, but what it allowed listeners to draw out.' The fact that listeners draw out different things at different times, depending on the context, offers sufficient proof of the impossibility of ever establishing any certainty of interpretation, despite the certain presence of multiple 'latent' meanings. In the final analysis, however, it is surely the multivalence and uncertainty inherent in Shostakovich's music which contributes to its enduring appeal.

If Richard Taruskin's article sets up the theme for the book as a whole, the following two authors examine the two languages Shostakovich worked in: the musical and the verbal. Shostakovich's ineluctable involvement with the politics of his time, and the frequent incorporation of literary texts into his works has inevitably led commentators to concentrate on the extra-musical qualities of his music. David Fanning's reminder that the Shostakovich 'industry' would not exist were it not for the millions of musical notes that Shostakovich wrote on staves is a timely one, however. Too much 'ideological mud-slinging' has led all too often to a trivialization of the music, which Fanning counters by bringing to the fore the complexity of Shostakovich's musical language. By dissecting the harmonic thinking in Shostakovich's scores, Fanning shows how it acts as a fundamental link in the chain of interpretation between the physical experience of hearing the music and the act of reading meanings into it. The context of performance offers another important way of bridging the gap between musical analysis and extroversive readings. Drawing our attention to the existence and continuing possibility of widely diverging performances of musical works, Fanning shows us how relevant an awareness of this can be, when it may lead to the discovery of widely diverging subtexts, making the starting-point for analytical or hermeneutic interpretation alike unusually hard to define.

Shostakovich was prolific not only as a composer of musical notes, but as an author of verbal texts, the numerous articles attributed to him notwithstanding. Svetlana Savenko focuses her attention on the *words* that Shostakovich wrote, choosing to treat them as works of art in their own right, like the music, and subjecting them to the same stringent methods of analysis. Interested in defining Shostakovich's literary style, Savenko compares the syntax of the composer's articles with that used in his private correspondence, with a view to exploring whether there is any correspondence with the musical language employed by the composer. Savenko charts the evolution of Shostakovich's literary style, revealing the apparent influence of his friend, the writer Mikhail Zoshchenko, and finding in it a similar dialectic between the author's 'natural' language and an 'alien' discourse intended as a parody on the encroaching engulfment of the Russian language by bureaucratic and politicized 'Soviet-speak'. Two specific devices, irony and tautology, are distinguished as being particularly prevalent in Shostakovich's writing, and Savenko's discussion of their usage casts another perspective on the role of irony in Shostakovich's work explored by Richard Taruskin. The sophistication and self-consciousness of Shostakovich's verbal language which Savenko reveals may in the end cause one to disagree with David Fanning's belief that the reality of Shostakovich's achievement can ultimately only be located in his music.

The remaining ten articles in this volume are arranged chronologically, and view Shostakovich's life from the perspective of biography, analysis, musical, cultural and political history, or sometimes a combination of these approaches. Laurel Fay concentrates on the circumstances surrounding Shostakovich's affiliation, as a young composer in the 1920s, to the Leningrad Association of Contemporary Music (LASM). She puts under scrutiny for the first time Shostakovich's important but complicated relationship with Boris Asafiev, a major figure in Soviet music. By reassessing the composer's later confusing statements about Asafiev's significance in his life, Fay shows how and why that relationship came to be so mythologized. Lyudmila Mikheyeva-Sollertinsky, daughter of Shostakovich's closest friend, the musicologist and critic Ivan Sollertinsky, picks up the story, at the end of the 1920s, to explore the more private context of personal correspondence. Shostakovich's revealing letters to Sollertinsky provide a unique chronicle of the path of the composer's fortunes as they soared in the 1920s and nosedived in the 1930s. The juxtaposition of Shostakovich's early letters to his friend, where he emerges as a witty raconteur, ebullient and caustic, with those written in the 1930s, makes chilling reading.

Inna Barsova discusses the tightrope Shostakovich had to walk in the 1930s between 'social demands' (the public) and 'grand passions' (the private), which culminated in the Fifth Symphony, in which the composer faced the challenge of preserving his artistic integrity, but at the same time placating Stalin. Setting Shostakovich's life at that time in its social context, with extensive reference to press coverage of political events and unpublished contemporary documents, Barsova paints a stark picture of the extreme fear in which Shostakovich had to operate when composing this work. She then proceeds to an analysis of the many semantic layers of the last movement, in which the '*auto-da-fé* of an entire nation' appears to be acted out in coded language to the overt accompaniment of triumphant marches.

Olga Komok's article on Shostakovich's friendship with the Russian Futurist Alexey Kruchonykh takes us into a quite different context: that of Shostakovich as a neighbour in the 1940s in Moscow, where he moved following evacuation in Kuibyshev. Basing her account on fascinating unpublished archival sources, Komok reveals a whimsical side to Shostakovich, and places the composer in the context of literary life of the period. At the same time that Shostakovich was getting to know Kruchonykh, he was writing his Eighth Symphony. David Haas reveals Shostakovich as a musical innovator in this work, in which he deliberately allies himself to tradition by writing in the same key as Beethoven's famous C minor symphony, but at the same breaks with that tradition by ending his work with neither triumph nor tragedy. In sympathy with David Fanning, Haas makes a plea for studying the score of this symphony (following Shostakovich's own exhortation to students to immerse themselves in the great works in the repertoire) rather than the possible sources of its inspiration, arguing how important it is to look beyond quotations to purely musical strategies of development, structure and dramaturgy.

In tracing in full for the first time the history of the composition of Shostakovich's *Anti-Formalist Rayok* (written between the late 1940s and the 1960s), and investigating its musical and literary antecedents, Manashir Yakubov addresses yet another dimension of Shostakovich's *œuvre*. Placing his lampoon of the functionaries of Soviet officialdom within the context of the thousand-year-long tradition of Russian musical satire, and paying particular attention to Musorgsky's *Rayok*, written a century earlier, Yakubov deciphers a vast field of references—political, historical, musical, and literary—which extends from Glinka and the national anthem of the Russian Empire, to Moscow gaols, the KGB, and certain notorious party apparatchiks.

Nelly Kravetz, who was the first person to bring to public notice a series of unpublished letters written by Shostakovich to Elmira Nazirova, turns our attention back to the symphonic repertoire. Her article investigates the biographical and musical context of Shostakovich's Tenth Symphony, and, in particular, the horn theme from the work's third movement, whose meaning can now be finally unravelled. Elmira Nazirova, a composer based in Baku, had studied with Shostakovich while he was teaching at the Moscow Conservatoire. In 1953 she became the addressee of a barrage of letters during the composition of the Tenth Symphony, and unwittingly played a major role in its composition.

The last three articles in the volume are comparative in nature. Lyudmila Kovnatskaya seeks to place Shostakovich more firmly in the context of twentieth-century European music by comparing the trajectory of his career with that of Benjamin Britten, one of his most beloved contemporaries, whom he met in the 1960s. The affection was mutual, of course. Britten found that he and Shostakovich (no matter how different their compositions were) seemed to have 'sprung from the same stock of forebears'. In her absorbing study, Kovnatskaya illuminates many surprising parallels and points of contact between the two composers that corroborate Britten's assertion.

Caryl Emerson examines Shostakovich's penultimate song cycle, the *Six Poems of Marina Tsvetaeva*, written in 1974, both on its own terms, and in a wider context: through the prism of Pushkin and Musorgsky's *Songs and Dances of Death and Survival*, written a hundred years earlier. In discussing which Tsvetaeva poems Shostakovich chose, and how he set about arranging them,

Emerson shows the composer creating a work, which, with its 'particularly dense cluster of Russian cultural myths about the appropriate life and death for poets' contributes to a tradition that goes back to Pushkin.

The last article in the volume (by myself) concerns Shostakovich's creative and personal relationship with the prose writer and dramatist Anton Chekhov, one of whose stories was read to him on the night that he died. It examines the importance of Chekhov as a figure of moral integrity during the bleakest years of Shostakovich's life, and the nature of Shostakovich's identification with the writer. After exploring the circumstances surrounding the completion of the opera *Rothschild's Violin* and the conception of *The Black Monk*, which Shostakovich embarked upon in the last months of his life, the article concludes with a discussion of Shostakovich as literary critic. This concerns the composer's sensitivity to the musical qualities inherent in Chekhov's methods of narrative construction, and his contention that a type of sonata form can be detected in 'The Black Monk'.

ROSAMUND BARTLETT

I

Shostakovich and Us

RICHARD TARUSKIN

I

'I wish, Ladies and Gentleman, I could cure myself of the habit of speaking ironically,' Max Beerbohm once teased a radio audience. 'I should *so* like to express myself in a straightforward manner.' Earlier, just as straightforwardly, he had written (in *Zuleika Dobson*) that 'one is taught to refrain from irony, because mankind does tend to take it literally'.[1] Every letters column, every writer's mailbag, overflows with corroboration. Recently, a Bay Area columnist tried kicking at the budget cuts that are hobbling the state of California's public library system with a burst of fulsome mock-approval. Her next column naturally consisted of apologies to all the book-lovers and librarians she had offended. 'I was being ironic,' she tried explaining to one. 'If you were, I would know it,' her caller retorted.[2] Surely one of the most striking features of the theatre historian Isaak Glikman's 1993 edition of Shostakovich's letters, the first major post-Soviet contribution to the literature on the greatest of all Soviet artists, is the frequency with which the editor (one of the composer's closest friends) intervenes to explain that Shostakovich, you see, was making a joke. A choice specimen is his commentary to a letter Shostakovich sent him from Odessa as a new year's greeting on 29 December 1957. This is the first paragraph:

I arrived in Odessa on the day of the nationwide celebration of the fortieth anniversary of Soviet Ukraine. This morning I went outdoors. You, of course, can well understand that it is simply impossible to stay at home on such a day. Despite overcast skies, all of Odessa turned out. Everywhere there were portraits of Marx, Engels, Lenin, Stalin, and also Comrades A. I. Belyayev, L. I. Brezhnev, N. A. Bulganin, K. E. Voroshilov, N. G. Ignatov, A. I. Kirilenko, F. R. Kozlov, O. V. Kuusinen, A. I. Mikoyan, H. A. Mukhitdinov, M. A. Suslov, E. A. Furtseva, N. S. Khrushchev, N. M. Shvernik, A. A. Aristov, P. A. Pospelov, Y. E. Kalinberzin, A. P. Kirichenko, A. N. Kosygin, K. T. Mazurov, V. P. Mzhavanadze, M. G. Pervukhin, N. T. Kalchenko.

---

[1] Quotations from Beerbohm via 'Aristides' (Joseph Epstein), 'Toys in My Attic', *American Scholar*, 61/1 (Winter 1992), 8.

[2] Adair Lara, 'Oh, I see, You're Making a Joke', *San Francisco Chronicle*, 9 Nov. 1993, p. D8.

And this is Glikman's annotation: 'The whole paragraph, seemingly borrowed from a standard newspaper account of those days, is full of pointed irony. Dmitry Dmitriyevich with deliberate comic pedantry lists the names alphabetically [*sic*], omitting neither initials nor surnames. Indeed the whole letter maintains a satirical tone.' Here, with apologies, is Shostakovich's second paragraph:

Everywhere there are flags, slogans, posters. All around are joyful, radiant Russian, Ukrainian and Jewish faces. Here, there and everywhere one hears salutations honoring the great banner of Marx, Engels, Lenin, and Stalin, and also in honor of Comrades A. I. Belyayev, L. I. Brezhnev, N. A. Bulganin, K. E. Voroshilov, N. G. Ignatov, A. I. Kirichenko, F. R. Kozlov, O. V. Kuusinen, A. I. Mikoyan, H. A. Mukhitdinov, M. A. Suslov, E. A. Furtseva, N. S. Khrushchev, N. M. Shvernik, A. A. Aristov, P. A. Pospelov, Y. E. Kalinberzin, A. P. Kirilenko, A. N. Kosygin, K. T. Mazurov, V. P. Mzhavanadze, M. G. Pervukhin, N. T. Kalchenko, D. S. Korochenko. Everywhere one hears Russian and Ukrainian speech. Now and then one hears the foreign speech of representatives of progressive humanity, who have come to Odessa to congratulate the Odessans on their great holiday. I walked around and, unable to contain my joy, returned to the hotel and decided to describe to you, as best I can, the nationwide celebration in Odessa.

And here is the commentary: 'Shostakovich ridicules the false rejoicing of the crowd of city-dwellers filling the streets of Odessa. The repetition, or in musical terms the recapitulation, powerfully reinforces the humorous effect.'[3]

Did we really need to be told? Did Glikman really think we did? He seems so eager to point out what we could never miss that he passes over, or maybe has not noticed, a joke that really is worth calling attention to. It was only because I had put myself to the trouble of transcribing the whole farrago word for word that I found the names Kirilenko and Kirichenko interchanged the second time around, identifying the pair as the Ukrainian nomenklatura's Dobchinsky and Bobchinsky, the Tweedledee–Tweedledum bureaucrats in Gogol's farce, *The Inspector General*. Since I got to tell about it, I feel my time was rewarded. But what was Glikman's reward? What was the point of instructing us that the letter contained a global irony so transparent and unsubtle?

One's first assumption is that the old Soviet habits die hard. Anyone who has worked with Soviet editions of primary sources such as composers' letters will recall similar schoolmasterly interventions—intrusive, mistrustful of the reader, seemingly needless, often verging on the comic in their own right. One that has been stuck in my memory now for over twenty years, owing to what I have to call its grotesque typicality, is the editor's prim retort, in a volume of selected articles by Cesar Cui, the nineteenth-century composer and critic, to a passing remark Cui made in polemic with his perennial antagonist Hermann Laroche. Cui wrote that 'unevenness in the work of artists who are devoid of critical

---

[3] *Pis'ma k drugu: Pis'ma D.D. Shostakovicha k I.D. Glikmanu*, ed. I. D. Glikman (Moscow and St Petersburg, 1993), 135–6. The commentaries have been somewhat abridged and conflated.

discernment, like Rubinstein or Tchaikovsky, can be startling'. The editor, writing in the wake of the so-called 'Zhdanovshchina' (after Andrey Zhdanov, the Politburo member who directed the post-war reimposition of strict Stalinist conformism in the arts), jumps in on Laroche's side—on the side, that is, of nineteenth-century Russia's most conservative critic—to caution the reader, in a footnote, that 'if this assertion can to some extent be justified in the case of A. Rubinstein, it is completely mistaken in the case of P. Tchaikovsky'.[4]

It often happened that the footnotes in Soviet publications kept up a sort of running feud with the text; a famous tragicomic instance was the hardliner musicologist Yury Keldysh's 1935 edition of some challenging memoirs by the ostensibly 'populist' composer Modest Musorgsky's aristocratic companion and probable lover, Count Arseny Golenishchev-Kutuzov.[5] Altogether painful was the footnote in which the editors—the Jewish editors, I note regretfully—of a 1971 edition of Musorgsky's letters sought to soften the impact of one of the composer's harsher attacks on the Jews: 'In spite of what might seem the blatant anti-Semitic character of these lines', they wrote, 'in the light of Musorgsky's world-view, as well as his personal friendships and his creative interests, this sally is to be explained not by any chauvinistic outlook on the part of the composer, but by a general aversion to the bourgeoisie and to the mercenary element.'[6] Leaving aside the part about some of the composer's best friends, could the editors have believed that their exculpatory equation of Jewishness with moneygrubbing was any the less blatantly an anti-Semitic slur than anything Musorgsky had to offer?

No, of course not; but one understands the need for all of these intrusions. They were the price of publication; the only alternative, under the conditions of Soviet censorship, was expurgation. (Indeed, the anti-Semitic passage from Musorgsky is expurgated not only in previous, but also in subsequent Russian editions of his correspondence.) But that does not explain Glikman's commentaries, which were written under no such constraints. Nor have we taken their full measure. For the problem of irony can cut the other way, too. People can be schooled and then overschooled in irony, as the boy who cried wolf found out some time ago. So just as often Glikman felt called upon to step in and explain that Shostakovich, you see, was not making a joke. In one of the earlier letters in the book, Shostakovich writes, 'I'm working a lot, but not composing anything.' As Glikman explains, this meant that Shostakovich was doing a lot of film-scoring, which he did not take seriously as creative work. Then

[4] Cesar Antonovich Cui, *Izbrannye stat'i*, ed. Izrail Lazarevich Gusin (Leningrad, 1952), 238, 592.

[5] A. A. Golenishchev-Kutuzov, 'Vospominaniya o M.P. Musorgskom', ed. Y. V. Keldish, in M. V. Ivanov-Boretsky, ed., *Muzikal'noe nasledstvo: Sbornik materialov po istorii muzykal'noi kul'turi v Rossii*, vol. i (Moscow, 1935), 5–49. For an analysis of the commentary see R. Taruskin, *Musorgsky: Eight Essays and an Epilogue* (Princeton, 1993), 26–34.

[6] M. P. Musorgsky, *Literaturnoe nasledie*, ed. A. Orlova and M. Pekelis, vol. i (Moscow, 1971), 354. The passage glossed is on p. 245.

Shostakovich writes, 'I hope that these are only temporary setbacks for my modest and insignificant talent.' Glikman insists that we take this literally: 'These words are not by any means a pose; he did not like posing.' And yet a great deal in the letter would seem to contradict this interpretation. For one thing, Shostakovich himself appears to mock the sentence in question, observing immediately afterwards that 'modesty becomes a person'. For another, the sentence parodies an earlier one in the letter, in which Shostakovich sympathizes with Glikman's reported illness by saying, 'I hope that these are only temporary setbacks for your mighty organism.'[7]

In any case, as revealed in the letters Glikman has made public, Shostakovich's modesty did not extend to self-denigration. One of the most moving letters of all, for me, and the one that if pressed I would single out as the most significant in the book, is the letter that ends with the following paragraph:

During my illness, or rather my illnesses, I picked up the score of one of my works. I looked through it from beginning to end. I was astonished at its quality. It seemed to me that having created such a thing I can be proud and serene. It was devastating to think that it was I who composed this composition.[8]

Glikman speculates that the composition in question was the Eighth Symphony, one of the works that were under a tacit but official ban (or 'idling', as the expression went) at the time of writing. 'And then one fine day,' he writes in his commentary, 'on the eve of the new year, there arose in [Shostakovich] the need somehow, in a letter to me, to answer his persecutors, tell them what he thought of their judgement, their verdicts and sentences, and what he thought about himself.'[9] What made the letter so moving—for Glikman, too, I would hazard a guess (though for some reason he does not say so), as well as for me—is not so much what is said within it as the date that stands above it. The 'one fine day' on which Shostakovich wrote with such intensity about the value of his work was in fact a day of days: 21 December 1949, Stalin's seventieth birthday, the grand apotheosis to which Solzhenitsyn devoted a whole surrealistic chapter in *The First Circle*, a day that was bloated up from end to end of the Soviet Union in an unprecedented discharge of bellowed, orchestrated lies.

This letter opens out into a much broader, more important interpretive terrain than the special, relatively (ahem) straightforward case of irony. I mean the general terrain of subtexts and multivalent meaning (what literary theorists like to call 'polysemy'). This is the interpretive space in which, for at least half a century, the vast majority of Shostakovich readings have taken place. As in the case of the letter I have just quoted, knowing the dates of things can be terribly important. Knowing, for example, that the first performance of the Fifth Symphony took place in November 1937, at the very height of the so-called 'Yezhovshchina' (after Nikolay Yezhov, the 'iron commissar' of internal affairs),

---

[7] *Pis'ma k drugu*, 72–3.   [8] Ibid. 85.   [9] Ibid. 86.

perhaps the bloodiest political terror the world had ever seen, provides an indispensable subtext for comprehending the palpable funereal imagery in the slow movement. Even if it should turn out that Shostakovich never intended any such thing (though I have no idea how such a fact could be established), perceiving the connection is essential to understanding the way in which the symphony was received—as all reports agree, the slow movement provoked a wave of open weeping in the hall—and why Shostakovich's music was valued the way it was.

That social value, which made Shostakovich's music as controversial outside Russia as it was precious inside, was precisely the result of the play of subtexts—the uncontrollable play of subtexts, I should add. It was one of the very few things the totalitarian regime was powerless to control short of banning the music, which it occasionally did. And that made it precious. 'I always sensed intuitively in it a protest against the regime,' says Solomon Volkov, the author of that shameless best-seller *Testimony*, a book that falsely purported to be Shostakovich's transcribed oral memoirs. (Its ruses were exposed a dozen years ago by the American Shostakovich biographer Laurel E. Fay.) But this time Volkov was speaking in his own voice, rather than through his little puppet Mitya, and we can believe him.[10] And we can agree: of course he sensed protest in Shostakovich's music, along with millions of his countrymen. They needed to sense such a thing; and music, with its blessed polysemy, afforded them a consolation no other art could provide under conditions of Soviet thought control.

Music was special. Music *is* special. Nothing could prevent Volkov and many other intellectuals—as he reports in the introduction to *Testimony*, again written in his own voice—from associating the violent music to the second movement of Shostakovich's Eleventh Symphony not with the events of 'Bloody Sunday' in 1905, as the Symphony's official programme stated, but with the more recent bloody events in Budapest, where Soviet troops had lawlessly put down the Hungarian rebellion. ('Never mind,' an ex-Soviet musicologist of Volkov's generation has assured me, 'we *knew* what it meant.') For Volkov, for my friend, and for many others, assembling in a concert hall and listening together to Shostakovich's music gave them an otherwise unavailable sense of solidarity in protest.

Did the composer intend it? The question, I submit, is irrelevant. A hundred years earlier, radical students had loved to foregather in the balcony of St Petersburg's old Great Stone Theatre to cheer Italian singers who reached their high notes in Rossini on words like *libertà*. There was nothing Tsar Nikolay I could do to prevent it. Does it matter whether Rossini intended it? Sometimes the composer's intention is manifestly irrelevant to the meaning of his work,

---

[10] 'Zdes' chelovek sgorel', *Muzykal'naya akademiya*, 3 (1992), 6. On *Testimony*, see Laurel Fay, 'Shostakovich versus Volkov: Whose Testimony?', *Russian Review*, 39 (1980), 484–93.

and insistence on limiting meaning to original intention only, and obviously, impoverishes it. The veteran Russian scholar Daniel Zhitomirsky recently called attention to a gripping instance of this sort of contingency involving the song cycle 'From Jewish Folk Poetry', long regarded as being, quite intentionally, one of Shostakovich's riskiest compositions.[11] Once again, knowing the date crucially affects not just interpretation but our direct apprehension of the work. 'From Jewish Folk Poetry' was written during the black year 1948. That was the year of the Zhdanovshchina, and of the Communist Party's infamous 'Resolution on Music', a document that subjected Shostakovich to his second bout of official persecution. It was also the year in which for the first time anti-Semitism, under the guise of a campaign against 'cosmopolitanism', became official government policy in the Soviet Union. The actor Solomon Mikhoels was murdered in Minsk. The Jewish Anti-Fascist Committee was liquidated and its leadership arrested. Over the next five years, practically every Jewish cultural activist in the country would be executed. Shostakovich's song cycle was the most demonstrative of his several appropriations of Jewish thematic and subject-matter, and when you connect the various events of 1948, even when Stalin's cynical recognition of the infant state of Israel that year and the triumphant arrival of Golda Meir (then Myerson), the Israeli ambassador, just in time for the High Holidays are weighed in the balance, it seems more convincing than ever to associate that appropriation of Jewish folklore with the composer's wish covertly to affirm solidarity with the persecuted. Indeed, it was a way of identifying himself and his colleagues, creative artists in Stalin's Russia, with another oppressed minority.

Obviously, at the time of writing this composition could not be performed except clandestinely (which, according to recent reports, it was, more than once, to tearful gatherings of Jews and artists). It was written 'for the drawer' as one said then, along with the Violin Concerto, whose Scherzo contains another Jewish theme in direct conjunction with the first tentative and somewhat ambiguous occurrence in Shostakovich's work of his musical monogram, DSCH (D, E flat, C, and B, as they are named in German), that would haunt his music from then on with increasing frequency. Yet even for the drawer, Shostakovich took precautions. He changed the words of one song, as the ex-Soviet Israeli musicologist Joachim Braun has pointed out, to name the Tsar explicitly as the force behind a Jewish father's exile to Siberia. And he followed the first eight songs, which paint a uniformly bleak picture of Jewish life in Russia, with a final optimistic trio depicting life in the 'Sovietishe Heymland' (to recall the name of that egregious showcase of a Yiddish journal that appeared briefly during the Khrushchev years).

Braun calls these last three songs 'tribute money', and tries, wishfully in my opinion, to portray them as a veiled, deliberate parody of the authentic Jewish

---

[11] See D. Zhitomirsky, 'Shostakovich', *Muzykal'naya akademiya*, 3 (1993), 29.

style elsewhere embraced in the cycle.[12] Whether or not a parody, the optimistic songs are definitely an emollient. Even so, the last of them, the exultant song of a Jewish mother about her children's prospects in the land of the Soviets, makes for a rousing, if conventional, finale.

That, at least, seems to have been Shostakovich's intention. But between 1948, when the songs were written, and 1955, when they were first publicly performed in the early days of the 'thaw', a great many events had taken place. Among them was the so-called Doctor's Plot, the loudly publicized arrest of six prominent Jewish doctors (plus two token Russians and a Ukrainian) on charges of murdering the Politburo members Zhdanov and Shcherbakov at the behest of the American Jewish Joint Distribution Committee (identified by *Pravda*, in the paranoiac jargon of the day, as an 'international Jewish bourgeois national organization'), and plotting to wipe out the rest of 'the leading cadres of the Soviet Union'. This was widely, and one can only think plausibly, read as a *provokatsiya* intended to justify the wholesale deportation or destruction of the Jews of European Russia, from which only Stalin's providential death a few weeks later saved them. (Among those briefly arrested in the immediate aftermath of the Doctor's Plot was one of Shostakovich's close friends, the Jewish composer Moisey Vainberg, who had fled to the USSR from Poland in the wake of the Nazi-Soviet invasion of 1939. Vainberg was arrested not because he was involved in any organized Jewish activities, but because he had the misfortune of being related by marriage both to Mikhoels and to Professor Miron Vovsi, one of the accused medical assassins.)

Thus, by the time Shostakovich's song cycle reached its first public culmination, its concluding words—'Our sons have become doctors! A star shines over our heads!'—had taken on a new and chilling meaning the composer never foresaw. They now pointed, with excruciating irony, to the utter betrayal of the hopes an oppressed people had once vested in the Russian Revolution. And the star! Instead of the red star atop the Kremlin one now thought of the stars sewn on the garments of the German Jews.

It is clear, I should think, that Shostakovich could never have intended this particular irony, which is now perhaps the most potent jolt his song cycle can administer to the appropriately attuned listener. It is equally clear, I hope, that it is now as much, and as legitimately, a part of the experience of the music as anything he did intend, and that he could only have welcomed it, if one may put it so, and the contribution it made to the effect of his work on the consciousness of its hearers, and to its value as testimony. As contexts change, subtext accumulates. What made Shostakovich's music the secret diary of a nation was not only what he put into it, but what it allowed listeners to draw out.

---

[12] Joachim Braun, 'The Double Meaning of Jewish Elements in Dimitri Shostakovich's Music', *Musical Quarterly*, 71 (1985), 74–5.

Glikman's book, like Zhitomirsky's article, contains many moving, indeed wrenching moments, and a wealth of biographical revelation, some of it directly relevant, as we have seen, to the apprehension of Shostakovich's works. And yet there is—I won't say a flaw because it arises out of such honourable circumstances—a pervading predicament about its commentaries to which I have already drawn perhaps ungrateful attention, but which I nevertheless feel I must pursue because it has such a bearing on our business not only as scholars and as critics, but as listeners to Shostakovich.

The power of the book, as well as its dilemma, is summarized when, taking leave of the reader, Glikman confesses that the memory of Shostakovich is sacred to him.[13] It was in order to protect the memory of his most cherished friend, and protect what *he* knew to be the meaning of his friend's words, that the editor felt called upon to interpose himself so often between the reader and the text. Irony, which is to say contradictions between the manifest sense of an utterance and its latent sense, inevitably became the primary object of his ministrations. In all cases, and regardless of which level of meaning he saw fit to espouse in a given case, his object was the same: to adjudicate and resolve the contradiction.

Like the Soviet readings to which I have compared them, Glikman's was thus an attempt to take possession of the meaning of the text, or perhaps, in his own view, to return possession to the rightful owner. It was an attempt to contain meaning and foreclose interpretation. In that sense it *was* an old Soviet habit, as I have suggested—or rather, it was an attempt to fight Soviet methods of appropriation with Soviet methods. What Glikman tried to do was to carry out a sort of pre-emptive strike not only against the old, opportunistic official view of Shostakovich, to which the reflexes of a lifetime had understandably rendered him permanently sensitive, but also against the equally opportunistic habits of secret nonconformist interpretation in which he knew his readers, in reaction to the very same coercive official construction, had been thoroughly trained.

But the efforts to resolve every contradiction and eliminate every ambiguity or multivalence inevitably produces inconsistencies and contradictions of its own. And the price of certainty is always reduction—reduction not only in meaning, but in interest and value. Glikman's presentation of Shostakovich's letters thus crystallizes in a microcosm, and with relatively unproblematic texts, the difficulties and the fascination that have always haunted the experience of Shostakovich's musical works, those vastly problematical texts, and our relationship to them—the problem, if you will, of 'Shostakovich and Us'.

The fact is that no one owns the meaning of the music, which has always supported—nay invited; nay compelled—multiple opportunistic and contradictory readings, and no one can ever own it. Under the old Soviet dispensation, of course, the Party claimed exclusive rights to it. Attempts by Volkov or

---

[13] *Pis'ma k drugu*, 311.

Glikman, among many others, to return exclusive ownership to the composer are futile at best, dishonest at worst. The 'Shostakovich' to whom ownership is returned is an *ex post facto* construction—as he would remain even if the authenticity of *Testimony* were confirmed—through which latter-day inter- preters, potentially including the composer, assert their own authority. Imagine Edgar Bergen making himself very small and trying to sit on Charlie McCarthy's lap.[14]

But that hopelessness of final arbitration is precisely what has given the music its enormous social value, its terrific emotional force, and its staying power. No other music—indeed, no other body of texts—so radically forces engagement with the most fundamental issues of interpretation. No other body of texts so compellingly demonstrates that meaning is never wholly immanent but arises out of a process of interaction between subject and object, so that interpretation is never wholly subjective or wholly objective to the exclusion of the other. And no other body of texts so fully convinces us that the meaning of an art work, indeed of any communication, is never wholly stable, but is the product of its history, a history that only begins with its creation. (Otherwise, one could maintain, the United States national anthem is not a patriotic song but only a drinking song.)

Add to all of this the incredibly high stakes of the creative and interpretive game as played within the frontiers, both temporal and geographical, of a brutal political tyranny. Whether viewed internally or externally, whether in terms of their content or their context, Shostakovich's works are fraught with horrific subtexts that can never be ignored. That is why they have always been, and will always be, objects of furious and manifold contention. We can never merely receive its messages; we are always implicated in their making, and therefore we can never be indifferent to them. It is never just Shostakovich. It is always Shostakovich and us.

II

The fact that not even Shostakovich's devoted confidant can entirely succeed in determining for us the extent to which the composer's texts contain irony, or even when they do, is all the evidence we need that irony, along with every other aspect of meaning, is not something that texts merely 'contain'. Irony, as Stanley Fish so pithily puts it, 'is neither the property of works nor the creation of an unfettered imagination, but a way of reading'.[15] I quote Fish because he is the soul of quotability, not because his view of irony is a new one, still less

---

[14] Edgar Bergen was a popular American ventriloquist whose most famous dummy was called Charlie McCarthy [ed.].

[15] Stanley Fish, 'Short People Got No Reason to Live: Reading Irony', in *Doing What Comes Naturally* (Durham, NC, and London, 1989), 194.

because it is the invention of recent literary theory. It may be new to formalized theory, but it is, and has always been, a standard aspect of informal critical practice. I mean the practice of ordinary, non-professional readers and, in the particular and especially pertinent case of music, listeners.

The familiarity of the notion is attested by any number of old jokes, like the one about the two Jews who meet in the Warsaw railway station. 'Where are you going?' asks one. 'To Minsk,' answers the other. 'Ha!', says the first, 'You say you are going to Minsk so that I should think you're going to Pinsk, but I happen to know you *are* going to Minsk, so what's the point of lying?' Or the one about the two psychoanalysts. 'Hello,' says the first. 'Hmmm,' thinks the second, 'what did he mean by that?' Of course it is no accident that these jokes are peopled by Jews and psychoanalysts, representatives of distinguished gnostic traditions—two traditions (or is it only one?) that radically distinguish between manifest and latent content and radically privilege the truth-value of the latent. Many such traditions—the mythographic, the symbolist, the occult—lurk in the background of modern art. Nor let us forget an occult science that used to be practice until quite recently, that of kremlinology, along with its sister discipline, 'Aesopian' discourse. All Soviet texts—regardless of their provenance, whether public or private, official or underground, whether the latest photo of the Politburo line-up atop the Lenin mausoleum or the latest tape of clandestine 'guitar poetry'—have always been doggedly scrutinized for their latent content. The assumptions have always been that such content is there, that it will contradict the manifest content, and that it is the true content. Armed with such assumptions, who could fail to find it? Thus it is no accident, either, that the theoretical literature on irony, such as it is, overlaps as much as it does with the literature on censorship and its complicated interactions with artistic expression. True hermeneuticists, though often confused with exegetes who merely investigate and defend 'original intention', have long been subversive readers who have realized the necessarily arbitrary nature of the choice between manifest and latent content. Hans-Georg Gadamer, for one, long in advance of post-structuralist or reader-response theory, recognized (in *Truth and Method*, his classic treatise on interpretation) that hidden meanings are as much the creation of the reader as of the writer.[16]

All of this is quite apart from the special status, and the special attributes, of music—especially music in the post-Beethovenian symphonic tradition of which Shostakovich was such a master. This type of music was perhaps the most potent medium of artistic expression ever devised. It was equipped with a sophisticated and highly ramified practice of melodic elaboration and directed harmony, which enabled it both to forecast and to delay points of melodic and harmonic arrival. Since by means of these techniques it was always portending its own future and recalling its own past, it could be said to possess a powerful

---

[16] See *Truth and Method* (1960; anon., trans. New York, 1982), 488.

internal sign-system—an introversive semiotic, Russian formalists would say—that enabled it to represent enormous tensions and cathartic releases that elicited corresponding affective responses in the hearer: responses that were controlled and directed more precisely, hence more powerfully, than those brought about by any other art medium. At the same time symphonic music was often laden with 'extroversive' symbols and portents as well. By Beethoven's time there were already many conventions for representing the wider world and its contents, all the way from primitive onomatopoeia to sophisticated 'intertextual' allusion. The repertoire of such devices grew rapidly over the next hundred years, with Tchaikovsky, Shostakovich's countryman and predecessor, making a signal contribution to its development. But—and this may be the key to its uncanny efficacy—such music resolutely eschewed the establishment within itself of any stable code by which its signs were to be read.

Thus, while its unfolding could simulate the manner and produce the effects of a drama or a narrative, music eluded conclusive paraphrase. Its inescapable assault on the senses and its dynamism, governed by a compelling syntax but unmediated by any established semantic canon, seemed to present and to evoke emotional intensity in a primal, inchoate fashion. 'Music', Schopenhauer was prompted thus to write, 'gives the innermost kernel preceding all form, or the heart of things.'[17] Wagner, under its (and Schopenhauer's) spell, called music that appeared to do this 'absolute music', and the name has stuck. But as originally conceived, the idea of absolute music did not imply abstraction, still less formalism. It meant something uncanny and sublime—something that names no names, and was therefore unattached to objects, but that was supremely attached to subjects, to the point where it could seem to take over its beholders' sentient lives for the duration, giving knowledge of a reality that went beyond the bounds of the sensory or phenomenal world, into the realm of gnosis or 'intuition'.

What this amounts to, in interpretive terms, is an overwhelmingly fraught surface or manifest content, consisting of the dynamically unfolding sound shapes with all their clamour of introversive and extroversive significance, but a symbology whose referents had to be sought in the realm of latent content. This gave rise to a persistent, heated, and fruitless debate that still rages on and off both in and out of the academy. On the one hand are those who would prefer to simplify matters, denying the very existence of a latent content, and claiming for music the status of an inherently or ideally non-referential medium, unattached to the wider world and beatifically exempt from its vicissitudes. Their outstanding nineteenth-century spokesman was Eduard Hanslick, on whom Wagner modelled the figure of Beckmesser, the eternal pedant in *Die Meistersinger*. The outstanding twentieth-century representative of this position

---

[17] Arthur Schopenhauer, *The World as Will and Representation* (1819), trans. E. F. J. Payne (New York, 1969), i. 263.

was the uprooted Russian nobleman and White émigré Igor Stravinsky, and in so identifying him I have identified the motivation for his aesthetic stance. In retrospect, it seems only predictable that the autonomist or formalist position should have achieved its completest ascendancy in the West during the cold war.

On the other hand were those who not only acknowledged the immanence of a latent musical content, but sought, or presumed, to define it, to fix it, to make it manifest, to have it name names and propound propositions, to subject it to paraphrase, which means subjecting it to limitation and ultimately to control. It is not difficult to see the political subtext informing this debate, or why the so-called referentialist side of the argument should have reached ascendancy in the twentieth-century totalitarian states at the same time that the autonomist position triumphed in the liberal democracies. But both of these extreme positions are impoverishing. The position that would eliminate a whole level of meaning from music impoverishes it literally and obviously. But the other side is hardly better. When fixed and paraphrased, the latent becomes blatant. And when the latent becomes wholly manifest, the manifest becomes superfluous.

For an astoundingly sustained demonstration of that blatancy, consider Ian MacDonald's book *The New Shostakovich*. Although published long after its subject's death, this travesty received its most trenchant critique from Shostakovich himself: 'When a critic, in *Worker and Theater* or *The Evening Red Gazette*, writes that in such-and-such a symphony Soviet civil servants are represented by the oboe and the clarinet, and Red Army men by the brass section, you want to scream!' That is what the composer said at a symposium, 'Soviet Music Criticism Is Lagging', held at the Union of Soviet Composers in 1933, and reported in its official organ, three years before he and all his colleagues were muzzled.[18] And here is what Ian MacDonald has written about a passage in Shostakovich's Fifth Symphony: 'Over the thrumming rhythm, flute and horn now converse in a major-key transposition of the second subject: two dazed delegates agreeing that the rally had been splendid and the leader marvellous.'[19]

There is MacDonald's book in a nutshell. The author musters all the methods of Soviet music criticism at its most lagging, vulgar, and biased in order to prove that Shostakovich was a 'scornful dissident' and that his creative achievement amounted to nothing less, and nothing more, than an obsessively sustained invective against the Soviet regime and against Stalin personally. The methods are familiar. There is trivializing literary or pictorial paraphrase: an ascending scale to a climax in the first movement of the Fourth Symphony depicts the imagined arrival chez Shostakovich of the NKVD, 'audibly climbing the stairs . . .

---

[18] 'Sovetskaya muzykal'naya kritika otstaet', *Sovetskaya muzyka*, 3 (1933), 121.

[19] Ian MacDonald, *The New Shostakovich* (Boston, 1990), 130.

and bursting in through the door on a triumphant crescendo [*sic*]'.[20] There is baby 'semiotics': every two-note motif says 'STA-LIN' (even when iambic) and every descending anapest means 'betrayal'. There is guilt by association: in defence of his thesis that Shostakovich was dissident from birth, MacDonald names a few anti-Utopian writers of the 1920s (Zamyatin, Olesha, Bulgakov, Zoshchenko) and points out that 'Shostakovich knew these writers personally . . . and socialized with them'.[21] There is the shifting burden of proof ('There is nothing to suggest that the composer . . . opposed the non-Party writers.') There is 'verificationism' or confirmation bias: evidence in support of preconceived conclusions is selectively culled and marshalled; contrary evidence is suppressed or damned. And there is pervasive browbeating: 'There can be absolutely no doubt' of the author's readings; all others are 'palpably ridiculous'. At their most triumphant and peremptory, MacDonald's exegeses might have served as confessions to be shoved under Shostakovich's nose by the State Procurator, Vyshinsky, together with a pen.

III

Where latent musical meaning is neither negated nor successfully administered—where, in other words, it is acknowledged but contested—the value of its vessel is much enhanced. Nietzsche grasped this truth better than anyone when he wrote, 'Music reaches its high-water mark only among men who have not the ability or the right to argue.'[22] The whole history of the arts in Russia (not just the Soviet Union), and the whole story of Shostakovich's life, are encapsulated in that sentence. In few countries have the arts ever mattered so much, and in few countries have they been subjected to more terrible stress, to a more terrible contest for ownership. As the pre-eminent modern master of the post-Beethovenian rhetoric (a rhetoric that declined in the West as the autonomist aesthetic triumphed) Shostakovich was willy-nilly the most important artist in the country where the arts were most important—and the most watchdogged, precisely because his was the medium with the most potential slippage between its manifest and its latent content. Because of this, Shostakovich was the one and only Soviet artist to be claimed equally by the official culture and the dissident culture.

He managed this feat, of course, by leaving interpretation to others. Not explaining his music—or any music—except under pressure, in the vaguest terms, became the Shostakovich defence, and a rule that he carried over even into his private life. That his letters to Glikman contained little about his music

---

[20] Ibid. 112.

[21] Letter to the Editor, *Times Literary Supplement*, 28 Sept. 1990, p. 1.

[22] Friedrich Nietzsche, 'The Wanderer and His Shadow' (1880), in *The Philosophy of Nietzsche*, ed. Geoffrey Clive (New York, 1965), 303.

beyond what Glikman calls 'statistics'—number of movements, timings, keys—
might have been expected; Soviet letters, after all, were public documents
whether or not they were published. But he was just as tight-lipped in
conversation. A much-repeated anecdote (prized because it brings together
two leading figures whose meetings were few) reproduces some summer shop
talk between Prokofiev and Shostakovich overheard by the musicologist
Grigory Shneyerson at Ivanovo, the Composers' Union retreat, immediately
after the war:

Prokofiev: You know, I'm really going to get down to work on my Sixth Symphony. I've
written the first movement [here follows a detailed description of its form], and now I'm
writing the second, with three themes; the third movement will probably be in sonata
form. I feel the need to compensate for the absence of sonata form in the previous
movements.
Shostakovich: So, is the weather here always like this?[23]

The later portions of Glikman's book, given over to a Boswellian or Robert-
Crafty chronicle of Shostakovich's last years, show the composer growing more
and more noncommittal even as circumstances seemed to favour the lowering
of his guard. On 24 February 1974, less than half a year before his death,
having listened to a symphony by his former pupil Boris Tishchenko and said
little, Shostakovich offered a sort of apology that might be taken as his Aesopian
credo:

I am generally close-mouthed. I have neither the wish nor the ability to analyse or
discuss the pieces I hear. I just listen to the music people give me to listen to. Either I like
it or I don't. That's all.[24]

Well, that's not quite all. There is more here than the doer's quarrel with the
talker, more than the artist's familiar insistence on sensory immediacy and
pleasure over secondary, rationalized response—though in this over-analytical
age of ours it's a hint we might do well to consider at times. There is simply too
much in Shostakovich's instrumental music that is strongly marked—too much
that resonates, like Beethoven's or Tchaikovsky's music, with characteristic and
functional genres, with the conventional iconicity of emotion, with intertextual
allusion, with sheer violence—for us to doubt that at bottom he shared his
society's faith in the reality of the latent content. Yet unlike the socialist-realist
critics who tried to catalogue and thus circumscribe his 'imagery' and
'intonations',[25] and unlike the more recent biographical paraphrasts (including

---

[23] Quoted in Zhitomirsky, 'Shostakovich', 26–7.

[24] *Pis'ma k drugu*, 306.

[25] For explication of these actually quite useful terms, which go back to Boris Asafiev
('Muzykal'naya forma kak protsess', 1930), and whose meanings are actually disguised by their
English cognates, see Malcolm H. Brown, 'The Soviet Russian Concepts of "Intonazia" and "Musical
Imagery"', *Musical Quarterly*, 60 (1974), 557–67. (Shostakovich's Seventh Symphony furnishes the
practical illustrations.)

the one who scandalously appropriates his name), Shostakovich insisted on keeping the latent content latent—and keeping it labile.

And there is more to that insistence than a mere wish to preserve what Admiral Poindexter notoriously called 'deniability'. As long as music is left to 'speak for itself', it can only speak truth. Janet Malcolm's study of Sylvia Plath's contending biographers contains a passage that cuts remarkably near to the Shostakovichian quick. Whereas 'the facts of imaginative literature are as hard as the stone that Dr. Johnson kicked', the author writes, there is always 'epistemological insecurity' in works of non-fiction, precisely because it is aiming at a whole truth that is inevitably beyond its grasp.[26] The aspiration to literal truth brings always with it the possibility, indeed the virtual certainty, of falsehood.

Just so, paraphrasts of Shostakovich's symphonies and quartets, who strive to reconcile the latent content of the works with the literal truth of lived experience (the composer's, the people's, their own), but who lack an omniscience that not even the composer could fairly claim, cannot hope to achieve a perfect fit, and hence, to the extent that they profess certainty, will always lie. For the composer's perfect silence we substitute a Babel of partial truths. History has decreed that this particular composer's works are fated to be read in part—but never impartially—as non-fiction. That is what accounts for the moral stature they, and he, have achieved—uniquely achieved, I think it is fair to say—in the annals of twentieth-century music. But there is tremendous irony in this, because it is a fate and a stature that Shostakovich could never have sought, but that were conferred on him—thrust upon him—by the powers that tormented him, and by the way in which he responded to his tribulations. There was no inkling as of 1936, when he was first denounced and humiliated (and, let us not forget, mortally threatened), that Shostakovich would be a composer primarily associated with the concert genres, that his reputation would rest chiefly on his symphonies and, even more improbably, on his string quartets. (Except for his cello sonata, by 1936 he had not yet written any important chamber music.) The infamous *Pravda* editorial that marked the clampdown, 'Muddle Instead of Music', was provoked by an opera, the extravagantly successful *Lady Macbeth of the Mtsensk District*. It was the 29-year-old composer's second opera, and the first in a planned Wagnerian (or anti-Wagnerian) tetralogy. It was clear that the stage was Shostakovich's chosen medium, as it had been for most Russian composers.

Lady Macbeth, the critic of the *New Yorker* dryly observed in 1935, was 'no great exercise in restraint',[27] and it was no great act of moral witness, either, though it posed as one. Like many operas in the 'new-objective' Weimar orbit, it contained a violent, voyeuristic, and utterly un-erotic sex scene, and it embodied a grotesque, if sincerely motivated, moral inversion that, I have

---

[26] Janet Malcolm, *The Silent Woman* (New York, 1994), 154–5.
[27] 'Musical Events', *New Yorker*, 21 Oct. 1935, p. 116.

argued elsewhere,[28] is alarmingly consistent with Stalinist ethics: the one character in the opera presented as positive or even human—that is, the title character—is the one that brutally murders all the others. (Having garnered my share of brickbats for expressing such an unpopular opinion about this much-mythologized work, I was cheered to find my impressions confirmed by Professor Zhitomirsky in the post-Soviet press.) For Shostakovich, though, there would be no more operas. He never dared risk another. His prudence was borne out of course, in 1948, when it was another opera, Vano Muradeli's *The Great Friendship*, that served the Zhdanovshchina as pretext and sacrificial lamb. But Shostakovich's sacrifice of what would surely have been one of the great operatic careers was a terrible loss, not only to him but to us.

The instrumental works Shostakovich had produced up to the year of his denunciation, including his first three symphonies, were all written against rather than in emulation of the canonical symphonic tradition, once again in the debunking spirit of the 'new objectivity' that had emanated in the 1920s from Germany. The first of Shostakovich's works to fit the canonical heroic-classical mould and the high ethical tone with which he is now so firmly identified was the Fifth Symphony, which was received by the powers as an act of contrition, and saddled by them with a quasi-autobiographical subtext, first enunciated in a review by the novelist Alexey Tolstoy that appeared in the newspaper *Izvestiya*, and soon thereafter echoed in an article that appeared in the newspaper *Vechernyaya Moskva* over the composer's name.[29] From that point on, two things were firmly established that would last until the end of Shostakovich's life, and continue to this day: first, the persistent tension between official and subversive readings; and second, the tendency for both official and subversive readings to take the form of biographical—which is to say, ventriloquistically autobiographical—narratives.

At first, contention was between the print and the oral media. In the beginning, for example, only the official interpretation of the Fifth Symphony—the he-loved-Big-Brother version dubbed by Alexey Tolstoy as the exemplary Soviet *Bildungsroman* ('personality-formation' narrative) in tones—could be published and circulated in writing. Other readings, rife from the start (especially as regards the grotesque march in the first movement and the stentorian finale), had to circulate as folk tradition. It is a fascinating study to trace the gradual emergence of counter-narratives in print—a study that amounts to a shadow history of Soviet, anti-Soviet, and post-Soviet historiographical revisionism.[30]

---

[28] In an essay that originally appeared in the *New Republic*, 20 Mar. 1989; an expanded and updated version in *Defining Russia Musically* (Princeton, 1997).

[30] See Alexey Tolstoy, 'Pyataya simfoniya Shostakovicha', *Izvestiya*, 28 Dec. 1937, p. 5; D. D. Shostakovich, 'Moi tvorcheskii otvet', *Vechernyaya Moskva*, 25 Jan. 1938, p. 30.

[31] See R. Taruskin, 'Public Lies and Unspeakable Truth: Interpreting Shostakovich's Fifth Symphony', in D. Fanning, ed., *Shostakovich Studies* (Cambridge, 1995), 17–56.

IV

The thickest aura and the loudest Babel—a true international Babel this time, in many tongues—have surrounded the Seventh ('Leningrad') Symphony, ever since the composer's autograph score was microfilmed and flown to New York by way of Teheran and Cairo in a great fever of war-hysterical publicity, for performance under Arturo Toscanini. (That autograph has been recently issued in facsimile by a Japanese publisher, with a provocative introductory note by Manashir Yakubov, the archivist of the Shostakovich family estate.) Toscanini's performance was broadcast on 19 July 1942 to an audience of millions, including Mr and Mrs Stravinsky of Hollywood, who, we learn from Mrs Stravinsky's posthumously published diary, stayed at home in order to listen in.[31] Aura attached in those days far more to the work and its circumstances than to the composer's person. As Toscanini put it in a letter to Stokowski, whom he had to fight for first-performance rights, 'I admire Shostakovich music but I don't feel such a frenzied love for it like you.'[32] Stravinsky's regard for Shostakovich likewise fell short of frenzied love, as he lost no opportunity to remind his legions of interlocutors. Yet the very fact that a composer of Stravinsky's stature felt compelled to position himself insistently and repeatedly *vis-à-vis* a composer universally accorded a lesser stature during Stravinsky's lifetime already suggests something of Shostakovich's emblematic status, and that of the Seventh Symphony among his works. Nor was Bartók immune—else why should he have been so enraged by the symphony that he went to the trouble of parodying its notorious 'invasion' theme? (There really can be no doubt about that, despite Bartók's wan claim, when pressed, that he was quoting 'Da geh' ich zu Maxim' from Lehár's *Merry Widow*, the tune that may in fact have served as Shostakovich's model for caricaturing the Nazis; the passages in question from Bartok's *Concerto for Orchestra* are in Shostakovich's key, not Lehár's, and follow Shostakovich's exact note sequence.) What has made composer and work into icons, and the symphony from the very first (though there has been little agreement as to what it is an icon of), is the way their careers have forced critical confrontation with so many cherished assumptions about art music, its values, and its relationship to the world.

Shostakovich, by turns abused and adulated by a totalitarian state to a degree that lies at both extremes beyond the power of his benignly neglected Western counterparts to imagine, was in the 1940s a vastly ambivalent emblem. Was he toady or victim? Secret voice of conscience or accomplice to deception? Nation's darling or party-propped demagogue? Keeper of the Beethovenian flame or cynical manipulator of clichés? He aroused pity and annoyance, envy and

---

[31] See *Dearest Bubushkin*, ed. Robert Craft (New York, 1985), 125.
[32] See Harvey Sachs, *Toscanini* (Philadelphia, 1978), 279.

condescension, admiration and scorn—but never inhabited the limbo of public disregard that has by and large been the fate of the modernist generations in the West. He lacked the freedoms of his counterparts in *laissez-faire* states, including the freedom to be indifferent and the freedom to be marginal. He accepted the civic obligations that were thrust upon him and the rewards that followed.

While now it is easy enough to see that he had little say in the matter, in the 1940s this was not so clear. Arnold Schoenberg (again: what compelled his avid notice?) reproached Shostakovich for having 'allowed politics to influence his compositorial style', finally exonerating him on terms that today can only seem callous: 'Heroes can be composers and vice versa, but you cannot require it.'[33] Yet having established which of them was the hero, Schoenberg could allow himself a certain *noblesse-oblige* generosity towards the Soviet composer that contrasted with Bartók's and Stravinsky's furious rejection. Linking Shostakovich with Sibelius after the habit of contemporary reviewers such as Olin Downes (who cried them up) and Virgil Thomson (who cried them down), Schoenberg made a pronouncement—'I feel they have the breath [did he mean breadth?] of symphonists'—that has been pounced upon ever since by writers eager to issue Shostakovich or Sibelius a passport to academic respectability.[34] And yet Shostakovich's relationship to the public, both at home and abroad, was at once a seeming vindication of the ostensible ideals of socialist realism and paradigmatic violation of one of Schoenberg's fundamental postulates: 'If it is art, it is not for everybody, and if it is for everybody, it is not art.'[35]

The Seventh brought it all to a head. This hulking programmatic symphony, this bombastic anachronism replete with onomatopoetical battle music and cyclic thematic dramaturgy, emerged like some sort of woolly mammoth out of the Stalinist deep freeze. Its rhetoric was shamelessly inflated: by a veritable stage band in its outer movements, by a theatrical travesty of Bach in its protracted Adagio (Passion chorales, massed violins soliloquizing a chaconne). Its path to grandiose affirmation opportunistically replayed Beethoven's Napoleonic scenario, and the crass methods by which its message was mongered assaulted fastidious taste just as brutishly as the invaders could be heard assaulting Russia with a mind-numbing march that brazenly appropriated the surefire formula of Ravel's *Bolero* (even down to the snare drum ostinato and surprise modulation at the end), the very cynosure of the middlebrow. Glikman's Shostakovich defiantly confirms the resemblance: 'I don't know what will become of this piece,' Glikman reports his friend saying after playing through the newly composed first movement in August, 1941. 'Idle critics will surely rebuke me for imitating *Bolero*. Well, let them; that is how I hear the war.'[36]

[33] Arnold Schoenberg, *Letters*, ed. Erwin Stein (Berkeley and Los Angeles, 1989), 219.
[34] Arnold Schoenberg, *Style and Idea*, ed. Leonard Stein (Berkeley and Los Angeles, 1984), 136.
[35] Ibid. 124.   [36] *Pis'ma k drugu*, 22.

The war. This debasement of musical values was being carried out in the name of the same holy humanitarian cause that dominated the daily headlines. Shostakovich's symphony was riding both cause's and headlines' coat-tails to worldwide acclaim. In fact it was making headlines of its own. Its performances, both at home and abroad, were as much political events as musical ones. Was music serving politics or was politics serving music? Was music exploiting politics or was politics exploiting music? Or, worst of all, was the very distinction between the two being undermined?

Toscanini's powerful advocacy of the music was at least partly due to its political implications. 'I was deeply taken', he wrote to Stokowski, 'by its beauty and its anti-Fascist meanings, and I have to confess to you, by the greatest desire to perform it. . . . Don't you think, my dear Stokowski, it would be very interesting for everybody, and yourself, too, to hear the old Italian conductor (one of the first artists who strenuously fought against Fascism) to play this work of a young Russian anti-Nazi composer?'[37] Performing the work would be another anti-Fascist credential for a conductor who, in America, was trading heavily on his political commitments. That 'extramusical' appeal was accounting for the symphony's success; and that 'extramusical' freight was what conditioned not only 'the special meaning of this Symphony', as Toscanini called it, and its special privileges, but also its very special blatancy.

Critics took revenge. Virgil Thomson launched his review in the *New York Herald Tribune* with a really memorable salvo: 'Whether one is able to listen without mind-wandering to the Seventh Symphony of Dmitri Shostakovich probably depends on the rapidity of one's musical perceptions. It seems to have been written for the slow-witted, the not very musical and the distracted.' And he ended by accusing the composer of cynicism: 'That he has so deliberately diluted his matter, adapted it, by both excessive simplification and excessive repetition, to the comprehension of a child of eight, indicates that he is willing to write down to a real or fictitious psychology of mass consumption in a way that may eventually disqualify him for consideration as a serious composer.'[38]

B. H. Haggin, less verbally astute but further out on a limb because he was writing for the *Nation*, then a Stalinist publication, hauled out all his doughtiest pejoratives: derivative, eclectic, unresourceful, crude, pretentious, and of course 'trashy'. What was particularly galling was the barbarization of musical values in the name of humanitarian ones, paradoxically embodied in 'an hour-and-a-quarter-long symphony concerned with the struggle and final victory of humanity over barbarism'. The Russians, Haggin warned, not very realistically, 'can escape this difficulty only by recognizing the unimportance of those external conditions [that is, the unimportance of the war against Fascism] in

---

[37] Sachs, *Toscanini*, 279.
[38] 18 Oct. 1942; repr. in Virgil Thomson, *The Musical Scene* (New York, 1945), pp. 101, 104.

relation to the greatness we are aware of in some music, the importance instead of the composer's personal and musical resources'.[39]

Aesthetics were thus pitted irreconcilably against ethics; transcendence against commitment; quality against currency; art for the sake of art against art for the sake of people. For so crystallizing the terms of the endless and fruitless debate, Shostakovich's Seventh Symphony surely deserves its status as icon, though again it is a status the composer could hardly have sought.

The debate has not been helped by its latest phase, carried out since Shostakovich's death. The objective has been a dual one: to show, first of all, that the blatant manifest content of these works was a protective screen camouflaging a hidden truth that only a musical or moral connoisseur could discern (so much for populism); and to show, second, that the hidden meaning was of a sort that would allow precisely the claim Schoenberg denied, namely the claim of heroism—or rather, in the Soviet context, that of dissidence.

In Volkov's *Testimony*, the first-person narrative included the startling assertion that 'the Seventh Symphony had been planned before the war and consequently it simply cannot be seen as a reaction to Hitler's attack. The "invasion theme" has nothing to do with the attack. I was thinking of other enemies of humanity when I composed the theme.'[40] From this evidence, Ian MacDonald has dependably managed to read the whole symphony ironically, as 'a poker-faced send-up of Socialist Realist symphonism' that satirizes precisely what it was formerly perceived as glorifying. By relating the march theme in the first movement not to Lehár (or to *Deutschland über alles*) but (fleetingly) to Tchaikovsky's Fifth Symphony, MacDonald identifies it as 'Russian rather than German', hence—like every other work of Shostakovich that MacDonald interprets—a mockery of Stalin, not Hitler.[41] (The resemblance to Tchaikovsky is as demonstrable as the others, but the asserted coincidence of keys is the product of MacDonald's inability to read an orchestral score.)

Like most *parti-pris* interpretations this one has to ignore many salient features of the object interpreted. To uphold the view of the Seventh as exclusively anti-Stalinist one has to disregard the imagery of actual battle, as well as that of repulsion (the horripilating climax of the first movement), and finally of victory (the cyclic return at the end of the finale, which reinstates in glory a theme that MacDonald wants to read as satirically insipid). These musical events can hardly be read out of the context of the war and its immediate, overriding urgencies, conditions that could not have been foreseen when Volkov's Shostakovich claimed to have had his first thoughts of the Seventh.

But of course there is something much larger at stake. The Volkov/ MacDonald reading merely substitutes one limited and limiting paraphrase

[39] B. H. Haggin, *Music in the Nation* (New York, 1949), 109, 113.

[40] *Testimony*, 155.   [41] *The New Shostakovich*, 160.

for another, in the face of the multivalence that has always been the most special, most valuable property of symphonic music. In a very late Soviet contribution to the Shostakovich debates, the distinguished music theorist Lev Mazel likens this multivalence to that of algebra, wherein a formula containing several unknowns can have various arithmetic solutions.[42] It is an analogy that arises naturally out of Russian historical conditions. 'The life experiences that serve as impulse toward the creation of an artwork', Mazel valuably reminds us, 'are not tantamount to its content'; nor does 'the objective result of an artist's work necessarily conform to its original plan'. Whatever Shostakovich may have thought he was signifying by means of his invasion theme, this means, wartime listeners were justified in hearing a representation of Nazis, and we are justified now, if we are still interested in anti-Soviet revisionism, in hearing a representation of Bolsheviks. Such a change in signification, Mazel contends, 'is nothing special: life itself had rearranged the emphasis within a generalized and compounded image'. (The veteran analyst complicates that image further by demonstrating in detail the derivation—one he does not venture to interpret, but is content 'to state as fact'—of the invasion theme not from Lehár, not from Tchaikovsky, but from the E flat major episode in the finale of Beethoven's piano sonata, Op. 10 No. 1.)

Yet so ingrained is the practice of hermeneutic ventriloquism that even Mazel, in seeming contradiction of his own enlightened premisses, resorts to documentation in order to invest his interpretation of Shostakovich's 'generalized and compounded image' with the composer's *ex post facto* authority. He reports that upon evacuation to Samara (then Kuibyshev), where he completed the Seventh in the late autumn of 1941, Shostakovich and his wife made friends with their neighbour Flora Yasinovskaya, a biologist who was the daughter-in-law of Maxim Litvinov, the early Soviet foreign minister (and the mother of Pavel Litvinov, a prominent dissident of the 1960s). In unpublished notes she made at the time, later made available to Mazel, Yasinovskaya recorded some comments Shostakovich made to her alone, late at night, after he had played the symphony through to an audience of fellow evacuees: 'Fascism, yes, but music, real music is never tied literally to any theme. Fascism is not simply national socialism, and this is music about terror, slavery, spiritual exhaustion.' Later, her notes relate, Shostakovich took her even more fully into his confidence: 'the Seventh (and also the Fifth) is not only about Fascism, but about our system as well, about any tyranny or totalitarianism in general.'[43] Thus, Mazel suggests, the varying readings of the Seventh may be harmonized. Within this broadened documentary purview all readings may be authenticated. The putative original identification of the invasion theme with Stalin does not preclude its later use as a symbol for the Nazi aggression. The two ideas are

---

[42] L. Mazel, 'K sporam o Shostakoviche', *Sovetskaya muzyka*, 5 (1991), 30–5.

[43] See also Elizabeth Wilson, *Shostakovich: A Life Remembered* (London, 1994), 159.

not necessarily in conflict; the same algebraic formula can support either arithmetic solution, or both.

In its allowance for a certain multivalence, and in its refusal to reduce the meaning of the symphony to the meaning of a single theme, or of both to a particular verbal paraphrase, Mazel's view of the Seventh is a distinct improvement over old-line Soviet readings and over the simplistic revisionism of the present day. And yet even it remains ultimately unsatisfactory, because like the other interpretations it insists on identifying meaning, whether of the theme or of the symphony, with the composer's explicit designs, and only admits multivalence in so far as the composer's intention may be so represented. The genetic fallacy remains in place.

V

However 'monologically' Shostakovich's works were read by the regime (to borrow an appropriate word from the vocabulary of the Soviet critic Mikhail Bakhtin), however passively the silent composer appeared to acquiesce in the readings thus imposed, and however great the consequent propaganda yield, the regime could never fully ignore the power of music (and Shostakovich's music above all) to harbour potentially anarchic folk hermeneutics. The issue was finally brought to a head in 1948, during the Zhdanovshchina. The Party stooges who were now recruited to vilify Shostakovich—mainly Vladimir Zakharov, the leader of the Pyatnitsky Folk Choir, who inveighed against Shostakovich at the open hearings, and the composer Marian Koval, who did so in a series of calumnious articles in the journal *Sovetskaya muzyka*, the organ of the Union of Soviet Composers—did so by attacking the monumental instrumental genres that Shostakovich now employed.[44] The overt, quasi-'Tolstoyan' charge now made against him was that such genres, being inaccessible to the broad public and thus élitist, were divisive of society, hence uncommunitarian, hence anti-Soviet. The covert motive, transparent enough but now documented through the recent efforts of the archivist Leonid Maksimenkov, among others, was to discourage genres that in their wordlessness were less than ideally subject to ideological control. As Maksimenkov writes, 'the ideologues from Agitprop demanded texted music, which could be submitted to censorship on a par with movies, literature and programmatic, socialist-realist painting.'[45]

Early drafts of the Central Committee's Resolution on Music contained

---

[44] For Zakharov's deposition, see *Soveshchaniya deyatelei sovetskoi muzyki v TsK VKP (b)* (Moscow, 1948), 20–4; for excerpts in English trans., see Alexander Werth, *Musical Uproar in Moscow* (London, 1949; repr., Westport, Conn., 1973), 53–5. For Koval's denunciations, see M. Koval, 'Tvorcheskii put' D. Shostakovicha', *Sovetskaya muzyka* (1948), nos. 2–4.

[45] L. Maksimenkov, 'Partiya—nash rulevoi', *Muzykal'naya zhizn'*, nos. 15–16 (1993), p. 9.

explicit formulations designed to render all musical genres safe for censorship—formulations that, had they been published, would have acquired the force of law. One read, 'Resolved: to liquidate the one-sided, abnormal deviation in Soviet music towards textless instrumental works'. A revision substituted the somewhat less baleful verb *osudit'* ('censure' or 'judge unfavourably') for 'liquidate'. Had these passed, one wonders what Shostakovich would have been left with. In the end, though, the formulation was vague and somewhat absurd; no specific genres were condemned, only the 'formalist tendency in Soviet music', which was 'anti-people and conducive in fact to the liquidation of music'.[46] Maksimenkov comments that 'the laconicism of the final version of the directive portion of the resolution bears Stalin's indelible stamp'.[47] It should be added that there was good reason, from the administrative point of view, for imprecision. Specific directives, after all, can be complied with. Compliance can be a defence. There can be no defence against the 'laconic', inscrutable charge of formalism.

So Shostakovich went on writing symphonies, and, increasingly, quartets. And they continued to attract ventriloquists from all sides. More and more prevalently, Shostakovich's post-Zhdanovshchina output was read as so many notes in a bottle. To some extent, the works obviously invited such a reading. Many of them contain signals that their latent content was private rather than public. The very shift, beginning in the 1950s, from symphony to quartet as the centre of gravity for Shostakovich's output was such a hint. It was manifestly an anti-Soviet move of a sort, for, as both the Soviet government and its citizens knew long before it became a trendy slogan in the West, the personal is political. To concentrate on chamber music was not just un-Soviet activity, it was un-Russian. There was never much of a tradition in Russia for chamber music. Under the Soviets it was always vaguely suspect as aristocratic or genteel, and in 1948 it was openly denounced. The official list of Soviet genres, drawn up for official promulgation in one of the superseded resolution drafts, included symphonic, operatic, song, choral and dance genres only; the final text specifically rejected all styles and genres that appealed only to 'narrow circles of specialists and musical epicures'.[48] There had never been a Russian composer before Shostakovich to concentrate the way he eventually did on quartets, or to write so many of them. (Nikolay Myaskovsky, another prolific composer who was frightened into abstraction, came closest, with thirteen; but since Myaskovsky wrote twenty-seven symphonies, the quartets do not bulk nearly as large in his output as they do in Shostakovich's. Besides, Myaskovsky's career

[46] Ibid. 9–10.

[47] Ibid. 10.

[48] Ibid. 9; for the text of the Resolution on Music ('Ob opere "Velikaya druzhba" V. Muradeli, Postanovlenie Tsk VKP (b) ot 10 fevralya 1948g.'), see *Sovetskaya muzyka*, 1 (1948), 3–8. An English translation is included in Appendix B, in Andrey Olkhovsky, *Music under the Soviets: The Agony of an Art* (London, 1955), 280–5 (the passage on chamber music is on p. 282).

was practically over by 1948, while most of Shostakovich's quartet-writing lay ahead.)

There are other hints of politically fraught preoccupation with the private and the personal in Shostakovich's quartets, and his late music in general. They include slow, ruminative, fading finales; the simulation of recitative (often in a demonstratively broken or halting mode, reminiscent of the end of the funeral march in Beethoven's 'Eroica' Symphony); or contrariwise, the simulation of voicelessness (the tapping bows in the Thirteenth Quartet) or of screaming (the piercing unison crescendo at the end of the same quartet). The transfer of musical ideas like the screams, or of whole passages of music, from one work to another, suggesting that different works are chapters in an overarching narrative, also puts us in mind of biography, the most overarching narrative of all. The obsessional quotations and self-quotations add the prefix 'auto-' to the biographical gesture. And of course there is the increasingly resolute denial of optimism, of 'life-affirmation', which is to say denial of the *sine qua non* of Soviet art. (Here is where the late Shostakovich's surprising recourse to a few superficial trappings of twelve-tone technique, officially denounced for its decadence and pessimism, seems to find its rationale.) As Shostakovich, a world-renowned and much-revered figure, reached the stricken and debilitated end of his road, and as the Soviet state stumbled towards its own debilitated end, the composer could afford to lessen his guard, if ever so slightly. Whereas in the Yevtushenko-inspired Thirteenth Symphony he was still manifestly wrestling with Soviet authority, in the Fourteenth Symphony, a fully-texted and explicit death-affirmation, Shostakovich spat in its face. In the Fifteenth Quartet—a racking medley of Adagios—he fashioned his personal pain and his pessimism into a *tour de force*.

VI

I speak of hints within the works, but they are hints that we read in hindsight, and with ever-increasing knowledge of the events of the composer's life. Ultimately it is difficult—no, it is impossible—to know whether he is forcing his autobiography on us, or we are forcing it on him. We did not need complacent post-structuralists to tell us that autobiography, too, is a way of reading.[49]

The first work of Shostakovich to end *morendo*, with the dying of the light, was the Fourth Symphony, on which the composer was at work at the time of his first denunciation, and which was withdrawn before its première (it is now known) not at Shostakovich's request but at the bidding of the Composers'

[49] See Paul de Man, 'Autobiography as Defacement', in *The Rhetoric of Romanticism* (New York, 1984), 67.

Union leadership.[50] This combination of circumstances made it inevitable that when the symphony was finally performed twenty-five years later, in 1961, it was received as the composer's first note-in-a-bottle. Reading the symphony as autobiography reached a predictable height of impertinence (that is, of trivial specificity) with MacDonald,[51] but there is something about it that does seem naggingly to foreground the issue, namely the extremes within the symphony of inwardness and extroversion, and the manifestly ironic way in which these extremes are juxtaposed and even interchanged.

What I am calling the issue is the one that was framed by the doomed poet Osip Mandelstam, who in the 1920s argued that lyric poetry, the novel, and what he called 'psychological prose' were inappropriate for Soviet art because the historical epoch no longer had any 'interest in the human fate of the individual'.[52] One could make a case that the young Shostakovich, the composer of those callous 'new-objective' early symphonies, operas, and ballets, shared that outlook, and it was an attitude by no means confined in those days to the Soviet state. But that was before Mandelstam discovered what, a couple of years later, Shostakovich, too, would learn: that when the Soviet state turned against you, you were indeed one man alone; and your individual fate mattered to you, if not to the epoch.

The last movement of Shostakovich's Fourth Symphony has two codas. The first, which seems a parody of the 'Gloria' chorus from Stravinsky's *Oedipus Rex*, may be the most raucous and deafening passage of symphonic music ever composed. The muted, drawn-out whimper that trumps it, though, is what stays in the mind, deliberate echo that it is (right down to the harp and celesta) of Mahler, the most self-absorbed bourgeois neurotic subject of them all. This music, which was almost certainly composed post-denunciation, seems palpably to set the inner and the outer, the public and the private, the manic, turbulent collective and the human fate of the bruised individual, in blunt, easily read (indeed, as it turned out, too easily read) opposition.

But this simple message from the bottle seems foreshadowed—ambiguously, enigmatically, uncertainly, not at all easily—in the first movement, which has not such an obvious *ex post facto* relationship to the events of the composer's life. After a rude raspberry of an introductory leitmotif, the stomping first theme gets under way in a series of aggressively revolting parade-ground colours: an octave pairing of trumpet and tenor trombone is answered by one of bass trombone and tuba, and finally by a pair of tubas, doubled flatulently by the bassoon and contrabassoon. Though not without detours, the first thematic group continually gathers sonority and stridency until it fairly explodes in a

---

[50] I. Glikman, '. . . Ya vse ravno budu pisat' muzyku', *Sovetskaya muzyka*, no. 9 (1989), 47; *Pis'ma k drugu*, 12–13.

[51] See *The New Shostakovich*, 109–17.

[52] Quoted in Jane Gary Harris, editor's introduction to *Autobiographical Statements in Twentieth-Century Russian Literature* (Princeton, 1990), 13.

crazy squawking. After a general pause, the second group begins in the tiny voice of the solo bassoon, accompanied by isolated grunts from the cellos and basses, the harp finally entering to mark off the cadence. This is public versus private with a caricatural vengeance. No one could miss it. But when the themes are recapitulated at the other end of the movement, the smug stability of the dualism is undermined. The theme that had been given to the solo bassoon comes back in the paired (and now doubled) trumpet and trombone over the stomping chords, and the theme that had represented the blustery parade-ground follows, played *pianissimo* by the solo bassoon, accompanied by the same low strings, but now with the addition of a quietly insistent bass drum.

I cannot really say exactly what this disquieting exchange of roles means. I have no ready verbal paraphrase with which to replace it, and I have no ready answer to a friend of mine, a composer, who asked, 'Why couldn't he just have been experimenting?' (except maybe Varèse's answer: 'My experiments end up in the wastebasket, not the score'). But my uncertainty may be one reason why the movement haunts me the way it does. Maybe incertitude—irreducible multivalence—is essential to the experience of the symphony as a work of art. There is more to an art work, one has to think, than there is to a note in a bottle.

I am pretty sure I do know what the Eighth Quartet is all about. Shostakovich has seen to that. This is the one composition of his that asks expressly to be read as autobiography, the one time Shostakovich did put an explicit note in a bottle. And, although my saying so may win me few friends, I believe that this melancholy, much admired work of 1960 reveals something beyond its intended message—something I, for one, would rather not believe. What it shows is that the need to communicate urgently and with specificity in an atmosphere of threat did at times shrink Shostakovich's creative options.

The wry relationship between the stated programme—a requiem for the 'victims of war and Fascism', allegedly prompted by the viewing of atrocity footage in Dresden—and the music, which consists almost wholly of the DSCH motif in thematic conjunction with allusions to Shostakovich's earlier works, the martyred *Lady Macbeth* especially prominent among them, was evident from the start. Shostakovich was clearly identifying himself as victim. The point is made over and over again. The motifs associated with the composer's musical monogram include a Jewish theme from the finale of the Second Piano Trio, which overlaps three of the four notes in DSCH, reinforcing the association Shostakovich had already proclaimed between his personal fate and that of the Jews, and also the first theme of the First Cello Concerto, which overlaps a different three of the four notes in the monogram. The Cello Concerto idea is confronted with a violent motif that had been associated in a film score, *The Young Guard*, with executions. In the final movement, the DSCH motif is played in exquisitely wrought dissonant counterpoint against the main continuity motif from the last scene of *Lady Macbeth*, which depicts a convoy of prisoners *en route* to Siberia.

All of this, as I say, is clear—and became clearer, in another instance of changing contexts and accumulating subtexts, when *Lady Macbeth* was restored to the active repertoire a year after the Quartet's premiere, with an expanded final scene. And yet, by hooking this self-dramatizing quartet onto 'his' side's most hallowed and heavily exploited official propaganda motif of the cold war— namely, that it was the Soviet Union that had saved the world from fascism— Shostakovich forced the work's official acceptance despite the clarity of its latent message (not to mention the incoherence of the manifest one), and even its official promotion. This was, in its way, an impressive political coup.

The most searing page in Isaak Glikman's book is the one in which he describes the actual biographical subtext to the Eighth Quartet, corroborating previous reports by Galina Vishnevskaya and Vladimir Ashkenazy, among others, but adding a wealth of poignant detail.[53] Shostakovich was being pressured to join the Communist Party as a trophy, and had not found within himself the fortitude to resist. It was in an agony of humiliation and self-reproach, as much as an agony of revulsion at Fascist atrocities, that he conceived this work, and it was offered as an apologia, in the first instance to his own conscience.

The central strategy, it now seems clear, was to contrive the pointed conjunction, which takes place near the end of the fourth movement, between the DSCH motif and the one extensive quotation that does not come from one of Shostakovich's own works, namely the famous song of revolutionary martyr-dom that begins with the words *Zamuchen tyazheloi nevolei*, which mean, literally, 'tortured by grievous unfreedom'. The citation was insulated from official suspicion by the fact, known to every Soviet schoolchild, that this was one of Lenin's favourite songs. Yet by appropriating it, Shostakovich was, as it were, giving his quartet not only a subtext but, literally, a text, proclaiming his unfreedom and disclaiming responsibility for what he judged in himself to be an act of cowardice, or rather, a craven failure to act.

The Eighth Quartet is thus a wrenching human document: wrenching the way Glikman's commentary to it is wrenching, or the way . . . well, the way a note in a bottle can be wrenching. But its explicitness exacts a price. The quotations are lengthy and literal, amounting in the crucial fourth movement to an inert medley; the thematic transformations are very demonstratively, perhaps over-demonstratively, elaborated; startling juxtapositions are reiterated till they become familiar. The work provides its own running paraphrase, and the paraphrase moves inevitably into the foreground of consciousness as the note patterns become predictable.

The compulsion to write in this virtually telegraphic or stenographic way was unquestionably an inner compulsion. Its sincerity compels a strong empathic response; and yet the work, I feel, is weakened by it nevertheless. I

[53] *Pis'ma k drugu*, 160–1; see also Jasper Parrott with Vladimir Ashkenazy, *Beyond Frontiers* (London, 1984), 55–6; and Galina Vishnevskaya, *Galina* (New York, 1984), 399–400.

do not find myself returning to it with renewed anticipation of discovery, and when I do find myself listening to it, I seem to be listening to it the way determined paraphrasts like Ian MacDonald evidently listen to every Shostakovich piece. MacDonald himself reveals the danger of such listening when he comes to evaluate the Ninth and Tenth Quartets, works to which the musical imagination—my musical imagination, at any rate—responds with less coercion and more imaginative energy. Finding in it nothing beyond the same anti-Stalinist programme he finds in every Shostakovich piece, MacDonald writes dismissively, 'one can be forgiven for thinking that we have been over this ground once too often'.[54] Having ears only for the paraphrase, he is unable to distinguish one quartet from another, or distinguish his own hectoring, monotonous voice from Shostakovich's.

Ultimately, what is wrong with MacDonald's approach, for all that one may sympathize with readings that respect the reality of the latent content, is the same thing that was wrong with many of the radically revisionist readings of Shostakovich that emanated out of the Soviet Union during the *glasnost* years that now seem so long ago. In both cases, Shostakovich has been assimilated to inappropriate ready-made models. In the failing Soviet Union he was cast as a 'dissident' of a sort that simply did not exist during the better (or rather, the worse) part of his lifetime. In the West, he has been cast as an alienated modernist. Both moves reduce him to a stereotype.

To read in MacDonald's book, for example, that the 'Leningrad' Symphony was just another exercise in sarcasm or mockery is painful. At a time when White émigrés like Stravinsky and Rachmaninov were raising funds and sending supplies for Russian war relief, and when even Anton Denikin, the White general who had led the attack on Moscow during the Russian Civil War, was calling upon the Allies to open up the 'second front' in support of the Soviet Union, Shostakovich is portrayed as heartlessly self-absorbed, obsessed with unassuageable feelings of personal resentment and disaffection.

It is here that Glikman's book, and others like it, can offer the most valuable corrective. The mature Shostakovich was not a dissident. Nor was he a modernist. The mature Shostakovich was an *intelligent* (pronounced, Russian-style, with a hard g, and the stress on the last syllable), heir to a noble tradition of artistic and social thought—one that abhorred injustice and political repression, but also one that valued social commitment, participation in one's community, and solidarity with people. Shostakovich's mature idea of art, in contrast to the egoistic traditions of Western modernism, was based not on alienation but on service. He found a way of maintaining public service and personal integrity under unimaginably hard conditions. In this way he remained, in the time-honoured Russian if not exactly the Soviet sense of the word, a 'civic' artist.

[54] *The New Shostakovich*, 234.

That was the ultimate irony, and the ultimate victory. Like the silenced Akhmatova and the martyred Mandelstam, Shostakovich, as the American Slavist Clare Cavanagh so movingly suggested at the Ann Arbor Shostakovich conference in 1994, managed to bear witness 'against the state on behalf of its citizenry'. This was perhaps the most honourable civic use to which music has ever been put, a use in which the composer and his audience acted in collusion against authority. Music was the only art that could serve this purpose publicly. Never was its value more gloriously affirmed.

And that is why Shostakovich's music, while easy for advanced musicians in the West to deride, has always tugged at their conscience, making it necessary for them to deride it. The extreme social value placed on this music—by official ideology, to be sure, but also by disorderly, 'carnivalistic' folk tradition (to borrow once again from Bakhtin's rich vocabulary)—has made the overweening technical preoccupations of the West look frivolous. The present rash of opportunistic efforts—by Volkov, by MacDonald, even by Glikman—authoritatively to define the meaning of Shostakovich's work can only diminish that value and work against the interests of composer and audience alike. Definitive reading, especially biographical reading, locks the music in the past. Better let it remain supple, adaptable, ready to serve the future's needs.

The significance of Dmitry Dmitrievich Shostakovich in and for the history of twentieth-century music is immense, possibly unparalleled, and, above all, continuing. Anyone interested in that history or alive to the issues his work so dramatically embodies will listen to it (*pace* Virgil Thomson) without mind-wandering, unless musical perceptions are wholly divorced from moral perceptions. The fact that his work still looms in our consciousness, while that of so many once better-regarded figures has receded unregretted into Lethe, suggests that the divorce is not yet final. The fate of the music, of its composer, and of the society from which they both emerged, have made it, quite apart from its composer's designs or those of any critic, precisely into a bulwark against that divorce. Smug paraphrasts notwithstanding, it is unlikely that we who live in more favoured times and places can ever fully come to grips with such a legacy. Given our scholarly and critical interests, this may seem lamentable. In the context of our lives as we live them, it is something to rejoice in.

2

Shostakovich in Harmony:
Untranslatable Messages

DAVID FANNING

I

The context *is* fascinating. Shostakovich's relationships with literary figures, with friends and fellow-musicians, with the power-brokers in the Soviet system, and, not least, with women,[1] are all pertinent to the many enigmas of his musical legacy; and it is vital, not only for our understanding of Shostakovich the Man but also for the general de-mythologizing of Soviet cultural history, that a lot more Russian material, including his voluminous correspondence, should become available in translation, properly commented on by writers sensitive to the way Russian minds work. But what is it that we are trying to get *in* context? Were it not for the music he created, we would not now be so avidly attending Shostakovich concerts, buying recordings, organizing conferences, and publishing books. Looking at recent trends in published commentaries, there is reason to fear that his career may become merely an arena for ideological mud-slinging, and however fascinating it may be to observe the swing of the Shostakovich reception history pendulum, we may not thereby be getting any closer to what makes the music tick. We surely need to remember that even the bravest composer, the most subversive, the most socio-politically challenged, the most politically correct composer, never gained immortality on that strength alone. Music commemorating the victims of pogrom, holocaust, terror, and atom bomb has to be more than anecdote or reportage if it is to survive; unless, that is, we are prepared to yield to emotional blackmail. And Shostakovich's major concert works, including the most overtly commemorative, survive, because they speak to listeners who have never heard of Stalin's Great Terror. They spoke to Western audiences long before the appearance of Volkov's *Testimony*. Do they really speak so differently now that the historical

I should like to acknowledge the valuable comments of my Manchester colleagues John Casken and Geoff Poole, and especially Jo Barber, on an early version of this article.

[1] See 'Zhenshchini v ego zhizni', in Sofya Khentova, *Udivitelnyi Shostakovich* (St Petersburg, 1993), 89–170.

background is so comparatively openly revealed? Do they not communicate, in significant part at least, by means of complexities of formal and harmonic language, the analysis of which is at the same time an analysis of that communication?

The question of what kind of analysis is now begged. But I want to approach an answer by way of a little further reflection on Shostakovich commentary. I am addressing here not only my frustration with the tendency to trivialize Shostakovich's music by 'reading' it in the manner of a pop-up story-book. I am also responding to the suspicion sometimes voiced that at least some of the music may indeed work that way, and that this is a sign of artistic weakness. For instance, Bayan Northcott, one of the most thoughtful British musical essayists, has lumped Shostakovich in with Schnittke as appealing 'primarily to the *zeitgeist* and never mind the notes';[2] and rather more subtly Richard Taruskin has written apropos Shostakovich's post-Fifth Symphony works:

> The changes wrought in him by his ordeals lent his voice a moral authority perhaps unmatched in all of twentieth-century music. But the impulse to communicate urgently in an atmosphere of threat did lead, at times, to an overreliance on extroversive reference as bearer of essential meaning, and a correspondingly debased level of musical discourse.[3]

'Extroversive' is a term originating in Russian literary theory of the 1920s, and it has been proposed in an influential study by V. Kofi Agawu as a useful jargon word for those aspects of musical meaning which derive from outside the work in question. Its complementary opposite is 'introversive', which denotes the meaning created by the structural processes of music *per se*.[4] Of course what constitutes 'over-reliance' or 'a debased level of musical discourse' is a moot point, and Taruskin's examination of irony in the present volume fleshes out his argument impressively. Nor would anyone want to deny that Shostakovich's music is unusually rich in extroversive reference, especially in works such as the Eighth String Quartet which provoke Taruskin's doubts. But the implication of a poverty of introversive design, coming from such an authoritative source, represents a challenge that Shostakovich commentators ignore at their peril.[5]

Of course there is an analytical literature which addresses the introversive

---

[2] *Independent*, Saturday 11 May 1991, classical music page.

[3] Taruskin, 'Public Lies and Unmentionable Truth: Interpreting Shostakovich's Fifth Symphony', in David Fanning, *Shostakovich Studies* (Cambridge, 1995), 55.

[4] V. Kofi Agawu, *Playing with Signs* (Princeton, 1991), chs. 2 and 3. There are, of course, many variations of terminology for defining this fundamental symbiosis in musical meaning. Similar helpful pairings are 'immanent/extrinsic' (see Patrick McCreless, 'The Cycle of Structure and the Cycle of Meaning: The Piano Trio in E minor, Op. 67', in Fanning, *Shostakovich Studies*, 113–36, and 'connotative/denotative' (see Vera Micznik, 'Meaning in Gustav Mahler's Music: A Historical and Analytical Study Focusing on the Ninth Symphony', Ph. D. diss., State University of New York at Stony Brook, 1989). Nowhere, arguably, is the distinction between and the interrelation of such complementary opposites so crucial and so problematic as with Mahler and Shostakovich.

[5] If responding to it appears to align me with what Rose Rosengard Subotnik has dubbed 'Anglo-American empiricists', who prefer to ignore the question of ideology and certainly never declare

aspect of Shostakovich, and it is by no means a negligible one. It includes a mountain of Russian studies,[6] two published British doctoral dissertations,[7] a few, (remarkably few!) unpublished American doctoral dissertations,[8] and one from Germany.[9] Between them the non-Russian studies have a fair amount to

Ex. 2.1

Lady Macbeth

[Dolzhansky, 'Aleksandriiskii pentakhord']

their own, as opposed to the 'Continental metaphysicists' (approved by her) who rarely get to grips with the musical text itself, so be it. Subotnik elaborates on the distinction in 'The Role of Ideology in the Study of Western Music', *Journal of Musicology*, 2 (1983), 1–12.

[6] The most recent extensive listings are in Laurel Fay's bibliography to the Shostakovich chapter in Gerald Abraham *et al.*, *The New Grove Russian Masters 2* (London, 1986) and in Ernst Kuhn (ed.), *'Volksfeind Dmitri Schostakowitsch'* (Berlin, 1997), 231–75. See also the bibliography in Ellon Carpenter, 'The Theory of Music in Russia and the Soviet Union, ca. 1650–1950', Ph. D. diss., University of Pennsylvania, 1988, iii. 1369–92, and 'Russian Theorists on Modality in Shostakovich's Music', in Fanning, *Shostakovich Studies*, 96–112.

[7] Richard Longman, *Expression and Structure: Processes of Integration in the Large-scale Instrumental Music of Dmitri Shostakovich* (New York and London, 1989); Eric Roseberry, *Ideology, Style, Content, and Thematic Process in the Symphonies, Cello Concertos, and String Quartets of Shostakovich* (New York and London, 1989).

[8] Laurel Fay, 'The Last Quartets of Dmitrii Shostakovich: A Stylistic Investigation', Ph. D. diss., Cornell University, 1978; Ellon Carpenter, 'The Theory of Music' (see note 6 above); David Haas, 'Form and line in the Music and Musical Thought of Leningrad: 1917–1932', Ph. D. diss., University of Michigan, 1989.

[9] Karen Kopp, *Form und Gehalt der Symphonien des Dmitrij Schostakowitsch* (Bonn, 1990).

say about form in the large-scale works and about thematic transformation, which are contributions not to be underestimated. Large-scale form is after all the arena for Shostakovich's musical dramas, and thematic transformation is in many instances the powerhouse. But most of these studies shy away from harmonic and tonal language, or if they do tackle it, they come seriously to grief. Yet it is precisely in this area, I would argue, that much of the power of Shostakovich's message—the musical, universal, and untranslatable message—resides. I have chosen three brief examples, spanning progressively longer musical paragraphs, to illustrate the problems scholars have encountered in this area and to outline some possible ways to engage with them more fruitfully.

The first is from the passacaglia in *The Lady Macbeth of Mtsensk District*, just after the death of Katerina's father-in-law in the middle of Act II (p. 152 in the Sikorski vocal score, Hamburg, 1979; pp. 250–1 in their unpublished full score; the first bar of Ex. 2.1 is an analytical reduction of Shostakovich's harmony). The East German scholar Eckart Kröplin tells us that the home key is D minor,[10] which is plausible enough until we notice the perfect cadences in C sharp minor which frame the theme. It is true that Shostakovich, like ground-bass composers from Purcell on, deliberately keeps the boundaries between statements of the theme fluid, but the continual harmonic and textural reassertion of C sharp minor (at five of the succeeding eleven rotations of the theme—figs. 286, 288, 290, 291, 292), suggests that Kröplin has made a straightforward misdiagnosis. Russian scholars from Alexander Dolzhansky onwards have argued far more persuasively that the pitch structure here is modal—rooted on C sharp, with flat second, fourth, fifth, and octave degrees as modifications to the minor scale, an extension of what Dolzhansky dubbed the Alexandrian pentachord.[11] Viewed in this perspective the affective quality of the theme has to do with the modal flattening of an extraordinary number of scale degrees. The expressive curve of the passacaglia as a whole is determined not only by its obvious relentless textural accumulation but also by the flux of relative 'flatness' in the scale degrees superimposed on the theme.

Kröplin is no soft target. On a musicological, as distinct from analytical, level his book is a masterly documentary study. But his discussion of *Lady Macbeth* is the only one in any language, so far as I know, which attempts to assign tonal areas to specific sections; its misdiagnoses are unfortunate (another is discussed below). They are also symptomatic of Western scholarship's generally shaky grasp of harmonic context in Shostakovich and of a deficient acquaintance with Russian theory. If we can get such initial diagnoses right, we stand a much better chance of commenting perceptively on the music's harmonic qualities,

---

[10] Kröplin, *Frühe sowjetische Oper* (Berlin, 1985), 224. His observation is repeated without acknowledgement in Michael Koball, *Pathos und Groteske: Die deutsche Tradition im symphonischen Schaffen von Dmitri Schostakowitsch* (Berlin, 1997), 261.

[11] Aleksandr Dolzhansky, 'Aleksandriiskii pentakhord v muzyke D. Shostakovicha', in Givi Ordzhonikidze, *Dmitri Shostakovich* (Moscow, 1967), 402.

and hence on its emotional qualities too. That goes not just for specific instances like the *Lady Macbeth* passacaglia, but also for larger musical time-spans.

That is precisely where Russian studies stop short. As Ellon Carpenter has commented:

> Modal language in Shostakovich's music has not been addressed in its totality, but only in part. Now that the unfolding of its diatonic basis has been examined [by Russian scholars], a more processive and all-inclusive approach needs to be applied, in order to reveal each piece's unique modal-tonal embodiment in and contribution to the thematic structure.[12]

Here is another important challenge—one I intend to take up with my next two examples. Kröplin is once again misleading in his analysis of the second scene in *Lady Macbeth*, that of Aksinya's molestation, where he diagnoses the opening as G flat (minor).[13] The first few bars are given at the beginning of Ex. 2.2, and a

Ex. 2.2

Lady Macbeth, Act 1

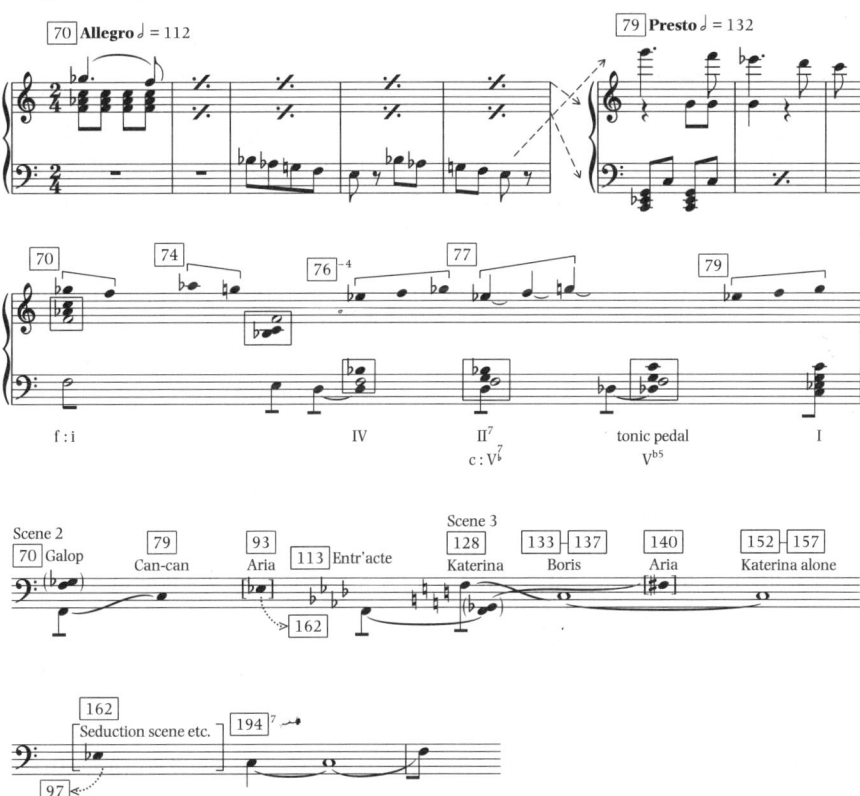

[12] Carpenter, 'Russian Theorists' (see n. 6), 112.   [13] Kröplin, *Frühe sowjetische Oper*, 222.

glance at the score confirms that the home key is clearly F minor, with G/G flat as a modally variable second degree of the scale.

What is then interesting, bearing Carpenter's challenge in mind, is to trace how Shostakovich spans the following 68 bars to the C minor of the next part of the scene, whose opening bars are given at the end of the top system of Ex. 2.2 (that is, how he links his galop to his cancan, to use Kröplin's helpful labels).[14] The second system of Ex. 2.2 shows one way of charting the process. Sketched here is a kind of middleground summary, showing an internal pedal-note on F, a top line focused on the modally variable second degree (G/G flat), a gradual stepwise bass descent, and a pivot harmony at fig. 77 from F minor to C minor.

Admittedly this does little more than point to harmonic continuity; the *character* of the music is established at the outset in a kind of Stravinsky *Les Noces* texture, fast-forwarded in silent film manner, giving an effect at once faintly ethnic and mechanically distorted. But the stretching out of the modulatory process indicated in Ex. 2.2 is in itself an important compositional resource. It elevates the manic, sado-primitive character of the musical texture to, or at least towards, the realms of high art; it gives medium-term directional focus to the 'linear polyphony' characteristic of Shostakovich's pre-1936 style;[15] it has the potential, should the composer choose, to mediate between, or shade into, more conventionally tonal, modal, or even atonal writing. In this instance it is also part of a larger framework of tonal coherence. As the last two systems of Ex. 2.2 suggest, the F minor to C minor progression underpins the entire key structure of Scenes Two and Three.

A detailed comparison of the ways in which that progression is effected would be no easy task, and its place would be in a specialist journal rather than here. But I believe it would tell us something significant about the way the structure of these scenes 'breathes'. That would help us to be more precise about how *Lady Macbeth* represents such a huge advance on Shostakovich's other theatre scores of the time, which contain so many similar thematic ideas to the opera without developing or exploiting them to the full.[16]

The still more general point here is that there are continuities in the middleground of Shostakovich's most carefully composed works, which do not immediately leap to the ear, which have not been researched (or at least written about), and which have much to do with the way we hold our breath, musically speaking, over long time-spans. And *that* is something I take to be one of the prime symptoms of great music.

An even more direct response to Ellon Carpenter's challenge may be possible

[14] Kröplin, *Frühe sowjetische Oper*, 222.

[15] For a discussion of which see e.g. Detlef Gojowy, *Neue sowjetische Musik der 20er Jahre* (Laaber, 1980), 122–32, 258–96.

[16] Notable in this respect is the music-hall review *Uslovno ubityi* [*Declared Dead*, or as it is commonly known, *Hypothetically Murdered*] in which the cancan music of scene two of the opera is used to represent a bacchanale.

with reference to the second movement of the Tenth Symphony, clarifying a number of thoughts I have set out elsewhere.[17] Here my example of an alarming diagnosis is from Richard Longman's published dissertation.[18] He contends that the movement ends in E flat major, from fig. 99 in the score (Ex. 2.3). That the E flat is in fact plagal to an actual ending on the movement's tonic of B flat minor can be verified by playing a recording and testing each of the two keys for tonic status after the movement has finished.

Ex. 2.3

In fact Longman proposes changes of tonal centre at ten points in the movement. Rather than arguing the toss in each instance I would suggest that these are *all* fictions, with no more key status than the intermediate chords boxed in my previous example. A more coherent and unified view of the pitch structure is shown in the top three systems of Ex. 2.4. These show three eight-note modes divided into minor-third scale segments, differentiated in the musical structure by deviations from pure octatony (square brackets) and by which of the third-segments is exploited thematically (shown by slurs). To show a little more detail, the middle of Ex. 2.4 rejigs Longman's key centres in terms of that same modal hierarchy, comprising pitch centres, modal supports, modal links, and non-modal notes. From this hierarchic notation may be gauged something of the psychological 'distance' of each phase of the music both from the 'tonic' B flat minor and from the controlling modes.

What I am trying to represent in this movement is nothing less than the essence of Shostakovich's long-range harmonic thinking. On one level I foresee the possibility of viewing a structure like this one in an important and still under-researched historical line—of composers who exploit the intersection between mode and major-minor tonality.[19] Nor do I think it is too much to claim that in elaborating on this topic we may uncover one missing link between the way we experience Shostakovich's music and what we so often read about it. In the case of the movement just analysed, the hypothesis would be that Shostakovich's shifts of interval content within one referential mode are

---

[17] *The Breath of the Symphonist: Shostakovich's Tenth* (London, 1988), 39–46.

[18] *Expression and Structure*, 132.

[19] For an investigation into the history of the octatonic mode see Richard Taruskin, 'Chernomor to Kashchei: Harmonic Sorcery; or, Stravinsky's "Angle"', *Journal of the American Musicological Society*, 38 (1985), 72–142; for modal techniques in Russian music of the 1920s see Peter Deane Roberts, *Modernism in Russian Piano Music: Skriabin, Prokofiev, and their Russian Contemporaries* (Bloomington, Ind., 1993). Major composers whose blend of modality and harmony deserves fuller investigation include Sibelius, Nielsen, Vaughan Williams, Ravel.

Ex. 2.4

Tenth Symphony, II

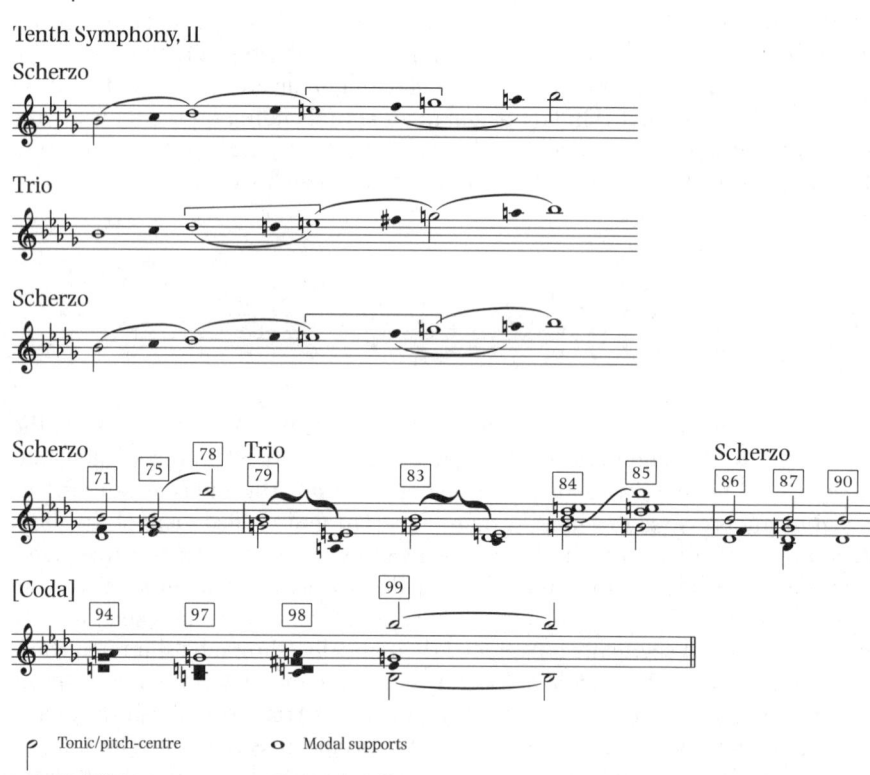

| ♩ | Tonic/pitch-centre | o | Modal supports |
| ● | Modal links | ■ | Non-modal degree |

a way of achieving motion within motionlessness—specific types of motion, in fact, within a specific type of motionlessness. That in turn helps to explain how the sensation of fruitless struggle, signalled extroversively in the main theme's often-noted reference to the opening of *Boris Godunov* and in the violent dynamics and scoring, is also conveyed introversively in the underlying structure. Maybe it was an injudicious leap on my part to suggest that this is all consistent with the 'portrait of Stalin' view in Volkov's *Testimony*.[20] But in principle I believe that the trend in recent musicology to look at the overlap of hermeneutics and analysis is a healthy one,[21] and for all the risks of subjectivity and bogus scholarship it entails, it certainly beckons invitingly to anyone seriously engaged with Shostakovich's music.[22]

[20] *The Breath of the Symphonist*, 44.

[21] See e.g. Lawrence Kramer, 'Haydn's Chaos, Schenker's Order; or, Hermeneutics and Musical Analysis: Can They Mix?', *19th-Century Music*, 16 (Summer 1992), 3–17. Kramer's first footnote lists further prominent examples of this tendency.

[22] For a further illustration see my editor's introduction to *Shostakovich Studies*, 9–12.

II

There is a further dimension which overlaps with the concerns of the theorist and the cultural historian and which tends to be overlooked by both. It is not unique to Shostakovich—far from it—but it is almost uniquely thought-provoking in his case. It concerns musical interpretation in the everyday sense of performance.

One reason for the continuing disagreements about the character, or even the ideology, of Shostakovich's music may simply be that we encounter it in such widely diverging performances. The finale of the Ninth Symphony is a case in point. Consider the Russian liner note to Kirill Kondrashin's recording: 'The bassoon introduces an uncomplicated melody, which is quickly caught up by the strings, and the music is once more possessed of a light, carefree atmosphere, speeding to the end with happy exhilaration.'[23]

Anyone with access to the recording in question (at the time of writing it is available on CD from BMG Classics/Melodiya 74321 19846-2, but not with the original liner note) can verify that Kondrashin's interpretation flies in the face of that description. But if we listen to Haitink in the same movement in 1985 the 'light carefree atmosphere' does indeed predominate (Decca 414 677-2).

Kondrashin's view of the finale is consistent with a description such as Ian MacDonald's (if we make allowances for his over-enthusiastic final sentence):

A dark whirlwind now seizes the movement, driving it to a climax of teetering expectation—but all that emerges is the clownish main theme, hammered out on the entire orchestra in a peroration of towering bathos. Shostakovich's contempt is scalding. Here are your leaders, jeers the music: circus clowns.[24]

It should be said that the two polarized descriptions I have quoted do not represent a consistent East–West division or even a then-and-now one. In many ways Russian commentators have been far more ready to discuss the blackness of the Ninth Symphony's humour than have Western ones.[25] And in Mariss Jansons'1992 EMI recording (CDC7 54339-2) all three liner notes, in English, French, and German, go along with the view of the work as essentially happy and serene—which is a bit disturbing, even if they do have the composer's own

---

[23] Semyon Shlifshteyn, liner note to EMI ASD 2409 [1966].

[24] MacDonald, *The New Shostakovich* (London, 1990), 179.

[25] For Russian summaries of the Ninth Symphony's reception history see Sof'ya Khentova, *Shostakovich: zhizn' i tvorchestvo*, ii (Leningrad, 1986), 210–18, and Marina Sabinina, *Shostakovich— Simfonist: dramaturgiya, estetika, stil'* (Moscow, 1976), 267–74; for Sabinina's own emphasis on the symphony's subtext [*podtekst*] see esp. p. 269. For shorter Western summaries see Boris Schwarz, *Music and Musical Life in Soviet Russia* (Bloomington, Ind., 1983), 210–11; Günter Wolter, *Dmitrii Schostakowitsch, eine sowjetische Tragödie: Rezeptionsgeschichte* (Frankfurt-am-Main and New York, 1991), 80–3; and Michael Downes, 'The Politics of Musical Criticism: A Study of Some Works by Dmitri Shostakovich', M. Phil. diss., Cambridge University, 1991, 61–7.

precedent for saying so.[26] But the point I should like to stress is that discrepant reactions may have to do not so much with different ideologies or climates of opinion as with genuine reactions to divergent styles of performance; such performance variations should perhaps make us all the more wary about the meanings we assign to this music.

Such permissiveness should not be the last word. There are at least some halfway-objective criteria for evaluating these interpretations. What makes Kondrashin's performance so very different and apparently so much more in touch with the *podtekst*, as identified by Sabinina and other Russian commentators? Arguably it is a case of surface detail allying character to structure, and hence the extroversive to introversive dimensions of meaning. For instance, Kondrashin's bassoonist adds insinuating crescendos to the long notes in the opening theme, pointedly leaves out the notated crescendo in bars 12 and 13 (the notated crescendos are then emphasized in the strings' immediate repetition of the theme), and slides drunkenly into the succeeding staccatos. All this highlights the instability of the theme's paradoxical slow polka character. But at the same time it anticipates the vehement aspect of the theme revealed nearly 300 bars later at the recapitulation (fig. 94). This and the high-profile dynamic nuances of the second and third themes (from figs. 72 and 77) serve to undermine the surface cheerfulness of subsequent returns of the main theme (figs. 75 and 81, the latter marking the beginning of the development section).

Virtually all performances of this movement have to decide how and where to increase the tempo (later publications of the score carry guiding metronome marks). Kondrashin manages to achieve the most compelling of overall accelerandos over the entire exposition and development sections, not by progressively pushing the tempo, but by details of phrasing, dynamic, and accentuation, which combine to suggest the sensation of driving on full throttle and gradually releasing the brakes. But he also adds a steep unnotated stringendo over the six bars leading to fig. 89, which just happen to be the point of maximum harmonic instability in the development section. This he subsequently balances with an exaggeration of the composer's ritardando over the four bars into the recapitulation (from fig. 94^{-4}), thereby preparing for the main theme itself to come in with a horrible swagger. Here again is interpretative licence in powerful alliance with introversive factors.

There is one more very concrete reason why Kondrashin's recording sounds so different from Haitink's. In 1961 a revised edition of the score was published, which is the basis for the current Collected Works score. It contains an apparently slight, but actually crucial rescoring of the recapitulation of the second theme (figs. $95–96^4$), adding violins to the woodwind to achieve a good balance without sacrificing the overall *fortissimo* dynamic (Ex. 2.5). The effect is

[26] For the composer's comments on the work see Lev Grigoriev and Yakov Platek, eds., *Dmitry Shostakovich about Himself and his Times*, trans. A. and N. Roxburgh (Moscow, 1981), 117.

that the swagger of the recapitulation can be prolonged and therefore the whole dramatic scale of the movement heightened. Where the reinstrumentation comes from is anyone's guess. Typically the Complete Edition commentary gives no clue, and the extensive literature on the work, including Shostakovich's and Kondrashin's own writings, sheds no light on the revision.[27]

Ex. 2.5

Personally I would be inclined to cite Kondrashin's contact with the composer as further circumstantial evidence of his superior insight. But to go into questions of authenticity or faithfulness to the composer would require looking at all sorts of other evidence, including Shostakovich's own recordings of such things as the Piano Quintet, the Second Piano Trio and the piano duet version of the Tenth Symphony.[28] That is another story. There are enough hazards already in the issues I have raised in this chapter. It may be true that quantifying and interpreting performance deviations from a score is more a matter for journalistic criticism than for scholarly discourse. And the dangers inherent in analysis and criticism are well known—that analysis tends to reify the text and criticism to fetishize the performance.[29] But the dangers of neglecting these dimensions are just as clear. By all means let us continue uncovering ideological, autobiographical, and documentary 'subtexts', but let us also not forget that musical meaning is just as important a part of the meaning of Shostakovich's music.

[27] See e.g. Kondrashin's 'Moi vstrechi s D. D. Shostakovichem' [My meetings with D. D. Shostakovich], in Grigory Shneyerson, ed., *D. Shostakovich: Stat'i i materiali* (Moscow, 1976), 86–97; for Shostakovich's attention to balance in rehearsal see esp. p. 92. On Kondrashin's 'decodings' of Shostakovich symphonies, with the composer's knowledge, see his 'Statement at Bucknell University', New York, 9 Sept. 1980, reprinted in *Behind the Mask*, unpublished typescript, ed. Alan Mercer and Ian MacDonald [1992]. On Shostakovich's disapproval of Koussevitzky's tempi in the first recording of the work (leading to a second recording taking the composer's wishes into account) see Khentova, *Shostakovich*, ii. 214. On Shostakovich's corrections after rehearsal, taking into account Mravinsky's interpretation, see ibid. 214–15.

[28] For details see entries for these works in Derek Hulme, *Dmitri Shostakovich: A Catalogue, Bibliography, and Discography*, 2nd edn. (Oxford, 1991).

[29] See the conference Round Table programme on 'Analysis and Interpretation in Musical Criticism', chaired by Joseph Kerman, summarized in *Acta Musicologica* 59 (1987), 30. For further stimulating thoughts on the importance of performance insights see Richard Taruskin, 'On Letting the Music Speak for Itself: Some Reflections on Musicology and Performance', *Journal of Musicology*, 1 (1982), 338–49.

3

Shostakovich's Literary Style

SVETLANA SAVENKO

The writings of composers represent material of enduring interest. As is well known, Schumann, Wagner, Tchaikovsky, Scriabin, Prokofiev, and a whole host of other musicians were also active as journalists, philosophers, poets, or librettists, and their literary legacies have traditionally been made the subject of scholarly enquiry along with their musical compositions. It is also hard to overestimate the importance of personal writings such as letters and diaries for establishing a rounded picture of the creative personality. It should be noted, however, that composers' writings are usually treated as biographical material rather than as works of art in their own right, and are only rarely subjected to scholarly analysis—of the kind which attempts to make a connection between the everyday, mainly colloquial, language of personal documents and the elevated style of deliberately artistic expression. Not all letters and diaries can sustain this level of close study, but in certain instances it can yield interesting results, and Shostakovich's writings certainly fall into this category.

As is well known, any study of Shostakovich's writings presents considerable, and specific problems. The first problem is that of authenticity. It is as though their author were not a man of the twentieth century, who died a mere twenty years ago or so, but some legendary medieval master whose ancient texts have first to be identified before they can be studied. All the more valuable then is recently published material, the authenticity of whose provenance is beyond doubt, such as the book 'Letters to a Friend: Dmitry Shostakovich's Letters to Isaak Glikman'[1] and also the small collection of Shostakovich's letters to Lev Lebedinsky.[2] It is upon these materials that this article is based. Objections may justifiably be raised regarding the incompleteness of the source material, but a narrow focus is actually appropriate for this kind of study.

Dmitry Shostakovich certainly possessed a highly individual literary style. This style had certain innate and, as it were, genetic qualities which appeared when he

---

[1] *Pis'ma k drugu: Pis'ma D.D. Shostakovicha k Isaaku Glikmanu* (Moscow and St Petersburg), 1993. Further page references to this edition are simply given in brackets in the text without additional identification.

[2] 'Dusha i maska: Pis'ma D. D. Shostakovicha L. N. Lebedinskomu', *Muzikal'naya zhizn'*, 23–4 (1993), 11–142.

was young and remained virtually unchanged for the rest of his life. These were above all his simplicity of vocabulary (more 'elemental' than plebeian) and simplicity of syntax, a partial result of which was a direct and unambiguous discourse. These qualities are to be seen clearly in articles where one seems to be able to discern not only the composer's genuine ideas, but also his words.

Shostakovich's literary style bears the stamp of the times he lived in, notably in his actual vocabulary (such phrases as 'in the sense of', 'the representation of fate' or 'resolved on the tragic plane' can safely be ascribed to the prevailing lexicon of the times) but also in the syntax. Note for example the conclusion of the article 'Tragedy-satire' written in 1932, which reads like a telegraphic dispatch from the artistic front line: '3 Acts written at the present time. There will be four altogether. Planning on finishing it in 3–4 months.'[3]

'This essay impresses the reader with its exceptional brilliance and richness,' or 'the brilliantly portrayed descriptions, the dramatic conflicts—all this gave me great pleasure', and 'the third act, with its greater social richness, departs somewhat from Leskov'.[4] The flatness of the descriptions, all those newspeak 'on the plane' and 'in the sense of' circumlocutions which Shostakovich liked to use, calling to mind the stultifying officialese of newspaper reports, may strike present-day readers as threadbare and emotionally commonplace. But this should not be regarded as proof of Shostakovich's deficiency as a writer, but rather as evidence of a kind of positivism which demands a straightforward correlation between a word and its subject, and allows for no ambiguity, subtext, psychological subtlety, or ellipsis. The language employed is in fact independent of the context. This style appears not just in newspaper articles but in documents of an entirely different nature such as correspondence with friends, including the most intimate of passages. These too contain turns of phrase like: 'Questions of creativity trouble me greatly' (Glikman, p. 31); 'the difficulties of her life cause me a great many sorrowful reflections' when writing about his sister (Glikman, p. 48); 'I wish you all possible strength and courage so as to weather this grievous loss with calmness,' concerning the death of the addressee's wife (Glikman, p. 55). All these examples come from the 1940s, and it is possible to find even later examples.

Sometimes this 'plain style' achieves a genuine expressivity owing nothing to lyricism or rhetoric, as in the following letter: 'Our life here passes uneventfully, calmly and quietly. Sometimes at night, tormented with insomnia, I weep [sic!]. The tears flow abundantly, bitterly. Nina and the children sleep in the other room, and so I just abandon myself to tears. Then I calm down. My nerves are playing up' (Glikman, p. 36). Or take the well-known letter on the death of Ivan Sollertinsky: 'Ivan Ivanovich passed away on the 11 February 1944. You and I will never see him again. There are no words to express the grief which is

---

[3] *Sovetskoe Isskustvo*, 1932, 16 Oct.; quoted in: *D. Shostakovich o vremeni i o sebe 1926–1975*, ed. M. Yakovlev (Moscow, 1980), 31.   [4] Ibid. 31.

tormenting my whole being. May his memory be immortalized by our love for him, our faith in his genius and by his phenomenal love for the art to which he dedicated his magnificent life—the art of music. Ivan Ivanovich is no more. It is very hard to bear' (Glikman, p. 64).

I make no generalizations about the role and character of the lyrical impulse in Shostakovich's work—appropriate though they may be in this context—but note that his particular 'plain style' is individual enough to be extremely hard to imitate or counterfeit. The convoluted and prolix style of the articles attributed to Shostakovich from the 1950s to the 1970s show a marked contrast with this precise syntax. Incidentally, on one occasion Shostakovich himself offered an oblique, but entirely unambiguous, comment on the problems which were later to arise in authenticating the texts he is supposed to have written (letter of 9 August 1971, Glikman, p. 279):

I absolutely agree with your judgement on Stravinsky's 'Conversations'. Some of his pronouncements can be excused by the fact that he was just rambling on, not thinking what he was saying, and then he put his name to them, not paying much attention, simply in order to be left in peace.

Such things have happened to other people as well as Stravinsky.

The unusual precision of Shostakovich's linguistic style, far from being diluted, is only reinforced by the literary associations it invokes. Chief among them, obvious to even the most inattentive reader, is an association with Mikhail Zoshchenko. In his Commentary to the Letters, Isaak Glikman on one occasion specifically cites Zoshchenko, although it has to be said that he has in mind more the subject-matter than the style. The reference is to a medical consultation as portrayed by Shostakovich in the style of an absurdist short story:

'If I were to have an X-ray done of me,' said this luminary, 'it would not look so very different from your X-ray. However, I have no trouble moving, while you find it very difficult. This shows that no two organisms are alike.' (p. 267)

Shostakovich knew Zoshchenko well and had a high opinion of his work. However in the present context this is not all that important, especially if one takes into account the fact that Shostakovich's 'plain style' was already formed by the end of the 1920s, that is to say before (or at least certainly not later than) Zoshchenko developed his own style. For Zoshchenko, the 1920s were the period of 'The Stories of Mr Sinebryukhov', of the 'alien speech' of plebeian discourse, which was absolutely foreign to Shostakovich. During the 1930s Zoshchenko's style underwent a radical change, moving closer to that employed by Shostakovich. Not for nothing does Marietta Chudakova draw attention to the 'deliberate poverty' of the writer's lexicon, the 'banality of his cliché-ridden phrases',[5] paradoxically presented as directly expressing his own 'natural' discourse. Here is some typical Zoshchenko: 'At the present time our

---

[5] Marietta Chudakova, *Poetika Mikhaila Zoshchenko* (Moscow, 1979), 174.

interest centres on different material—the construction and prosperity of our country . . .'; '. . . to play an important role in the sense of reforging one's character'; 'one man has died, one small worker, individually insignificant in the brilliance of our days' (in this last phrase there is something reminiscent of Andrey Platonov, whose stylistic evolution was, despite their many other differences, very akin to Zoshchenko's). This is the Zoshchenko of 'Recaptured Youth', 'The Lenin Stories', 'Story of a Life'. However the attempt to 'accommodate his own literary personality within the narrow confines of this already formed language', having suppressed even the merest echo of any 'alien speech', results in a paradox: 'his "natural" language . . . appears as the most alien'.[6] As one perceptive contemporary observed, Zoshchenko's style can at times be interpreted as 'mocking the sort of person who would write like that seriously'.[7] The text seems to emancipate itself from the 'completely serious' intentions of the author.

As is well known, this playful dialectic between one's 'own' language and that of the 'other' was exceptionally important to Shostakovich, not merely in his writings but also in his music. It is worth looking closely at its origins. As far as one can tell, it did not take shape immediately, but was certainly fully developed by the 1940s. In passages where this dialectic is deployed, his style loses its artless straightforwardness, and turns into something with a hidden compartment, almost like an optical illusion. There are many such gems scattered throughout the letters to Isaak Glikman and to L. N. Lebedinsky; I will cite just two examples:

Freedom-loving peoples will eventually throw off the yoke of Hitlerism, peace will reign throughout the world, and once again we shall live our lives in peace warmed by the sun of Stalin's Constitution. Of this I am deeply convinced and therefore experience feelings of great joy. (31 December 1943, p. 62)

I have just heard on the radio that Comrade N. A. Mikhailov has been appointed Minister of Culture of the USSR. I am very happy about this. No one could forget how energetically he implemented the Historic Decrees. Progressive music circles, who have always placed great hopes in Comrade Mikhailov are particularly pleased. (21 March 1955, p. 110)

The ambiguous and parodic meaning of passages like these is unfailingly decoded in the footnotes to the published edition of the letters, which at first can seem somewhat excessive and inappropriate. On reflection, however, it has to be admitted that the footnotes might be completely necessary to future generations.

These little islands of the highly contextualized 'other' language, which now and then appear in otherwise completely neutral surroundings, use a highly

---

[6] Chudakova, *Poetika Zoshchenko*.

[7] T. Volpe, 'O vozvrashchennoi molodosti Mikhaila Zoshchenka', quoted in Chudakova, *Poetika Zoshchenko*, 173.

individual technique of alienation [*ostranenie*]. Two of its devices are particularly noticeable. The first is tautology, which we frequently find sprinkled throughout the more highly wrought passages: 'I have no doubt that the discussion [of the Eighth Symphony by the Union of Soviet Composers] will give expression to valuable critical observations which will spur me on to further creativity, and will cause me to review all that I have composed hitherto, enabling me to go forward rather than step backward' (8 December 1943, p. 61). Tautology is also employed in a direct, unvarnished way: 'her true-to-life portrayal in a true-to-life film' (8 October 1943, p. 60); 'a musically active figure by the name of Geronimus has asked me to write an article about his musical activities' (24 April 1967, p. 229); 'for a short time I stopped reacting acutely and painfully to all kinds of acute and painful events' (14 June 1967, p. 230); and finally, from a letter to Lebedinsky, 'calumnious calumny'.[8] Clearly the heart of this device is the play on words—the tautological phrase is itself the expression of its own absurdist debunking; it runs round like a squirrel in a treadmill, gloomily affirming the unvarying monotony of existence. By way of contrast, compare this extract from the young Zoshchenko (taken from the story 'A Dog's Smell', 1923), which is also constructed on the coincidence of meaning and phonetics, but of a quite different kind:

The merchant Yeremey Babkin blinked, looked around, then pulled out some money and gave it to the agent. 'Here', he said, 'take your doggone cur off to those swinish sons of bitches. And never mind the raccoon coat. It will have to go to the dogs . . .'[9]

The second device which Shostakovich makes use of is enumeration, a baroque piling-up of lists, usually of proper names appropriate to the context: 'You have the instincts of a real folk minstrel, and among the glorious pleiad of Dunayevsky, Pokrass, Kruchinin, Kheif, Zinovy Dunayevsky, Kats and many others you could take, if not the first place, certainly not the last' (23 December 1942, p. 51). This extract also happens to be a parody of a phrase by Sollertinsky about Scriabin, but the quotations in Shostakovich's correspondence are a subject for a separate study. There is a monstrous example of this device of making long lists in the letter of 29 December 1957, in which Shostakovich repeats a whole list of names ('I arrived in Odessa on the day of the nationwide celebration of the fortieth anniversary of Soviet Ukraine . . .'; p. 135). The letter, quoted earlier in this volume by Richard Taruskin (see pp. 1– 2) contains not only tautology but other distancing effects. But the hidden meaning is not always crystal clear. Sometimes it almost seems as though the

---

[8] 'Dusha i Maska', 13.

[9] Mikhail Zoshchenko, *Izbrannye proizvedeniya*, i (Leningrad, 1968), 90. Translator's Note: Zoshchenko's double pun here is untranslatable, since it depends first upon the adjective swinish (literally bitchy) having in Russian a slang meaning closer to the American 'a bitch of a day' than the English 'malicious' or 'catty', and secondly upon the expression 'to the dogs' meaning 'to hell with' rather than indicating collapse or decay.

mask has become grafted to the face it conceals, and the meaning fluctuates between two possible interpretations. Take, for example, the following passage: 'Yuri Grigoryevich Bryansky, whom you probably know well, has died bravely fighting for our Soviet Motherland. It is a sad and painful end to a young life. But he carried out his duty with honour, and we shall always revere his memory' (3 January 1944, p. 63). An unambiguous interpretation of this fragment, which is couched in such obviously official language, is scarcely possible if one thinks about its subject-matter. Unambiguous interpretations are similarly impossible with 'Good Fortune', the final song of the cycle 'From Jewish Folk Poetry', with its refrain 'The stars shine on our heads, oy-oy' (in his 'Requiem', to words by Anna Akhmatova, Boris Tishchenko quotes this motif and gives it a very specific meaning by associating it with Akhmatova's line 'And an enormous star threatens imminent catastrophe').

This parallel with a musical work brings us inescapably to an important topic: is there a correspondence between the language Shostakovich used in his life and that which he used in his music? I believe that there is, although as Marietta Shaginyan pointed out, there are striking differences between the handwriting in his musical scores and that in everything else he wrote: 'Words made up of nervous, untidy and jagged letters, but precise and steady writing in the scores, which do not suggest a shaking hand . . .'.[10] The correspondence consists first and foremost in the nature of the texts chosen by Shostakovich—not all of them, of course, but many of them. A composer who so consciously absorbed into his own individual writing style the hackneyed phrases of Soviet-speak, 'the hideous regimentation of language',[11] might quite naturally turn to this linguistic source in his creative work. This relates principally to the unpoetic raw material of the 'Krokodil' cycle,[12] but it is also partially true of the 'Four Verses of Captain Lebyadkin'. The Krokodil texts also display an ability to transcend the limits imposed by the musical work and continue their real life 'pre-opus'; the borders of artistic convention are here observed at their most transparent. This wandering back and forth between art and life can be seen to brilliant effect in an anecdote, more like a short story, which is related by Shostakovich in his letter dated 8 May 1966 (p. 215), and which has to be quoted in full:

There was one intellectually minded singer who decided to perform my humoresques from Krokodil. He came to see me and sang them through—not at all badly. Being not merely a singer but an intellectual singer, he asked me a question. Here I must digress a little and quote from the song 'Irinka and the shepherd':

'The shepherd cannot see Irinka. Thickset, broad-shouldered, he sits with his back to her peeling the shell from an egg.

---

[10] M. Shaginyan, 'Dmitry Shostakovich', in *D. Shostakovich: stat' i materialy*, ed. G. M. Shneyerson (Moscow, 1976), 42–3.

[11] E. Poliganov, 'Za marksistskoe yazykoznanie' in *Sbornik populyarnikh lingvisticheskikh statei* (Moscow, 1931), quoted in Chudakova, *Poetika Mikhaila Zoshchenko*, 159.

[12] Five Romances on texts from *Krokodil*, Op. 121.

But Irinka is dying for a squeeze.'[13]
This was the singer-intellectual's question to me: 'I don't quite understand. Is it the shepherd or the egg that Irinka wants to squeeze?'
This was my answer: 'Oh, our audiences are very attentive these days. I don't think they will have any trouble working out what it is that Irina wants to squeeze.'
The singer-intellectual agreed with me, but he wasn't at all sure about it.

There is one instance of Shostakovich directly transferring linguistic features to a musical opus, although it is of a very particular kind. In his 'Preface to My Complete Collected Works and a Brief Reflection upon this Preface', we find not only tautological excesses (which begin with the title) but also over-indulgent enumeration. The parodic manipulation of the 'alien' musical and literary language is something familiar to those who study Shostakovich's music. But there is another side to it, exemplified in the 'plain style' of the distinctly un-literary text chosen for the songs 'From Jewish Folk Poetry'. The words 'Me without you, you without me—is like a door without a handle', for example, come from one of the songs. The phrases 'I miss you very much' and 'We shall never see him again', on the other hand, come from the letters. The 'poor poetry' of the Jewish cycle which Anna Akhmatova was so shocked by is actually very close to Shostakovich's natural style.

Clearly, the composer's aesthetic standpoint could not but have an influence on the way he approached 'high' poetry. This standpoint was defined first of all by the meaning of the poetry, and only afterwards by qualities such as intonation, form, phonetics, and associations. This characteristic explains his attraction to Yevtushenko's poem 'In the Store', or Rilke's poem 'Conclusion' in the finale of the Fourteenth Symphony.

Two more quotations by way of conclusion. Shostakovich is certainly not the author of the first, although it seems that he was, in some awful way: 'A true son of the Communist Party, a distinguished public and state figure, the artist and citizen D. D. Shostakovich devoted his entire life to the development of Soviet music, the affirmation of the ideals of socialist humanism and inter-nationalism, the struggle for peace and the friendship of nations.' Thus reads the composer's obituary notice in *Pravda*. The second quotation is taken from his letter to Isaak Glikman of 24 September 1968 (p. 243):

Tomorrow will be my 62nd birthday. People love to be coy when they are asked questions like: 'if you could have your 62 years all over again, would you spend them in the same way?'. They always reply: 'Well, I've had some pretty bad times over the years, and one or two disappointments, but on the whole, yes, I would do it all over again.'
If I were to be asked this question, my answer would be: 'No! A thousand times No!'

---

[13] Translator's note: The Russian word for egg (*yaitso*) also has the vulgar meaning of testicle. The play on words depends on there being no distinction between the neuter genitive pronoun and the masculine ('ego'), which is used in the original.

4

Shostakovich, LASM, and Asafiev

LAUREL E. FAY

I

Biographers have tended to tread gingerly around the issue of Shostakovich's relations with the Association of Contemporary Music (ASM). While many history books routinely include his name in a long list of ASM's members, his activities as a member and the extent of his allegiance to the ideals of the organization—at least as those ideals came to be articulated *ex post facto* in the mid-1930s—are frequently minimized; the fact of his membership in ASM is mitigated by his contributions to the proletarian cause, chiefly through his work in the Teatr rabochei molodezhi (TRAM). That this subject remains shrouded in confusion and misunderstanding, however, is demonstrated by the unequivocal declaration in a recent study that Shostakovich 'was never an ASM member or even a close associate'.[1]

If Shostakovich was not a member of ASM—and I believe the assertion is technically correct on this score—there is a very simple explanation. ASM was a Moscow-based organization, and Shostakovich—a 17-year-old Conservatoire student when it was established in 1923—lived in Leningrad. If he had been a Muscovite he would certainly have become a member of ASM, as did his close friend Vissarion Shebalin and most other aspiring modernists of the period. When, after much effort, ASM's Leningrad counterpart, the Leningrad Association of Contemporary Music (LASM) was established in early 1926, Shostakovich took his own inclusion among its founding members for granted.

As it happens, in an important series of as yet unpublished letters, Shostakovich provides clear evidence of his involvement in and attitude towards the creation of LASM. The letters in question were written to the prominent Moscow theorist Boleslav Yavorsky, whom Shostakovich met during his Moscow trip in March 1925 and who quickly took on the multiple functions of confidant, father-figure, mentor, and patron in the young composer's life. Preserved in the Glinka Museum in Moscow are more than sixty letters from Shostakovich to Yavorsky—who was Shostakovich's senior by nearly thirty

---

[1] Sheila Fitzpatrick, 'The Lady Macbeth Affair: Shostakovich and the Soviet Puritans', in *The Cultural Front: Power and Culture in Revolutionary Russia* (Ithaca, NY, 1992), 194–5.

years—the vast majority of them dating from mid-1925 to mid-1927.[2] Unfortunately, Yavorsky's responses are not preserved. Nevertheless, Shostakovich's side of the correspondence, candid and chatty, offers invaluable insights into a crucial period of his development.

Shostakovich deemed the story of the founding of LASM curious enough to recount it, in some detail, in a letter he wrote to Yavorsky on 20 January 1926. As he told it, rumours about the impending establishment of a Leningrad Association of Contemporary Music had been circulating since the previous summer. Recently, Maximilian Steinberg, his composition teacher at the Leningrad Conservatoire, had informed him exultantly that an organizational meeting was imminent and that, as a member of the Association, he, Shostakovich, should expect to receive notice of this meeting. So, as he told Yavorsky, it had come as quite a surprise to Shostakovich when he subsequently read in a local paper that the Leningrad Association had already been formed and its presidium selected. That this had transpired without his knowledge or participation was bad enough. What miffed him even more was the ultra-conservative make-up of the presidium: chaired by Yurgis Karnovich (a minor composer, former student of Steinberg and a Conservatoire pedagogue), with the composer Yuliya Veisberg (composer, student, and daughter-in-law of Nikolay Rimsky-Korsakov) as second-in-command, critic Nikolay Malkov as secretary and a comrade Bortkevich as head of the Party cell. An artistic council consisting of Steinberg, Alexander Zhitomirsky, Boris Asafiev, Alexander Ossovsky, and Vladimir Shcherbachev was also announced.

Mystified by the developments, Shostakovich happened to run into Karnovich at the Conservatoire, who informed him that as a member of the Association he would be expected to demonstrate some of his works. While agreeing in principle, Shostakovich became increasingly puzzled and decided to call Asafiev, with whom he had recently come into personal contact. Asafiev told him that he himself had only just returned from Moscow, knew nothing, and was just as confused as Shostakovich. He agreed to find out what was going on. Not without some bitterness, Shostakovich observed to Yavorsky that what this constituted was an object lesson in how the heirs of Rimsky-Korsakov snatch at power.[3]

From his subsequent communication to Yavorsky, on 30 January 1926, it is clear that Shostakovich had anticipated some sort of demonstration or protest that had failed to materialize. He was upset because neither of the two most progressive musicians on the presidium of LASM, Asafiev and Shcherbachev, had resigned; they remained members. He complained that the only really contemporary musicians in this erstwhile association of 'contemporary' music were its lowly members (i.e. those not in position of authority). He felt shut out.

---

[2] RMMK f. 146. Since the completion of the present article, excerpts from this correspondence have appeared in *Muzykal'naya akademiya*, 4 (1997), 28–40.   [3] RMMK f. 146, ed. khr. 3250.

Not for the first or last time in his career, he groused that he was unappreciated, that he thought he would soon leave music.[4]

Shostakovich's analysis of the situation helps to explain the rivalry that manifested itself between the newly established LASM and another group that came into existence simultaneously, the Circle for New Music. As it turned out, Asafiev's allegiance to LASM proved fragile. Although he had close ties with ASM in Moscow, and had long pursued the goal of establishing a branch in Leningrad, the friction in Leningrad music circles—specifically between the reactionary forces entrenched at the Conservatoire and reform-minded pro-gressives, including Asafiev, whose frontal assault on the outmoded educational system was only beginning—hampered his efforts. By late December 1925, Asafiev must already have realized the ominous turn developments were taking. In a letter to Myaskovsky, he admitted he was tired and his heart just was not in LASM, that it would be awkward to refuse to join, but he would not be active.[5] Even though formally he may not have withdrawn from LASM, however, after its presidium was co-opted by the 'heirs of Rimsky-Korsakov', Asafiev devoted his own energies to his Circle for New Music, an extension of the new music concert series that he had initiated at the Institute for the History of the Arts several years earlier.

In his memoirs, the musicologist Mikhail Druskin—who was an active member of both organizations—provides important correctives to some pre-vailing misconceptions about the ideological basis of and rivalries between the two organizations.[6] Among Druskin's chief points were the following: LASM was an independent organization that had no direct affiliation with ASM in Moscow or with the International Society for Contemporary Music (ISCM); LASM was a legally constituted, officially recognized organization, registered with Glavnauka, with a dues-paying membership; the Circle had no such administrative status; it was a voluntary, informal group of no more than two dozen musicians who gathered to explore new music chiefly in private gatherings and offering only occasional public concerts. Juxtaposing the concert programmes of both organizations, Druskin demonstrates that, con-trary to the textbook characterization of the Circle as a radical, 'leftist' organization focusing the bulk of its attention on the latest novelties from the West,[7] there was actually little to distinguish between LASM and the Circle

---

[4] RMMK f. 146 ed. khr. 3251.

[5] Quoted in M. Druskin, *Issledovaniya. Vospominaniya* (Leningrad, 1977), 199.

[6] Ibid. 189–219. Druskin's claim, incidentally, that Asafiev and Shcherbachev were not included as members of LASM's original governing board (p. 201) is contradicted by Shostakovich's account, as is the official period history of the organization; see V. Bogdanov-Berezovsky, 'Leningradskaya Assotsiatsiya Sovremennoi Muzyki', in *Novaya muzyka; sbornik 1: Pyat' let novoi muzyki* (Leningrad, 1927), 37.

[7] See, for instance, Y. V. Keldysh, ed., *Istoriya muzyki narodov SSSR*, 1, 1917–1932 (Moscow, 1970), 142.

in the balance of contemporary Russian and Western fare on their concerts or
in the scope of their aesthetic reach. Judging from his own descriptions,
Shostakovich seems to have viewed what was going on, albeit dimly, more
in terms of personalities and political intrigues than in terms of legitimate
aesthetic or ideological debate. According to Druskin, incidentally, Shostakovich was not one of the members of the Circle, but he did attend their open
concerts.[8]

If he was initially disappointed with the institution of LASM and did not find
in it an ideal community of truly 'contemporary' musicians, Shostakovich did,
none the less, derive conspicuous benefit from his membership in the organization. The première performance of his graduation piece, the First Symphony—the consummation of a crusade that had obsessed Shostakovich for
an entire year—took place under the auspices of LASM on its first symphonic
concert on 12 May 1926. The triumphant success of the young composer's
symphonic début and its importance in launching his compositional career
have become axiomatic.

By the autumn of 1926, the senselessness of trying to sustain in Leningrad
two parallel concert-producing organizations devoted to contemporary music
had become apparent, leading eventually to the merger of the Circle with
LASM. Here again, Shostakovich's spin on events is instructive. On 3
November 1926, he wrote to Yavorsky that he had recently received a
notice from the Association for Contemporary Music containing one question:
Should they merge with the Circle for New Music? At this point in his letter
Shostakovich inserted the following: '(Asafiev!!!)'. Shostakovich confessed that
he had rejoiced when he read the notice because, he said, it would mean
peace and the two organizations would unite into one strong one. But, he
complained, the union had been scuttled by Andrey Nikolayevich Rimsky-
Korsakov and Maximilian Steinberg and, as a direct result, some members
had resigned from LASM; in his letter Shostakovich cited Alexander
Kamensky, Vladimir Deshevov, Druskin, and himself among the defectors.
Shostakovich said that he had been scheduled to perform in LASM concerts
on 25 November and 15 December but had backed out. When he informed
Steinberg, his teacher had taken personal offence and had yelled at him on
the phone. But Shostakovich concludes in his letter to Yavorsky that he will
'transfer to the Circle for New Music because that is where all the high-
quality musicians have gathered'.[9]

Whether it was due to Steinberg's yelling, to another's sober counsel or to
enlightened self-interest, by the time Shostakovich typed up and submitted his
(exceedingly) formal notification of resignation from LASM three days later, on
6 November, he had changed his mind about reneging on his prior commitment: 'Notwithstanding a certain fatigue brought about by recent events, I do

---

[8] Keldysh, ed., *Istoriya muzyki*, 1, 192.   [9] RMMK f. 146, ed. khr. 3269.

not consider it permissible to take back my promise as far as my appearance with my Sonata, on 25 November this year, is concerned. . . .'[10]

Bogdanov-Berezovsky noted that as a consequence of the failure of the merger initiative, its supporters were obliged to resign from LASM's governing board and were replaced by new members, including Andrey Rimsky-Korsakov.[11] But continuing internal turmoil and the walk-out staged by the younger members must have had an effect. The merger of the Circle for New Music into LASM was officially ratified on 6 February 1927.[12] There is no record of LASM concerts taking place on 25 November or 15 December, but on 2 December 1926, Shostakovich—who a month earlier had officially resigned his membership in LASM—gave the first public performance of his new Piano Sonata at a concert sponsored by LASM.

In its new incarnation, under the titular chairmanship of Yury Shaporin and the functional leadership of Druskin occupying the post of secretary, along with Semyon Ginzburg and other young associates of Asafiev—with Asafiev the *éminence grise* behind the scenes—LASM flourished for another year. During this period, the calendar year of 1927, LASM's only publications, six thematic issues of *Novaya muzyka*, edited by Asafiev and Ginzburg, appeared, and LASM sponsored four chamber music concerts and a second symphonic one. In a letter written to Yavorsky in May 1927 from the hospital, where he was recovering after his appendix operation, Shostakovich mentioned that if he was strong enough, he planned to perform his piano suite, *Aphorisms*, at a LASM concert on 19 May, but it is not clear whether this performance actually took place. Shostakovich's name also figured among the composers whose music was featured on what was apparently the last event sponsored by LASM, a 'concert-exhibition' in honour of the tenth anniversary of October on 25 November 1927.[13]

This is not the place to debate the real or imaginary ideological sins of LASM, questionable though they most certainly were. For Shostakovich's part, his aloofness from the leading personalities in Leningrad's musical life and his disdain for their petty intrigues and vanities seem to have guaranteed that the ambitious young composer viewed LASM, during its two-year existence, chiefly as a means to an end, as a natural outlet for promotion of his music. There is no indication that the activities of LASM as such exerted the slightest influence on his creative development. In any event, as Druskin indicates, by 1928 LASM was already in the process of disintegration, chiefly through inertia, not from

---

[10] TsGA(SPb) f. 2555, op. 1, d. 1097, i. 43. I am grateful to Paul Mitchinson for first bringing this letter to my attention. For the complete text, as well as a more detailed background, see L. Kovnatskaya, 'Shostakovich v protokolakh LASM', *D.D. Shostakovich; sbornik statei k 90-letiyu so dnya rozhdeniya*, ed. L. Kovnatskaya (St Petersburg, 1996), 59–60.

[11] Bogdanov-Berezovsky, 'Leningradskaya Assotsiatsiya Sovremennoi Muzyki', 40.

[12] Ibid. 41.

[13] A facsimile of the handbill can be found in Druskin, *Issledovaniya*, 209.

any conspicuous outside interference from the Russian Association of Proletarian Musicians (RAPM) or elsewhere. LASM did not simply fade away; the chairman Shaporin and secretary Druskin devised a document to disband it officially and the latter took great pains to make sure it was filed with the proper administrative authorities.[14] By the time the oppressive domination of RAPM forced the liquidation of the Moscow-based ASM in 1931, LASM—and Shostakovich's affiliation with it—was a matter of ancient history.

II

As mentioned earlier, Shostakovich came into personal contact with Boris Asafiev a few months before LASM was launched, in the summer of 1925, in connection with his campaign to secure the performance of his First Symphony. The circumstances of their early association are illuminated, once again, in Shostakovich's letters to Yavorsky. On 27 June 1925, still busy writing out the full score of the symphony he had submitted for his final examation at the Conservatoire seven weeks earlier, Shostakovich told Yavorsky that Asafiev had expressed interest in seeing it; he had given him his phone number but so far had been unavailable.[15] More than four months later, after he had screwed up his courage to approach Nikolay Malko about a performance of his symphony and had been encouraged by the positive response, Shostakovich admitted that the hardest thing in life for him was to ask something for himself. He had tried it once before with Asafiev, he had asked him to look at the symphony, but although he had phoned him five times, Asafiev was always 'terribly busy'. As Shostakovich confided in Yavorsky, 'I always fear busy people.' Later in the same letter of 3 November 1925, Shostakovich called Asafiev a very cautious fellow; when Shostakovich had informed him he had a score from Moscow to deliver to him, Asafiev had told him to bring it to the Conservatoire.[16] The way the over-sensitive youth interpreted it was that Asafiev obviously did not want Shostakovich to come to his home, lest he take it into his head to bother him with his symphony. Acknowledging his own excessive pride a few days later, Shostakovich told Yavorsky that the Asafiev experience had taught him not to stick his neck out; 'I am afraid of rejection. Terribly afraid. And I will always fear people with status.'[17]

Six months after initially expressing interest in hearing it, Asafiev finally found time to audition Shostakovich's symphony, on the evening of 7 December, 1925. The young composer subsequently wrote to his friend Lev Oborin, 'It was clear from the way he greeted me that he wasn't expecting much good to come

---

[14] Druskin, *Issledovaniya*, 214–15.

[15] RMMK f. 146, ed. khr. 3239.

[16] RMMK f. 146, ed. khr. 3243.

[17] From a letter dated 9 Nov. 1925; RMMK f. 146, ed. khr. 3244.

out of it. For some reason there are people in this world who don't know me and my wares at all, or if they know, they know very little and none the less consider me, with respect to music, if not nil then of very minor magnitude. Asafiev belonged to that number. He greeted me extremely politely. He poured tea. He spoke of the decline of interest in music. Then he sat me at the piano and said, "Very often I don't get my bearings in musical compositions immediately, so if I don't say anything to you, don't be offended. Somehow, when the opportunity presents itself, I will convey my opinion".'[18] Shostakovich admitted that this had thrown him into a panic; he feared that if Asafiev were to convey an indifferent opinion to Malko, the conductor might lose interest in performing the symphony. After playing the work to him, however, Shostakovich said he had been reassured by Asafiev's warm praise and his assertion that it was not only essential to perform the symphony, but to arrange for its publication as well.[19]

Elated by the acquisition of an influential new supporter, Shostakovich experienced a change of heart towards Asafiev. Two months earlier, he had made fun of him in a letter to Oborin. Elected for a third year to the academic council of the composition department at the Conservatoire, Shostakovich described to Oborin how he had been passing the time at its innumerable beginning-of-the-year meetings; 'sometimes I yawn, sometimes I say some-thing, sometimes I chuckle at a successful witticism and, during the speeches of Igor Glebov [the pseudonym Boris Asafiev wrote under], I think "My God! how rotten life is. When will he finish".'[20] By mid-December Shostakovich assured Yavorsky that he had come to value the Conservatoire more since Asafiev had appeared there, that he had always respected him as a musician, and that, after showing him the symphony, he thought the ice was broken.[21]

Over the next few months, Shostakovich maintained good, if not close, relations with Asafiev. This was the period when he felt comfortable enough to phone him with his questions about the founding of LASM. It was also a period when Asafiev promised to help Shostakovich land a teaching job. He was prodded in this by Yavorsky, Myaskovsky, and other Moscow musicians, all anxious to help rescue Shostakovich from the drudgery of working as a film accompanist. Asafiev wrote to Myaskovsky in early March that although he was sceptical about Shostakovich's aptitude for teaching—Shostakovich's own mother also had her doubts—he was prepared to do everything possible to help him and that he brought up the need to assist him at every leadership meeting

[18] Letter dated 16 Dec. 1925; in M. G. Kozlova, ed. 'Mne ispolnilos' vosemnadtsat' let . . .', *Vstrechi s proshlym*, vyp. 5 (Moscow, 1984), 254.

[19] Ibid.

[20] Ibid. 250. Interpolated at this point in the published text of the letter is an ellipsis which might well represent the suppression of more scathing comments about Asafiev.

[21] Letter dated 16 Dec. 1925; RMMK f. 146, ed. khr. 3248.

at the Conservatoire, to no avail.[22] Shostakovich eventually took up a job teaching sight-reading in the autumn of 1926.

The honeymoon ended on 12 May 1926 when Asafiev failed to attend the première of Shostakovich's First Symphony. Shostakovich, for whom this was an event of the utmost significance, an anniversary he would celebrate for the rest of his life, could not forgive him. In a footnote in volume one of her two-volume biography of Shostakovich, Sofya Khentova cites a letter to Sergey Protopopov in Moscow, in which Shostakovich informs him that 'Asafiev didn't come after all. He didn't come to hear my symphony because of his relationship to Veisberg, and so on.' Here there is an ellipsis in Khentova's version before the quoted portion concludes with the unequivocal statement, 'Everything between Asafiev and me is finished.'[23] Khentova has recently published a slightly more extended extract from this letter: 'Asafiev didn't come after all . . . Not to come and hear my symphony *on principle* because of his relationship with Veisberg, and so on, is the height of stupidity and formalism . . . Everything between Asafiev and me is finished . . . I only beg you not to spread my comments about Asafiev.'[24] Not having examined the original of the Protopopov letter, I can only assume that the comments Shostakovich did not wish circulated continue to be camouflaged by Khentova's ellipses.

In his letter to Yavorsky written the day after the première—Yavorsky at that time was travelling in Europe—the deeply offended Shostakovich made the situation clear. He claimed that the reason Asafiev had not come was because the concert was held under the auspices of the Association for Contemporary Music with whom he had ostensibly fallen out. Correctly or incorrectly, Shostakovich interpreted Asafiev's behaviour as an egotistical display of pique at the fact that he was not chairman of LASM. Shostakovich swore, 'By his not coming yesterday he has alienated me forever. He's a dirty intriguer and nothing more.'[25]

As categorical as this resolution sounds, it would be dangerous to assume from this that Shostakovich never found it in himself to forgive Asafiev. These words were written in the heat of the moment by a highly strung, phenomenally gifted 19-year-old. Shostakovich's surviving correspondence, and memoirs of those who knew him at that period, show him to have been moody, impulsive, an immature youth still trying on his convictions for size, eager to find acceptance. We have already seen that after Asafiev—his senior by twenty-two years—praised him and offered his encouragement, his stock took a sharp upward turn in Shostakovich's eyes. In her biography, Khentova cites the Protopopov letter mentioned above chiefly to explain why Shostakovich

---

[22] Letter dated 7 Mar. 1926; in O. P. Lamm, *Stranitsy tvorcheskoi biografii Myaskovskogo* (Moscow, 1989), 175.

[23] S. Khentova, *Shostakovich: zhizn' i tvorchestvo*, i (Leningrad, 1985), 142 n. 1.

[24] S. Khentova, *V mire Shostakovicha* (Moscow, 1996), 291.

[25] Letter dated 13 May 1926; RMMK f. 146, ed. khr. 3254.

experienced a brief cooling off in his relations with Asafiev. Brief is the operative word here. Khentova, and Shostakovich's other biographers, have been uniform in their treatment of the Shostakovich–Asafiev relationship as, on balance, one of mutual respect, professional admiration and, for the young Shostakovich, one of formative musical influence.[26]

Beyond the natural urge of the biographer to forge constructive links between Leningrad's two most illustrious musicians of the Soviet period, the chief evidence for Asafiev's formative influence on Shostakovich comes from Shostakovich himself. On the occasion of his fiftieth birthday, a seven-page autobiographical sketch was published in *Sovetskaya muzyka*, entitled 'Thoughts about the Path Traversed' that has become a standard source of information about the composer. Among the topics discussed, Shostakovich singles out his relationships with Asafiev and with Ivan Sollertinsky. His comments about Asafiev deserve to be quoted in full:

I met Asafiev and Sollertinsky in 1926. Both these musicians played an important role in the formation of my artistic world-view. In those years Asafiev was mad about the extremes in modernist art, he worshipped Stravinsky, Schoenberg, Kvrenek, the composers of the French 'Six'. To a lesser extent he was attracted by Bartók and Hindemith. Under Asafiev's influence I wrote the opera *The Nose* and the suite for piano, *Aphorisms*, works singled out for their mistaken aspirations to 'originality' and rational experiment. Later, Asafiev's and my paths diverged. I had more than one opportunity to be persuaded of the inconstancy of his positions in artistic matters, although I did not cease to respect him as a major musical scholar.[27]

It is, at best, an equivocal tribute, but one that has consistently been construed by Shostakovich's biographers in its most straightforward, positive vein.

The ten references to Asafiev attributed to Shostakovich in the revisionist memoir, *Testimony*, are uniformly unflattering. Ironically, Asafiev is one of the few targets of Shostakovich's scorn in the book on whose behalf his interviewer

---

[26] In a formal interview with Shostakovich conducted in Repino in May 1967, Khentova asked a series of probing questions about his relationship with Asafiev, but she suppressed most of the information elicited until 1996. See Khentova, *V mire Shostakovicha*, 24–5. Khentova noted that in this interview Shostakovich responded to her questions about Asafiev with pauses, searching for the right words and that, at a certain point, he began speaking more quickly 'as if he was in a hurry to relieve himself of unpleasant memories' (ibid. 24).

[27] D. Shostakovich, 'Dumy o proidennom puti', *Sovetskaya muzyka*, 9 (1956), 11. Shostakovich's memory for dates is not infallible. As we have already seen, his relationship with Asafiev dated from the summer of 1925. And, although he had encountered Sollertinsky earlier, his friendship with him dated from the summer of 1927. In his interview with Khentova in 1967, Shostakovich reaffirmed his lifelong respect for Asafiev's scholarship and diplomatically credited Asafiev with having advised him to study the music of Stravinsky and Hindemith—composers who were not included in the Conservatoire curriculum—but he made no claims for Asafiev's influence on specific works. He reiterated the explanation for their paths having diverged as owing to the fickleness of Asafiev's opinions. See Khentova, *V mire Shostakovicha*, 24–5.

Solomon Volkov felt compelled to intervene. Himself a product of a Leningrad musical tradition deeply indebted to Asafiev, Volkov appended an explanatory footnote to the first Asafiev reference:

It would be no exaggeration to say that Asafiev is the most important representative of Russian thought on music throughout the country's musicological history. (His work is only now becoming known in the West.) Unfortunately, high scruples were not among the character traits of this brilliant scholar and critic. It is important to stress Asafiev's significance because the reader of this book might easily come away with an inaccurate picture of his impressive accomplishments. Some of the best pages ever written about Shostakovich belong to Asafiev, though the two men's relationship varied at different times. Shostakovich could not forgive Asafiev for the position he took in 1948, when he allowed his name to be used in an attack on the 'formalist' composers. Shostakovich told me that he destroyed his correspondence with Asafiev. . . .[28]

It would be foolhardy to challenge the scope and significance of Asafiev's contribution to Russian musical thought or even to deny that he penned some eloquent, even insightful words about Shostakovich's music. None the less, what is remarkable for a musician of his acumen, his extraordinary fecundity, his drive to explore and promote the best in new music, Western and Soviet, is how little Asafiev actually wrote about Shostakovich.[29] He was never a pathbreaking champion of Shostakovich's music. Unlike Sollertinsky, he did not promote it aggressively and wholeheartedly; his admiration was tempered with qualifications.

Asafiev's expressions of support for the composer generally came after the fact. For example, in 1934 he lamented the fate of Shostakovich's first opera *The Nose*, writing that 'When the youthful composer dared to expose authentic

---

[28] *Testimony: The Memoirs of Dmitri Shostakovich, as related to and edited by Solomon Volkov*, trans. Antonina W. Bouis (New York, 1979), 41–2. Elsewhere, Volkov clarifies his own acceptance of the seminal importance of the relationship for the composer: 'One of Shostakovich's most influential advisers after he graduated from the conservatory was the inveterate modernist music critic, Boris Asafiev.' See S. Volkov, *St Petersburg; A Cultural History* (New York, 1995), 370.

[29] While Asafiev referred to Shostakovich elsewhere, during his lifetime he published only three essays of any substance devoted to his music: 'O tvorchestve Shostakovicha i ego opere Ledi Makbet', *Ledi Makbet Mtsenskogo uyezda* (Leningrad, 1934); 'Tri imeni', *Sovetskaya muzyka*, 1 (1943); 'Vos'maya simfoniya Shostakovicha', *Moskovskaya filarmoniya* (Moscow, 1945). All of these essays are reprinted in *Akademik B. V. Asafiev: izbrannye trudi*, vol. v (Moscow, 1957). An appreciation of the composer, 'Redkyi talant', written in 1947 for the journal *Novyi mir*, was published only posthumously in *Sovetskaya muzyka*, 1 (1959). To be fair, it should also be mentioned that Shostakovich was credited with the authorship of two newspaper articles about Asafiev, both published in the autumn of 1943, in support of the latter's nomination for membership in the Academy of Sciences. Both are standard boilerplate for this type of testimonial. Neither betrays any sense of personal intimacy, special indebtedness, or, for that matter, any clue that Shostakovich was in fact the author. See D. Shostakovich, 'Boris Asafiev', *Literatura i iskusstvo*, 18 Sept. 1943, p. 3, and 'B. V. Asafiev', *Vechernyaya Moskva*, 21 Sept. 1943. When asked by Khentova why he had written positively about Asafiev during the war, Shostakovich responded: 'He was a hero, in blockaded Leningrad. A hero.' See Khentova, *V mire Shostakovicha*, 25.

Gogolian existence in music and through it to "settle accounts" with the "images of the past" troubling his imagination, then instead of painstaking evaluation, they "shafted" him, simply accused him of formalism. . . .'[30] Four years earlier, when his advocacy might actually have benefited the embattled opera—one of the works Shostakovich later credited him with inspiring— Asafiev remained silent.[31]

Despite his later claims, I can find no contemporary evidence to suggest that Shostakovich experienced any thawing of relations with Asafiev in the period following the première of the First Symphony. Rather the contrary: in a letter to Yavorsky dated 6 March 1927, Shostakovich says that he is very much alone, a fact his mother explains by the boorishness of his nature, that is, his too great openness in criticizing people who are close. To illustrate, he relates the following incident. Someone had come to visit recently and when the word 'Asafiev' had come up, Shostakovich had remarked, 'Asafiev is the most vulgar fellow [poshlyak] I know.' His mother had been offended by his words because, the way Shostakovich figured it, Glebov [Asafiev] had written something nice about her son somewhere.[32] Earlier in this same letter, Shostakovich informs Yavorsky that he has just completed the fourth number of his piano suite, subsequently titled *Aphorisms*, one of the works he would later credit to Asafiev's influence. Shostakovich kept Yavorsky informed of his progress on the composition of *Aphorisms* and on the suite's completion in early May, he sent him an autographed score. Nowhere in the correspondence does he make any reference to Asafiev or his purported contribution.

Similarly, in the summer of 1927, when Shostakovich confirmed—in response to Yavorsky's evident incredulity—his intention to write an opera on Gogol's *The Nose*, there is no indication of any involvement at all on Asafiev's part.[33] This occurred just as Shostakovich was becoming fast friends with, and the inseparable companion of Sollertinsky, at which point the volume of his letters to Yavorsky drops off sharply, leading to the unavoidable conclusion that Sollertinsky quickly replaced Yavorsky as Shostakovich's mentor and confidant. This new friendship would scarcely have contributed to reconciliation with Asafiev, who did not share nor is likely to have appreciated Sollertinsky's notorious sense of humour. The brilliant Shostakovich–Sollertinsky duo—

---

[30] B. Asafiev, 'O tvorchestve Shostakovicha i ego opere Ledi Makbet', 27.

[31] Asafiev's puzzling failure to participate in the debate over the future of Soviet opera fuelled by the production of *The Nose* may have been due, in part, to his preoccupation with defending his own professional position from the vicious attacks launched by RAPM in the journal *Proletarskyi muzykant* in 1929. See E. Orlova and A. Kryukov, *Akademik Boris Vladimirovich Asafiev; monografiya* (Leningrad, 1984), 181–3.

[32] RMMK f. 146, ed. khr. 3277.

[33] RMMK f. 146, ed. khr. 3284. Shostakovich did, however, subsequently credit Asafiev for effecting his introduction to Alban Berg at the Leningrad première of *Wozzeck* on 13 June 1927. See S. Khentova, *V mire Shostakovicha*, 25.

brash, cocky, irreverent—did not sow in its wake universal feelings of goodwill in Leningrad artistic circles in the late 1920s.[34]

Still thin-skinned and sensitive to criticism, the young Shostakovich must surely have bristled at Asafiev's condescending assessment—as sincere as it may have been—of his First Symphony in a November 1927 retrospective of Russian symphonic music: 'Even one of the most talented of Leningrad composers, Dmitry Shostakovich . . . is unrepresentative as the author of a symphony, despite the merits which are always to be found in the youthful work of an undeniably gifted musician beginning to find his language. However, in this symphony there is a rare quality: laconism and, at the same time, understanding, the ability to grasp an idea by its characteristic qualities and display it deftly. But all the same, Shostakovich's symphony belongs to those first compositions that one sympathizes with because they promise more than they deliver.'[35] In mentioning his own personal dislike of Shostakovich's music in a letter written to Asafiev in late 1927, Nikolay Myaskovsky nevertheless felt compelled to concede: 'He's a disagreeable boy, but a really major talent.'[36] Given his own personality, I think this is a sentiment we can assume Asafiev probably shared.

Why then would Shostakovich, at the age of 50, single out Asafiev as the guiding spirit behind two of the formative works of his youth if it were untrue? To understand this we need to re-examine the source of the claim. In 1956, when Shostakovich's autobiographical sketch was published, the Central Committee Resolution of 10 February 1948, in which Shostakovich was condemned as one of the foremost representatives of formalist tendencies in Soviet music, was still very much in force. It would be nearly two years before another Central Committee Resolution 'corrected' the mistakes of the first and the stigma associated with Shostakovich was officially removed. It would be another ten years before *Aphorisms* was back in print for the first time in forty years and not until 1974 that *The Nose* was rehabilitated in Russia. By naming Asafiev as the source of inspiration behind these compositions—long branded as the epitome of 'formalist' decadence—Shostakovich was deliberately tarnishing the image and stature of the great Soviet musicologist. The smear would have been plain to the knowing reader, aware of Asafiev's perfidious role in the First Composer's Union Congress in April 1948, when he contributed his

---

[34] Asafiev was himself a man of complex, contradictory impulses with a fragile ego. As his student Druskin recalled, his strong character traits attracted some musicians and repelled others. Druskin also attributed the chill that came over Asafiev's attitude to him in the early 1930s in some measure to the blossoming of his own friendship with Sollertinsky. See Druskin, *Issledovaniya*, 170–1, 173. For additional insights into the relationship between Asafiev and Sollertinsky, see L. Mikheyeva, *I. I. Sollertinsky; zhizn' i nasledie* (Leningrad, 1988), 85–8.

[35] Igor Glebov [Boris Asafiev], 'Russkaya simfonicheskaya muzyka za 10 let', *Muzyka i revolyutsiya*, 11 (Nov. 1927), 28.

[36] O. P. Lamm, *Stranitsi tvorcheskoi biografii Myaskovskogo*, 187.

considerable prestige and authority to the persecution of the leading Soviet composers and, in turn, was elected Chairman of the Composer's Union. In the first half of the keynote speech (the second half was delivered by Tikhon Khrennikov) that framed the debate for the ensuing Congress, Asafiev targeted Shostakovich for censure: 'Shostakovich has quite a few "confederates" and outright imitators, infected by the most unhealthy formalist pseudo-innovation. And these representatives of the anti-people formalist direction have occupied the leading positions on our musical front.'[37] In his 1956 memoir, Shostakovich reminds his reader that Asafiev's own past was far from unblemished; he shifts the responsibility for the dissemination of 'formalism' squarely to Asafiev's shoulders. Malicious and untrue as this testimony may have been, Shostakovich knew it could do no real harm: Asafiev had been dead since 1949.

There is another instance of Shostakovich's alleged attribution to Asafiev of influence on one of his works, a truism that has also become entrenched in the Shostakovich literature. In the notes from her interview with Shostakovich in December 1940, Marietta Shaginyan jotted down: 'Asafiev advised him to read Leskov's *Lady Macbeth*, he read it, was bowled over, and in a jiffy wrote the opera.'[38] At the time of the interview, Shaginyan was a celebrated Soviet writer, newly captivated by Shostakovich's music, and fascinated by its creator. This interview, in which she was gathering material for a commissioned article, marked her first acquaintance with the composer. By 1940, Shostakovich's second opera had been consigned irredeemably to the dustbin of formalism. Always an avid reader, Shostakovich would hardly have required Asafiev's guidance to steer him to Leskov. Shostakovich's mentioning of him in this context resonates with the same accusatory tone as it does in the 1956 autobiographical sketch.[39]

---

[37] B. Asafiev, 'Tridtsat' let sovetskoi muzyki i zadachi sovetskikh kompozitorov', in *Pervyi vsesoyuznyi s"ezd sovetskikh kompozitorov; stenograficheskyi otchet*, ed. M. V. Koval (Moscow, 1948), 13. In Asafiev's absence, which was attributed to illness, his speech was read at the Congress by Vladimir Vlasov. It is noteworthy that, of the six composers singled out in the infamous Resolution of 10 February 1948 as the leaders of the 'anti-people formalist movement'—Shostakovich, Prokofiev, Khachaturian, Shebalin, Popov, and Myaskovsky—Shostakovich was the only one identified in Asafiev's speech by name. Attempts to comprehend Asafiev's conduct in and around 1948 continue to stir up discomfiting reflections in Russian musical circles. For a recent perspective on the issue, see V. Vasina-Grossman, 'Professiya—Istorik', *Muzykal'naya zhizn'* 16 (1988), 8; idem, 'Boris Asafiev: Posledniye gody', *Muzykal'naya zhizn'*, 7 (1989), 12–13.

[38] M. Shaginyan, '50 pisem D.D. Shostakovicha', *Novyi mir*, 12 (1982), 130.

[39] There are other clues in the notes Shaginyan made at this meeting indicating that Shostakovich had found it expedient to reinvent himself after the 1936 crisis. For example, she quotes the favourite composers he had listed: 'before Conservatoire—Chopin, after Conservatoire—Glinka, Borodin, Rimsky-Korsakov, Tchaikovsky'. After completing the Conservatoire and up until 1936, Shostakovich never cited the 19th-cent. Russians as among his favourites. When he fielded this common question during these years Shostakovich quite consistently named contemporary composers including Berg, Schoenberg, Hindemith, Křenek, and especially Stravinsky as exerting the most influence on his current development.

Why might Shostakovich have felt enough resentment towards Asafiev in 1940 to indict him as the initiator of the composition of the most infamous piece in Soviet music history, the exemplar of the degeneracy of artistic formalism? In 1934, Asafiev's first publication on Shostakovich, a thoughtful appreciation of *Lady Macbeth* in the context of the young composer's development, had been featured in the programme booklet of the Maly Theatre's production of the opera. The unexpected *Pravda* editorial of 28 January 1936 attacking the opera—together with a second editorial of 6 February assailing Shostakovich's ballet *The Limpid Stream*—touched off a rapacious witch-hunt for 'formalists' that eventually engulfed the entire cultural front. Initially, the Leningrad music critics failed to recognize the imperative behind the *Pravda* editorial. Some, most notably Sollertinsky, voiced their disagreement with the tendentious attack on Shostakovich. By the time Leningrad musicians were reconvened on 21 February to 'discuss' the issues *Pravda* had raised, the true situation was clear; there was no longer any question about the authority of the editorials. For this occasion, Asafiev penned a formal statement, read for him at the meeting and subsequently published in *Sovetskaya muzyka*,[40] in which he endorsed the *Pravda* editorials unequivocally, calling them timely and excusing his own prior evaluation of *Lady Macbeth* as having being blinded by the indisputable fact of Shostakovich's great talent to the ideological shortcomings of his music.[41]

In the frenzied search for scapegoats that infected the Soviet arts world in the succeeding months, Sollertinsky's name became indistinguishable from an apologist of formalism, aggressive propagandist of bourgeois Western tendencies and wilful perverter of Shostakovich and other Soviet musicians from the true course of socialist realism. Alone among the prominent figures of ASM and the progressive musical modernists of the 1920s, Asafiev was not called publicly to account for the 'errors' of his past; he emerged from the crisis virtually unscathed, with his professional and ideological credentials unchallenged. How he managed to accomplish this, a feat worthy of Houdini given his background, is a fascinating question in itself, one that Shostakovich might well have been hinting at in his comment to Shaginyan in his 1940 interview.

In a diary entry for May 1954, Edison Denisov describes an evening spent at Shostakovich's, who had taken the aspiring young Siberian composer under his wing: 'We spoke about Asafiev. D. D. says that he is antipathetic to him. Glazunov called Asafiev a "musical rogue". Originally *Lady Macbeth* was dedicated to Asafiev, but later D. D. struck out the dedication. He calls him

---

[40] B. Asafiev, 'Volnuyushchiye voprosy (vmesto vstupleniya na tvorcheskoi diskussii)', *Sovetskaya muzyka*, 5 (1936), 24–7.

[41] Ibid. 26. A detailed analysis of the inconsistencies and obfuscations in Asafiev's apologia with reference to his earlier activities, published writings, and personal correspondence is beyond the scope of this study.

"a Great Russian chauvinist".'[42] Denisov, incidentally, repeated these anecdotes and enlarged on them in a 1988 interview: 'When I was a student I read Asafiev's books and every time I mentioned Asafiev's name, Dmitry Dmitrievich bristled. He would repeat: "I have met many good people and many bad people in my life, but never anybody more rotten than Asafiev".'[43] The composer's older sister, Mariya, recollecting the rare exceptions to Shostakovich's habitually placid and forgiving disposition, noted: 'He also didn't forgive Asafiev his pusillanimity in 1936 and 1948.'[44]

Perhaps at one time Shostakovich really did intend to dedicate *Lady Macbeth* to Asafiev, although until recently Denisov provided the only detectable evidence.[45] The definitive dedication of Shostakovich's second opera was to his wife, Nina Varzar.[46] In 1954, when Shostakovich made this remark to Denisov, *Lady Macbeth*, like *The Nose* and *Aphorisms*, was still censored. There is at least a reasonable possibility that, after Asafiev's shameful performance in 1948, Shostakovich might have invented the dedication story out of spite.

There are other matters not discussed here that would also have served to drive a wedge between the two men; Asafiev's aspirations as a composer,[47] for

---

[42] The entry is dated 5 May 1954. E. Denisov, 'Vstrechi s Shostakovichem', *Muzykal'naya akademiya*, 3 (1994), 90; German trans. in D. Gojowy, 'Dmitri Schostakowitsch: Briefe an Edison Denissow', *Musik des Ostens*, Bd. 10, ed. H. Unverricht (Kassel, 1986), 204–5.

[43] Elizabeth Wilson, *Shostakovich: A Life Remembered* (London, 1994), 303. Denisov goes on here to relate how, at the insistent entreaty of Asafiev's wife, Shostakovich returned to her a letter Asafiev had written that, were it to be made public, would have destroyed his reputation forever. Unfortunately, there is no indication when this incident might have taken place. As quoted earlier, Solomon Volkov noted that Shostakovich told him he had destroyed his correspondence with Asafiev. The significance of this statement, however, must be considered in light of the fact that Shostakovich habitually destroyed all his correspondence.

[44] M. D. Shostakovich, 'Vspominaya Shostakovicha', *Muzykal'naya zhizn'*, 8 (1994), 31.

[45] Contemporary documents yield no trace of such an intent. In her publications before 1996, Sofya Khentova offered no source other than Denisov for accepting this second-hand report as fact. See, for instance, Khentova, *Shostakovich: zhizn' i tvorchestvo*, i. 285; idem, *Udivitel'nyi Shostakovich* (St Petersburg, 1993), 23. As it now turns out, in 1967 she had asked the composer point blank if it was true he had wanted to dedicate *Lady Macbeth* to Asafiev. Shostakovich's response: 'I wanted to, but changed my mind, you know, I changed my mind . . .' See Khentova, *V mire Shostakovicha*, 24.

[46] Although no dedication appears in the piano score of the opera published in Moscow in 1935, or in the 1979 publication of the 'original' 1932 version of the opera, the dedication to Nina Varzar appears on the first manuscript page of the autograph score. See RGALI f. 2048, op. 2, ed. khr. 32. For a review of the publications of the opera, see Laurel E. Fay, 'From *Lady Macbeth* to *Katerina*; Shostakovich's Versions and Revisions', in David Fanning, ed., *Shostakovich Studies* (Cambridge, 1995), 162.

[47] In his 1967 interview with Khentova, Shostakovich conceded that Asafiev wrote some 'good' ballet music, citing specifically *The Fountain of Bakhchisarai* and *The Flame of Paris*. He did not rate Asafiev's other music that highly, although he admitted he had heard little of it. See Khentova, *V mire Shostakovicha*, 25. In memoirs published in the same volume, Alisa Shebalina recalled that Shostakovich always retained something of the urchin in his demeanour. To alleviate the boredom of official meetings, he passed humorous notes to her husband. She quotes one such note which must have dated from after 1945: 'I sat down opposite him [Boris Vladimirovich Asafiev]; my

example, and, just as important, their conflicting assessments of Musorgsky's orchestration of *Boris Godunov*.[48] After Shostakovich's early disenchantment with Asafiev, the weight of credible evidence suggests that, beyond the observance of civilities that would have been necessary in the confined community of Leningrad's cultural sphere, Shostakovich and Asafiev never found common ground on which to build a mutually rewarding relationship, either professional or personal. Mediation by Solomon Volkov notwithstanding, the subject of Asafiev is one of the areas in *Testimony* where the voice and opinions of Shostakovich ring true. Once all the ellipses are filled out, and more of the primary sources become accessible, I think we will find that the issue of Asafiev's constructive role in Shostakovich's development, and perhaps in the history of Soviet music as a whole, has been as carefully mythologized as so much else in Shostakovich's biography.

loathsome . . . mug reminded him of the meeting at M. B. Khrapchenko's where I unsuccessfully criticized his ballet, *The Peasant Princess*. When I sat down, Boris Vladimirovich's hands began to tremble, and comrade Bogdasarov's speech overfilled his cup. Having moved to another seat from which my loathsome, drunken mug wasn't visible, B. V. calmed down perceptibly.' See Khentova, *V mire Shostakovicha*, 131.

[48] The remarks on this issue in *Testimony* (p. 227) echo opinions Shostakovich expressed in an interview he gave on 25 July 1970. See B. Gurevich, 'Shostakovich v rabote nad *Khovanshchina*', *Voprosi teorii i estetiki muzyki*, vyp. 11 (1972), 86.

5

Shostakovich as Reflected
in his Letters to Ivan Sollertinsky

LYUDMILA MIKHEYEVA-SOLLERTINSKAYA

The letters written by the great composer to his close friend Ivan Ivanovich Sollertinsky form a unique document. To begin with, there is the fact that they exist at all. Shostakovich and Sollertinsky lived in the same town, indeed for many years on adjacent streets, and parted company only after the beginning of the Second World War. One would have thought they had enough direct contact with each other, yet over one hundred and fifty of Shostakovich's letters to Sollertinsky have survived, which shed light on many hitherto unknown details of the composer's life, and often on particular traits of his character. So far as we can judge from the published correspondence, nothing comparable is to be found in any of the letters he addressed to the wide circle of his other correspondents—family members, friends, and acquaintances. In their sincerity, candour, and level of detail, their flashes of frequently ironic humour, their tone by turns bitter, anxious, and solicitous, they reveal just how dear and intimate a friend was their addressee, and how close the ties of friendship that bound them together.

We can confidently ascribe to early May 1927 the date on which this friendship began. In a special notebook in which he noted the significant dates of his life, Sollertinsky wrote: 'At the beginning of the summer—"Bruderschaft"[1] with Shostakovich.' The first of Shostakovich's letters are also from this summer; the composer, on holiday at Tsarskoye Selo, writes in them of the work he was engaged on at the time. The next batch of letters comes from Moscow, where Shostakovich had gone at the invitation of Meyerhold. Here is the first of these, dated 10 January 1928:

Dear Ivan Ivanovich,
I did not write to you straightaway, because I am only now beginning to get back to normal. I have still not got over my acute longing for Leningrad. The only thing that consoles me is that work is going well here. I've made really good progress with *The Nose*. I start work in the theatre[2] tomorrow. Will something come of it, do you think? I expect

---

[1] Russians use the German word to denote the mutual agreement, usually symbolized by the drinking of a toast with linked arms, to address one another in the intimate second person singular. (Translator's note)

[2] Meyerhold had invited Shostakovich to join his theatre company as music director.

you have heard, or will hear, from N. A. Malko about my symphony.[3] Before the concert there was an entertaining 'episode, very typical of my 'friend' M. V. Kvadri. I was told the story yesterday evening by somebody I know.

I arrived half an hour before the concert and went to buy a ticket. Having bought it, I went to my seat, which was in Row 16, and with the specific object of avoiding meeting M. V. Kvadri—in which I was successful—covered my face with a newspaper. But when I had to go up to 'take a bow', there he was, suddenly popping up and giving me a warm embrace with three slobbering kisses, Russian style, yelling 'Go up on stage! Take a bow!'

The way he got himself in to the concert was characteristic of the man. He went to see the administrator and to the accompaniment of loud laughter from onlookers demanded two complimentary tickets on the grounds that 'Shostakovich's symphony is dedicated to me!' One of the orchestral musicians who knew him backed him up, insisting: 'Look here, this is Mr Kvadri! Shostakovich's spiritual father!' He got his complimentary tickets. And then in the interval, with everybody round congratulating me, up comes the administrator, very apologetic that he had not given Kvadri comps at once. I was somewhat surprised by this, but graciously gave him my 'forgiveness'. Then yesterday I had the whole episode related to me by my acquaintance, and I realized what had happened.

Well, that's the news from here.

Here I am living surrounded by brilliant people (a brilliant theatre director, a 'brilliant' actress—'Oh Zinka! What a performance you gave yesterday! It was brilliant'), a composer and a poetess, both 'brilliant'. The last two being in point of fact the children of the 'brilliant' poet Yesenin and the 'brilliant' actress herself. . . .

'Well done all of you. You're all great' says V.E.[4] 'Eh, Shostakovich? Aren't they great? Don't you think so?'. 'Yes, indeed.'

Raikh:[5] 'I'd like your opinion, Dima (that is what they all call me here). Obviously Tanya has inherited her talent from her father, but where can Kostya have got his tremendous musical talent from?'

Meyerhold: 'From you, of course.'

Raikh: 'Why me? I'm an actress after all, not a musician.'

Meyerhold: 'Yes, you are indeed an actress. You have profound cognition of the Word. And as Heine said, where the Word comes to an end, there begins Music. Don't you think so, Dima?'

He feigns slight diffidence. He is always asking me 'What do you think, Dima? Eh? Come on now, tell me!' I maintain a sullen silence and nod agreement.

That is what my life is like here. Very amusing. Yesterday I was at the Kerzhentsevs— he used to be Ambassador in Rome and has now become Vice- president of the Bureau of Statistics. I met some interesting people there, including Raskolnikov and Eisenstein. But generally it is all rather bleak. I miss my own folk, and I miss you. Do write.

D. Shostakovich, Moscow 69, 32 Novinsky Bul'var, apartment 45.

---

[3] The reference is to the performance in Moscow of the First Symphony conducted by Nikolay Malko.

[4] Vsevolod Emilievich (Meyerhold). (Translator's note)

[5] Meyerhold's wife was the actress Zinaida Raikh. (Translator's note)

Even this, one of the first letters, gives us new information—first of all about Kvadri. The oldest of the group of five young Moscow musicians with whom Shostakovich developed a close association (Shebalin,[6] Oborin,[7] Staroka-domsky,[8] Nikolsky,[9]) Kvadri saw himself in the role of Balakirev to a new 'Mighty Handful'. (This must be where the remark about a 'spiritual father' comes from.) However, Shostakovich did not dedicate any of his works to him, certainly none of the symphonies. Furthermore, their relations sharply deteriorated after Shostakovich gave Kvadri a copy of his Piano Trio No. 1 to take with him to Moscow to give to Tanya Glivenko,[10] to whom he had dedicated the work. Kvadri failed to deliver the work as agreed; in other words, he simply stole it. Naturally, after this there could be no question of a close friendship between Shostakovich and Kvadri, as has been suggested by some commentators.[11] In any case, had there had been any substance in this view of their relationship, the composer would hardly have written in such terms. Where true friends were concerned, Shostakovich always spoke with great warmth, and many fond references to them can be found throughout the correspondence with Sollertinsky, Shebalin, Oborin, and other musicians with whom he was in contact.

There is also a received opinion in Shostakovich studies about the composer's attitude to Meyerhold, for whom he always had boundless respect and an unwavering admiration. But the relationship between them was far from simple. In some of the later letters the ironic tone which pervades the lines cited above turns to sarcasm. (Nevertheless, it is worth noting that Meyerhold is the only one of these pen portraits to be described as brilliant without inverted commas!) Only much later, in 1936, after Meyerhold's courageous public defence of the disgraced composer in the wake of the infamous newspaper articles headed 'Ballet Falsehood' and 'Muddle instead of Music', did Shostakovich's opinion of him definitively change. In the letters to Sollertinsky, Shostakovich gives details of his life away from Leningrad, his impressions of musical, theatrical, literary happenings, of new acquaintances, or encounters which in some way or other left their mark. From time to time such letters become almost short stories, in which actual facts are whimsically interwoven with striking flights of fancy in a way which was clearly intended to amuse his

[6] Vissarion Yakovlevich Shebalin (1902–63), composer and professor of composition at the Moscow Conservatoire. Shebalin was the only person to speak in Shostakovich's defence at the 'discussion' on *Lady Macbeth* organized at the House of Writers after the article in *Pravda*. (Translator's note)

[7] Lev Nikolayevich Oborin (1907–74), pianist and professor at the Moscow Conservatoire. Oborin was awarded the First Prize at the 1927 Chopin Competition in Warsaw in which Shostakovich participated. (Translator's note)

[8] Mikhail Leonidovich Starokadomsky (1901–54), organist and composer. (Translator's note)

[9] Yury Sergeyevich Nikolsky (1895–1962), composer and conductor. (Translator's note)

[10] Tatyana Ivanovna Glivenko, the young Shostakovich's first love. (Translator's note)

[11] S. Khentova, *Shostakovich: Zhizn' i tvorchestvo*, i, (Leningrad, 1985), 131, 132–3.

friend, or they are often conveyed in a deliberately exaggerated way. A letter dated 10 February 1930 from Rostov-on-Don, where Shostakovich was on tour, is interesting in this connection:

Dear Ivan Ivanovich,

I am sitting in my hotel room feeling bored. So I have decided to write to you. . . . There are a few things which have happened to me, and for want of anything better to do I thought I would set them down for you.

A young man who belongs to the breed of 'sons of bitches' travelled with me all the way to Rostov in my sleeping compartment. After Moscow we got talking, but of that more anon. When we got to Moscow, knowing that the train would be stopping there for about four hours, I rushed off to see Grabber Meyerhold. When I arrived the Grabber was asleep. Along with me, the painter Ulyanov was waiting to see him; an old fellow very shabbily dressed. After a while the Grabber emerged and engaged me in conversation. I formed the impression that he was not wildly pleased to see me.

I returned to the station in good spirits. All was well in the sleeping compartment; all my things still there. Soon Sonofabitch came back in. He informed me that he was a final-year engineering student on his way to a job in Rostov, and that he suffered from neurasthenia. He enquired about me. I told him who I was. My heart missed a beat when he said: 'Shostakovich? The composer?' (This had, of course, had been preceded by: 'Excuse me. What is your name?') 'Well,' I thought, 'that means he must have heard of me.' I assumed a self-deprecating air . . . 'No, I don't know you, never heard of you. I've heard of Vasilkovsky (?), but Shostakovich, no, I haven't heard that name before.' Awkward pause. I muttered something about probably being better known in musical circles than in engineering ones, upon which the bitch's offspring announced: 'No, no! I'm very interested in music. I go to the opera and I go to concerts but I have never heard your name. Wouldn't recall it even if you were to put a pistol to my head.' At all events we got safely to Rostov, where Yakobson met me—not the choreographer, another Yakobson—and took me to my hotel. So I went to my room, which has two beds in it, and got undressed for bed. All of a sudden, there is a knock at the door. It's already eleven o'clock. 'Well,' I think, 'perhaps someone has come to inverview me.' I start preparing a few phrases: 'music today, at this point in time . . .'—that sort of thing. I open the door, and who should be standing there but our bitch's son! 'You know, they haven't any rooms vacant, so would you mind if I came in with you for the time being, especially as (glancing at the second bed) I see there are two beds in here?' 'By all means, but I'm not sure how Yakobson will react. After all, I'm not paying for the room, it's the State Symphony Orchestra. I am not sure this is quite ethical.'

After a brief discussion of ethics, Mr Sonofabitch lugged in his suitcase. When Yakobson came in he raised no objection to my offering hospitality for the night to my 'friend'. Then he asked me who he was, and had I known him long? I replied that I had. 'Well, you need to watch out, you know. There are a lot of crooks about.' I insisted that this was a friend, but all the time cats were sharpening their claws inside me. 'What', I thought, 'if he runs off with my trousers?' Happily the S.O.B. only stayed one night and the next day went to Novocherkassk, where he had a job waiting for him. Nothing of mine was touched, not my trousers nor my condoms—well, in fact, originally I did have 6 condoms and when I looked there were only 5, but anyway that's a trifle . . . The orchestra is not bad, but the conductor (Yakobson) is hopeless. Despite this the concert (my performance anyhow) was a great success, I got a lot of applause and played 3 encores. In tails I look like an elegant footman. Several times I caught myself saying: 'May I help you, sir?' instead of 'Good evening' or 'Good bye', just like Court Counsellor Lakeyich (look up Chekhov's story Romance with a Double Bass) . . .

Taken as a whole, this flippant letter hardly stands in need of commentary, but it may be appropriate to add a small explanatory note about the 'permanent epithet' attached to Meyerhold. Evidently in conversation Shostakovich and Sollertinsky used to characterize people in this way. Thus the composer Lipatov is never referred to as other than 'old chap', while the conductor Gauk[12] is invariably 'petty bourgeois Gauk'. Many of the letters contain references to or paraphrases of characters and ideas drawn not only from Chekhov, but also from Zoshchenko and Gogol. Thus in a letter from Ivanov, where the composer was on holiday in April 1934, we read: 'I ran into our friend Shkolnikov down here. Six weeks ago his wife gave birth to an excessively bouncy little chap; he'll turn into a conductor like his father.'[13] Or, from the same letter: 'The weather is wonderful. The sun is shining and the snow is melting. The brooks are gurgling, the breezes are gently wafting, and the hills stand all around. I find myself in complete agreement with I. A. Khlestakov[14] when he expresses himself so eloquently in praise of nature.'

Naturally, by no means all Shostakovich's letters to his friend confine themselves to this sort of amusing and inconsequential banter. There is much discussion of news about music, everyday problems, and newspaper articles from which, as often as not, pessimistic conclusions are drawn. In a letter from Moscow dated 10 March 1935 a completely unexpected, and evidently for Shostakovich a deeply disturbing theme is broached:

Dear Ivan Ivanovich,
It looks as though it is going to be some time before I can get away from here. It may even be that I shall not be coming back to Leningrad at all, since the question of my moving here is now unexpectedly being discussed with some vigour. I am to speak to Voroshilov on the 16th. It has already been settled that I will go on the trip abroad. It will be for about one month, and in the mean time an apartment (which I have already been to look at) will be got ready for me. I am very sad to be leaving Leningrad, but there is nothing to be done about it, that is what the Government wants. If I had some real support in Leningrad, then I would stay, but the business with the room for N.V. has shown me clearly that I am regarded there with nothing but cold indifference. Now everything is being sorted out. I shall transfer the apartment to N.V. and will move to Moscow myself, with Mama. Please do write to me and tell me about yourself. How are you? What are you doing, and how do you feel? Write to

---

[12] Alexander Vasilievich Gauk (1893–1963), principal conductor of the Bolshoi Symphony Orchestra, professor at Leningrad and Moscow Conservatoires. (Translator's note)

[13] Shostakovich here parodies lines by Bobchinsky, a character in Gogol's play *The Inspector General* (Act I, scene iii).

[14] The anti-hero of Gogol's play *The Inspector General*.

me c/o Atovmyan. . . .[15] If I do move to Moscow I shall just have to drag you along with me, because I should be very unhappy to part from you. I kiss you warmly. Yours, D. Shostakovich.

In contrast to the preceding letters quoted, this letter (not given in full) demands rather more extensive annotation. The foreign trip to Turkey was undertaken by a large group of Soviet artists. Besides Shostakovich the group included the pianist Lev Oborin, the violinist David Oistrakh, the singers Valeriya Barsova, Mariya Maksakova, Alexander Pirogov, and Panteleimon Nortsov, the dancers Nataliya Dudinskaya and Azaf Messerer, and the conductor Lev Shteinberg. Shostakovich wrote several letters to Sollertinsky from his travels, in which he relayed his impressions of the sea voyage, of Turkey, of a reception at the Soviet Embassy (then officially styled Plenipotentiary Mission), and so on. More importantly, however, the letter contains the only specific reference to the personal drama that was currently being played out in the composer's family. It concerned the divorce from his wife, Nina Vasilievna. Shostakovich had married her in 1932, once it had become clear that his relationship with Tatiana Glivenko, the paramour of his youth, was irrevocably over. It was just at this point that Glivenko had a child, having married shortly beforehand.

There is a final echo of this domestic drama in the postscript of a later letter from Moscow written at the end of 1935: 'There can be no question of divorcing Nina. Only now have I come to realize and appreciate in my heart what a wonderful woman she is, and how dear she is to me.' However this letter, the precise date of which is not known, is the only one of its kind, and merits detailed consideration. Unlike Shostakovich, who meticulously destroyed all letters immediately after reading them (which is why none of Sollertinsky's letters to him have survived), Sollertinsky carefully preserved every single one that he received, and not just letters and telegrams, but also notes scribbled on scraps of paper, sketches of ideas or notes for librettos, etc. It is all the more revealing, therefore, that this letter, written at the time of the Moscow preparations for the première of the ballet *The Limpid Stream* should have apparently been torn in half, so that only the lower half of the piece of paper on which it was written has survived. This letter is of such importance that it seems appropriate to quote here the whole of the text we have, with the exception of the PS cited above:

[because] of my democratic tendencies I decided to invite these splendid fellows over and treat them to a glass of vodka. They have all worked tremendously hard on *The Limpid Stream*. I'm feeling rather wretched, as I still feel that *The Limpid Stream* is going to be scrapped soon. I didn't talk to you about it in Leningrad, because I didn't want to upset my family, who love me very much and will be upset by my 'flop'. At present, matters stand as follows: today we had the first stage-orchestra rehearsal. It went very well. Everybody is delighted. But the canker of doubt is gnawing at my soul, and I am gearing

---

[15] Levon Tadevosovich Atovmyan, member of the Union of Composers, a figure active in musical circles with whom Shostakovich was on friendly terms for many years.

myself up to 'agree' to the withdrawal of the ballet, which I am convinced is going to happen within a few days. I implore you not to hasten this eventuality, and not to speak anywhere to anybody about this. At least it has been a good lesson for me. I am sure you completely understand how I am feeling. I think you know perfectly well that *The Limpid Stream* is an ignominious failure for me, and that that has always been precisely my attitude to it from the very first. The only thing I want is that you should believe me when I tell you this was my attitude, and that having believed it, you should forgive me. It is impossible for me to do now what I did when I was writing *The Bolt*; I know that very well and curse myself mercilessly for it. I would be enormously relieved if you would answer this letter immediately and put my troubled mind at rest. Only please don't give me any recriminations; I should hate that, although in any case I think you have known me long enough to understand my feelings about this work [the page is torn off at this point] . . . [in that] case I absolutely count on you not to abandon me at this exceptionally difficult time of my life, because if there is one person whose friendship I treasure like the apple of my eye it is you.

So, please for God's sake write. I kiss you. Yours, D. Shostakovich.

(We should note in parenthesis that Ivan Sollertinsky was the only individual to whom the great composer, fully aware of the true extent of his gifts, deferred as the junior to the senior; to whom, without in the slightest compromising his own worth, he could make confession and ask absolution, and to whom he turned in his 'hour of need'. At no other time and to no other person, it seems, no matter what ties of family or friendship or professional collaboration might link them, are there parallel examples in Shostakovich's life. And this is the only communication to reveal the depth of their intimacy, their need for one another and the trust that each reposed in the other.)

We can assess more fully the significance of the surviving parts of this letter if we turn back to 1930, to the following passage from the letter of 10 February already quoted:

the director of the Moscow Art Theatre II, Comrade Smirnov, read me the libretto of the ballet *The New Machine*. The subject is most topical. There is a machine. It has gone wrong (problem of wear and tear on materials). They fix it (problem of amortization), and at the same time buy a new one. Finally everybody dances round the new machine. Apotheosis. All of this takes up three acts.

In this caricature can be dimly discerned the outlines of the libretto of *The Bolt*. Even when substantially reworked, it was not much better, and naturally the composer fully appreciated what a contrived and artificial piece of work it was. Nevertheless, he composed music for it, and magnificent music at that. This was a different situation. We have also to bear in mind that Sollertinsky had reacted unfavourably to the Leningrad performances of *The Limpid Stream* in the production by Fyodor Lopukhov, one of the leading Soviet choreographers of the day. In his review he had written:[16]

[16] I. Sollertinsky: ' "Svetlyi ruchei" v Malom opernom teatre', *Rabochii i teatr*, 12 (1935), 14, 15.

If success is to be measured by the volume of applause, it was undoubtedly a great success for the theatre. The victorious are not usually subjected to criticism. But on this occasion we are obliged to depart from this honourable practice. By all means let the victors remain victors, but the fact is that the victory won by this theatre was fought on uncommonly slippery ground. On ground that rejects any meaningful development of the action. The audience is treated to three acts of continual divertissement. Taken on its own, each number is fine, sometimes even outstanding, but the whole problem is that any one of them could be detached from the ballet to stand on its own in a variety bill, or inserted into a completely different ballet.

Further on, Sollertinsky outlines the action of the ballet, prefacing his account with a barbed phrase: 'In Adrian Piotrovsky's not terribly successful libretto, what might with a little indulgence pass for the plot unfolds as follows . . .' The synopsis concluded, he turns his attention to the music, about which he similarly has some serious reservations:

D. Shostakovich's music also lacks inner unity. Much of it is built from bits taken from the score of his earlier ballet *The Bolt*. Soviet music-lovers will be familiar with the general characteristics of this music from frequent concert performances—it is lively, full of temperament, and very simple in construction. It is orchestrated throughout with virtuosity, at times mordant and razor-sharp, at times gently mocking, not over profound, occasionally guilty of 'self-plagiarism' and a certain strident oversimplification, but always engaging and cheerful. *The Limpid Stream* is not the best music Shostakovich has written for the ballet, and falls well short of the mastery he displayed in the score for *The Golden Age*.

If one takes into account the fact that Sollertinsky always spoke out in support of his friend's works, and took particular care not to damage him in print, one can easily imagine how much more strongly he would have expressed his views on the ballet in private conversation, while feeling obliged in this commissioned review at least not to act against his conscience. The mood of Shostakovich's letter clearly reflects this and the clouds that were gathering over the Moscow production of the ballet. Fate decreed that his premonitions should come true, and they did so in the most dismal manner: we know that it was this production that resulted in the *Pravda* article of 6 February 1936 entitled 'Ballet Falsehood'. As the letter shows, the composer was aware that some of the responsibility for the negative opinions the ballet aroused must lie at his door, although of course nobody could foresee how extreme was to be the frenzied persecution of him that ensued.

The next letter, dated 17 November, pursues the same theme:

My dear friend Ivan Ivanovich,
I hope you got my telegram telling you that the Shakespeare conference is to take place on 25 November. I do hope that we shall be able to meet here and talk about this and that.
    Meanwhile, a brief account of my doings. There was an almost full rehearsal of *The Limpid Stream* today. I sat through the first act and then left. I'll tell you why later on. This

evening I telephoned Fayer[17] to ask him how things were. Both from what he said and from the tone of voice he said it in, I understood that things are not particularly good. The only thing that seems to arouse general approval is my music. Anyhow, he is coming to see me at 12 o'clock tonight and will give me the details. I also telephoned Lopukhov. He told me in a cheerful voice that '36 Moscow factory workers were there, and they were delighted. Arkanov is categorically opposed to the production. Mutnykh is categorically for it.' In any case I will go to see him at 10 o'clock this evening and he will fill in the details for me. I expect that the Arkanov line will prevail, as he has the support of 'the aggrieved'. On the 21st I. A. Akulov will be coming to see *The Limpid Stream*, and it will be up to him to decide whether it goes ahead or not. So, the 21st is the day when everything will become clear. I am quite relaxed about all this. I don't believe there is any point in whipping up a campaign in *Izvestiya* or any other paper. The only aspect of it that really upsets me is Lopukhov. I shall feel acutely sorry for him if this whole project were to collapse. He is a very good person and I am genuinely fond of him. *I beg of you not to speak to anybody at all about any of this.*

One more piece of news from the Bolshoi Theatre: V. L. Kubatsky, Honoured Artist of the Republic, has been sacked. Sacked as conductor and as Director of the Studio. I went to see him yesterday and tried my best to console him.

That's the end of the gloomy part of this letter.

Today I had the enormous pleasure of attending the closing session of the Congress of Stakhanovites.[18] On the podium I saw Comrade Stalin and Comrades Molotov, Kaganovich, Voroshilov, Ordzhonikidze, Kalinin, Kasior, Mikoyan, Postyshev, Chubar, Andreyev, and Zhdanov. I heard speeches from Comrades Stalin, Voroshilov, and Shvernik. I was utterly captivated by Voroshilov, but when I heard Stalin speak I completely lost all sense of proportion, joined the entire hall full of people in shouting 'hurrah', and could not stop applauding him. You will read his historic speech in the newspapers, so I will not set it out for you here. Naturally, today is the happiest day of my life: the day on which I have seen and heard Stalin.

The congress began today at 1 o'clock; that was why I left the rehearsal at the Bolshoi
. . .

As we see, this letter falls into two distinct parts. The first part is written in the style the two friends usually used to address one another and deals with the same subject as the preceding letter, namely the circumstances surrounding the production of Shostakovich's ballet, which were giving the composer so much cause for concern. Moreover, the first paragraph is extremely revealing: Shostakovich's mention of the forthcoming meeting may be taken to mean that he had something to discuss that could not be confided to paper and could only be discussed in a private conversation. Expressions like this crop up frequently in the letters to Sollertinsky, and one can but speculate how interesting and trenchant their actual exchanges must have been. The

[17] Yury Fyodorovich Fayer was for forty years (1923–63) a conductor at the Bolshoi Theatre and naturally he conducted performances of *The Limpid Stream*.

[18] The Stakhanovite movement was named after a worker in the steel industry who became a carefully fostered symbol of the Soviet worker's zeal to over-fulfil his production quota. (Translator's note)

second part of the letter, the style of which can perhaps best be described as 'semi-official', is pervaded by an irony which, while instantly appreciated by both friends, would escape the 'extraneous readers' for whom it was intended, by virtue of the composer's having switched to the familiar language of the press of the time. Needless to say it would have been far more important to Shostakovich to stay for the remainder of the rehearsal, but nobody chosen to receive an invitation to attend a Stakhanovite Congress had any choice but to accept.

The letter contains one other extremely important detail regarding the sacking of Viktor Kubatsky, the outstanding principal cellist and sometime conductor of the Bolshoi orchestra. This was a telling, and ominous, harbinger of the gathering storm of persecution that was beginning to threaten the musical profession. There were only in fact a few weeks remaining before the appearance of the infamous editorial article 'Muddle instead of Music' in *Pravda*, the official organ of the Central Committee of the Party. The next few letters from the composer to his friend[19] concern themselves with all the circumstances surrounding this article and the performances of *Lady Macbeth of the Mtsensk District*, which served as the pretext for the publication of the article. That these performances really were just a pretext may be judged from the fact that even Sollertinsky in Leningrad began to suffer deeply unpleasant consequences. We do not know the details, but matters grew so serious that Sollertinsky contemplated leaving his job at the Philharmonia and returning to his former profession of literary critic. Hearing of this, Shostakovich wrote in great alarm: 'Whatever happens I strongly advise you not to contemplate changing your profession. I don't just advise you, I implore you. Russia has many linguists but very few musicians. And to lose someone like you would be a catastrophe. Carry on with your important and valuable work (9 January 1936).

From Arkhangelsk, where the composer was on a concert tour with the disgraced Kubatsky, a circumstance which naturally only served to exacerbate an already miserable situation, he did not return home to Leningrad but to the capital, from where he sent Sollertinsky a letter uncharacteristically brief but of great import:

Dear Ivan Ivanovich,
I am living very quietly here in Moscow, sitting at home and not going anywhere. I am waiting for a phone call. I don't have much expectation of being received, but have not entirely given up hope. I hardly see anybody. Shebalin drops in from time to time. In *Sovetskoe iskustvo* there is a report of the discussion at the House of Cinema, in which it states: 'Continuation of the discussion of 3rd March. Participants included Comrades Eisenstein, Alexandrov, Shostakovich.' It is not clear to me what this can mean, since I

[19] Shostakovich's letter of 28 Jan. 1936 from Arkhangelsk is quoted in L. Mikheyeva, 'Istoriya odnoi druzhby', part 2, *Sovetskaya muzyka*, 9 (1987), 79.

have never in my life been inside the House of Cinema and consequently there can be no question of my having participated in anything.

In the person of Honoured Worker in the Arts Professor Golovanov[20] I have acquired a first class enemy. This is how it came about: I happened by chance to attend a regular rehearsal of *Quiet Flows the Don*. When it was over, the Artistic Committee, the Theatre Directorate, and so on all had a discussion about it, at which I was present. I made some sharp criticisms of Honoured Worker in the Arts Professor Golovanov. He got positively hysterical, and without waiting for the conclusion of the hysterics, I left. This is the only 'event' that has taken place during my stay in Moscow. Otherwise I am just sitting at home and waiting.

Well, good health and happiness to you, my dear and only friend. Greetings to Irina Frantsevna.[21] D. Shostakovich (29 February 1936)

As we may deduce, the composer had asked to be on the guest list for a reception to meet Stalin, but in vain. No-one wanted to speak to him. As was the custom when a person fell from favour, so-called friends either turned their backs, or waited to see how things would ultimately turn out. Shebalin alone proved himself a true friend. Throughout their whole lives the relations between the two composers were of the warmest and most loyal, although Shostakovich was not as close to Shebalin as he was to Sollertinsky. This can be seen from letters Shostakovich wrote to them both on the same subject, often on the same day: those to Sollertinsky are more candid and contain more detail. Evidently the row with Golovanov also played its part in the events of 1936, as the conductor was a person of considerable influence in official circles.

The next substantial clutch of Shostakovich's letters covers the summer of 1938. Up until that time the two friends had not spent long periods apart, so there had been no need for an intensive correspondence. But in 1938 Sollertinsky fell seriously ill and spent a long time in hospital. Shostakovich wrote regularly to him there, telling him the news and generally trying to cheer him up. Many excerpts from these letters, and from the final, wartime, letters, when the friends were forced to suffer a long separation, have been published in the above-mentioned article 'History of a Friendship'.[22] They will be published in full with annotations at a future date.

---

[20] Nikolay Semyonovich Golovanov (1891–1953), composer, pianist, and conductor at the Bolshoi Theatre and of the Radio Symphony Orchestra, professor at the Moscow Conservatoire. (Translator's note)

[21] Irina Frantsevna Gabar was at that time Sollertinsky's wife.

[22] See n. 19.

6

Between 'Social Demands' and the 'Music of Grand Passions'

The Years 1934–1937 in the Life of Dmitry Shostakovich

INNA BARSOVA

The problem of the relationship between Soviet artists and the authorities in the 1930s is still a long way from being completely clarified. Many things complicate the picture of cultural life during that period. First of all there is the contradictory way in which the regime itself behaved with regard to the implementation of its cultural policy, since it at times created an impression of possible liberalization (a phenomenon analysed in detail in Lazar Fleishman's article on Pasternak and Bukharin in the 1930s).[1] Secondly, there was no unanimity of feeling on the part of the Soviet people: the faith in the ideals of communism cherished by some was very far removed from the bitter insight of others. A third complication is the closed nature of people's behaviour in the 1930s, which expressed itself in particular in the 'verbal theatre' that permeated their everyday speech. Adopting verbal 'masks' was one of the most important ways in which people communicated with representatives of authority and with each other. A final complication is due to the coded nature of existence at that time, and the presence of a subtext in the language of art itself in certain specific cases where there was no possibility for operating differently. Such artistic works are now viewed rather simplistically as attempts to co-operate with the regime, as they are interpreted with hindsight, and from the point of the view of the omniscient and fearless present.

Beginning in 1927 and 1928, when the 22-year-old Shostakovich wrote the opera *The Nose*, the Soviet Union was shaken by an avalanche of false political show trials against 'enemies of the people'. It was by these means that Stalin cleared the way to unlimited power for himself over the country. At first these events remained on the periphery of Shostakovich's life, but gradually they closed in on him. This was the route of Soviet society's journey to Golgotha:

1928   The miners' trial of engineer-saboteurs
1929   The trial of the historians Evgeny Tarle and Sergey Platonov

[1] L. Fleishman, 'Pasternak i Bukharin v tridtsatie gody', *Druzhba narodov*, 2 (1992), 249–59.

1930   The trial of the bacteriologists; the trial of the Industrial Party

1931   The trial of the Union Menshevik Office, and of the Peasant Labour
          Party

1932–3   General 'purging' (the replacement of directors and all leaders in
          regional and provincial areas, and in people's commissariats; the
          dissolution of artistic groupings and the organization of centralized
          artistic unions; the eradication of 'nationalists'; the trial of agricul-
          tural leaders)

1934   The Leningrad trial of saboteurs of the Izhorsk labour department in
          January and the murder of Kirov in December

1935   The mysterious death of Kuibyshev in January; the application of all
          forms of punishment, including the death penalty, to children over
          the age of 12 in April[2]

1936   The mysterious death of Gorky in June; the trial of Zinoviev and
          Kamenev in August; the appointment of Yezhov in place of Yagoda
          to the position of National Comissar of Internal Affairs

1937   The trial of Pyatakov in January; the mysterious death of Ordzhon-
          ikidze in February; the trial of marshals and generals, and the mass
          executions of high ranking servicemen in the military in June
          (among the executed is Marshal Mikhail Tukhachevsky, a friend of
          Shostakovich)

1938   The trial of Bukharin in March; the removal of Yezhov from the
          political arena in May; the appointment of Beria.

It was probably towards the end of the 1920s that Shostakovich came to a complete understanding of the incompatibility of a life without lies and Soviet power, of genius and power, and simply of life and power. This understanding became a deeply concealed tragedy for him, and contrasted ominously with his high standing in the Leningrad artistic world, and the recognition of his genius by the intelligentsia. Shostakovich enjoyed immunity until January 1936. It should be remembered that his colleagues who were part of the musical avant-garde of the 1920s were subject to severe repression. Alexander Mosolov was branded in the press as an 'enemy of the people', and both performance and publication of his compositions was prohibited after 1929. He himself became a victim of repression in November 1937. After its première by the Leningrad Philharmonic under the direction of Fritz Stiedry, Gavriil Popov's First Symphony was banned from further performances in June 1935 by order of the Leningrad Repertoire Committee, for 'reflecting the ideology of hostile classes'.[3] Composers moved away from writing serious music and turned to writing

---

[2] 'O merakh bor'bi s prestupnost'yu sredi nesovershennoletnykh: Postanovlenie TsIK i SNK SSSR ot 7 aprelya 1935 goda', *Svod zakonov SSSR*, xix (Moscow, 1935), 155.

[3] Quotation from the Tur brothers: 'Chrezmernaya lyubov'', *Izvestiya*, 2 June 1933. Quoted in Gavriil Popov, *Iz literaturnogo naslediya. Stranitsi biografii*, ed. Z. A. Apetyan (Moscow, 1986), 403.

music for the cinema and the theatre, and arranging folk music in order to make a living.

Shostakovich's unique situation may be explained in part by the geographical distance between Leningrad and the Kremlin. The erection of a bust of Shostakovich (sculpted by Gavriil Glikman) in the foyer of the Philharmonic Hall is evidence of that, since it was organized by his admirers without the knowledge of the authorities. But the main reason probably lies in the fact that Stalin initially wished to preserve the talents of certain oustanding artists in order to have at his disposal court portraitists who could sing his praises with odes, songs, operas, novels, and films. Shostakovich basically continued to write music with the same kind of avant-garde orientation, and, with the exception of the Fourth Symphony, it was performed. Nevertheless, he had to pay for this blessing by providing a running commentary on his works in the newspapers. There is a clear discrepancy between the meaning of his music and the commentary he made on it. He used the latter to cover his traces and defend his music with ambiguous statements.

Shostakovich's journalistic writings in the 1930s can now be perceived in different ways. One may read them according to the laws of straightforward 'authorial discourse', evaluating them as a simple kind of accommodation with the authorities. But one can also discern in them a skilful lexical dissimulation—the 'verbal theatre of masks' which is so characteristic of the language of expression in totalitarian society. It was particularly noticeable in Shostakovich's journalistic writings, but also manifested itself in his letters and conversation, as Isaak Glikman has affirmed.[4]

Shostakovich's newspaper style is striking in its shocking collision of 'verbal masks', whereby the 'alien discourse' (in Bakhtin's terminology) coexists with the 'authorial discourse'. The 'alien discourse' is imposed by official party jargon. This was the typical rhetoric of the Stalin years which Shostakovich, however, offered up either in 'high' style, or in parodied and sometimes confusing ways. The serious 'authorial discourse' juxtaposed with it is also unexpectedly replaced sometimes by self-parody. This mosaic of indistinguishable verbal masks makes Shostakovich's journalistic writing very piquant reading.

The defensive function of this 'verbal theatre' may be truly evaluated in the political context of the voices of the press. Let us take, for example, the Leningrad evening newspaper, *Krasnaya Gazeta*, in January of 1934, where we can find the following newspaper headlines:

13 January, No. 11, p. 3: 'Lady Macbeth of Mtsensk'. In rehearsal at the Maly Opera Theatre (MALEGOT).

14 January, No. 12, p. 3: 'To the Party Congress'; p. 2: 'Saboteurs. The trial of the

---

[4] *Pis'ma k drugu: Pis'ma D.D. Shostakovicha k Isaaku Glikmanu* (Moscow and St Petersburg, 1993), 68–9 and others. I. Glikman refers constantly to verbal 'masks' in the letters.

Kolpinsk embezzlers (from the supply unit of the Izhorsk Factory)'. Seventy-one people were called a 'gang of class enemies'.

16 January, No. 14, p. 2: 'Saboteurs' (the continuation of the trial).

19 January, No. 16, p. 1: 'Address to the 5th Regional and 2nd Municipal Conference of Leningrad and the Leningrad Region Bolsheviks: To Comrade Stalin, Leader of the World Proletariat'; p. 4: 'Saboteurs'.

20 January, No. 17, p. 3: N. Svirin, 'Writers, Journalists and the Creative Environment'; p. 2. 'The Trial in Kolpin'.

21 January, No. 18, 'Special Lenin Edition', p. 4: 'Lady Macbeth of Mtsensk at the Maly Opera Theatre (MALEGOT). The composer talks about the opera and the production'.

23 January 23, No. 19, p. 3: 'The Première of Lady Macbeth'. The article reads: 'The performance was an exceptional success . . . Tomorrow the theatre will be performing "Lady Macbeth" for the delegates of the regional and municipal Party Conference'; p. 2: 'The Affair of the Saboteurs of the Izhorsk supply unit' (the judge's verdict was that seven people were sentenced to 'the highest measure of social defence', in other the words the death penalty, while the rest were were given 2, 3, or 10-year jail sentences).

25 January, No. 20, p. 3: Z. L. Orlova, 'Composers to the 17th Party Congress. Ahead with mass repertoire.' The article reads: 'Leningrad composers have joined the creative campaign in the name of the 17th Party Congress. Seventy composers have promised to take on the urgent task of writing musical works which will reflect the life of the Soviet nation on the eve of the 17th Congress.'

The middle of the third page of this issue is taken up with Shostakovich's article 'A Composer's Creative Report'. He writes:

With this production I am reporting to the 17th Party Congress . . . I have a lot of work still to do on my general outlook, but thanks to the correct and deeply sensitive leadership of our party, much has already been done in this respect . . . There has been a hiatus in my composition of chamber and popular music. This has occurred due to a certain underrating of these genres. It seems to me that Soviet composers underestimate the need for works in different genres. What a mistake! Just look at what such great masters as J. S. Bach and Mozart wrote, and for what purposes. It is necessary for us to follow their example in this respect. We cannot restrict ourselves exclusively to symphonies, operas, ballets or the like.

Shostakovich's article was published alongside a positive review by Ivan Sollertinsky, and a verse parody by Alexander Flit with the prophetic title 'The Life and Death of "Lady Macbeth of Mtsensk"'.

The murder of Kirov on 1 December 1934, which was incited by Stalin, introduced a new theme into the end-of-year reports by artists and made an already bloodstained situation even more cruel. Take, for example, *Leningradskaya Pravda* of 28 December, p. 3. In an article entitled 'We shall be the trumpeters of a great age', Shostakovich writes of his future Fourth Symphony:

This will be a monumental and programmatic work of grand ideas and grand passions. And, consequently, of great responsibility. I have been bringing it to fruition for many years now. And yet I have still not found the right form or 'technology' . . . The base and foul murder of Sergey Mironovich Kirov obliges me and all other composers to produce works worthy of his memory. It is a particularly onerous and difficult task. But responding to the 'social demands' of our remarkable era with works that meet its requirements, and acting as its trumpets is a matter of honour for each Soviet composer.

It is worth noting that in the above quotation Shostakovich puts the words 'social demands' in inverted commas, which is a rare example of him demarcating 'alien' language. By the 1930s, the phrase 'social demand' [a political term, meaning 'demand formulated by a social class', trans.] was already read as as social 'order' or 'command'. On page 2 of the same newspaper, a certain V. Bobrov published on behalf of workers a response to the verdict on the 'Leningrad Centre' pronounced the day before: 'Eternal damnation to them and death! . . . They must be immediately wiped from the face of the earth'.

Shostakovich nevertheless remained free until 1936, both in terms of ideas and musical technique. In 1935, Gavriil Popov, himself dreaming of exploding the 'banality of public taste' in his Second Symphony, and making a 'leap into the future', wrote with admiration in his diary about Shostakovich's music: '31 October. Detskoe Selo. Shostakovich's Fourth Symphony (I heard the first movement on the piano up to the reprise and have read the score of half of the first movement) is very astringent, strong and noble.'[5] At a time when the ideology of government optimism was beginning to propagate itself in art, Shostakovich really did write 'works of grand ideas and grand passions', assuring the reader all the while that he was thus meeting 'social demands'. He dared to speak through the music in *Lady Macbeth of Mtsensk* and his Fourth Symphony of man's suffering and his passions, of fear and catastrophe. The blow against Shostakovich in the editorials of 1936 ('Muddle Instead of Music' and 'Ballet Falsehood' in *Pravda* of 28 January and 6 February) is largely explained by the incompatibility of such music with the universally proclaimed official style, and the incompatibility of Shostakovich's genius with the regime's desired ideal of the unified Soviet artist.

In 1936 Shostakovich was faced with a test of his moral strength and courage. He had to answer the editorials with a new composition. It is quite possible that the leader expected something from the composer along the lines of Boris Pasternak's grateful verses to Stalin, which had appeared not long before (1 January, 1936) in *Izvestiya*.[6] Stalin could in any case hope for a 'Cantata about Stalin' or a 'Cantata about the Party'. But Shostakovich answered with a symphony without a text. Music's multivalence was the escape route which allowed him to preserve his freedom in secret. The composer faced two problems at this point: a moral one and a stylistic one. The 'Soviet

[5] Gavriil Popov, *Iz literaturnogo naslediya. Stranitsi biografii*, 261.
[6] Pasternak's stand during that period is analysed in L. Fleishman's article (see p. 255).

Artist's Answer' would after all be heard by both the tyrant (or his servants) and his real audience, as well as by eternity. At the same time he had to avoid 'the formalistic', 'chaos', 'wild harmonies', the 'screeching and scraping of the orchestra'. Shostakovich's musical language had to attain 'greatest simplicity' but remain worthy of the Master. It was no coincidence that the composer wrote that the 'composition of this work was preceded by an extended period of inner preparation'.[7] Let us examine further the moral problem.

One of the most tortuous aspects of this 'inner preparation' was probably the overcoming of fear. Leningrad at that time was paralysed by fear of torture-chambers and executions. The unpublished and little-known diary of Lyubov Yakovlevna Shaporina,[8] from the circle close to Shostakovich, provides an interesting revelation of the psychological climate at the time of the Fifth Symphony's première:

2 November 1937. If I stop to think about everything that's going on I have no strength left to live . . . On the 29th when I came back from work Natasha and Vasya opened the door and threw themselves on me—Evgeniya Pavlovna has been arrested. Ira is here . . .
20 November. Ira has gone to the public prosecutor, Shpigel, having obtained permit to see him the day before . . . Shpigel threw her out, saying 'There's no point in you hanging about here. Clear off, or we'll put you in an orphanage.'
21 November. Shostakovich's Fifth Symphony was performed at the Philharmonic Hall. The audience was beside itself and gave him a frenzied ovation in recognition of all the persecution to which poor Mitya has been subjected. Everyone kept on repeating the same phrase: he has answered, and answered well. D.D. came out [to take a bow] biting his lip, and looking incredibly pale. I think he was on the verge of bursting into tears. Shebalin, Alexandrov, and Gauk came from Moscow—only Shaporin wasn't there . . . I met up with [Gavriil] Popov, who said: 'You know, I've become a total coward: I'm so afraid of everything that I even burned your letter.'
6 January 1938. Yesterday morning they arrested Vera Dmitriyevna . . .
21 March. They have taken E.M. Tager . . .
19 February 1939. A. I. Rybakov has died in prison. Mandelstam has died in exile. People are dying all around us, and are permanently ill. It feels as if the whole country is exhausted to the point of collapse, to death almost. But it's better to die than to live in constant fear, in endless wretchedness, half-starving . . .

Fear gripped everyone, obviously Shostakovich included. Only a few had the strength to force it out of their systems. Art and creativity were the last refuges. As Anna Akhmatova wrote: 'I've had enough of freezing in fear | Far better to

[7] 'Tvorcheskie poiski, plani, mechti: beseda s kompozitorom D. Shostakovichem', *Vechernyaya Moskva*, 11 Dec. 1940.
[8] Lyubov Yakovlevna Shaporina, unpublished diary, 2 Nov. 1938 to 26 Oct. 1939, RNB (Russian National Library), op. 1086, ed. khr. 6. Lyubov Shaporina, neé Yakovleva (1879–1967), an artist and translator, and Y. A. Shaporin's first wife, kept a diary on and off from 1 Mar. 1917 until 23 Nov. 1956. In it she describes without aposiopeses the events of the two Russian 1917 Revolutions, the hunger of 1918, the Civil War, the terror of the 1930s, the blockade, the terror of the 1940s and 1950s, and Stalin's death.

call forth the Bach Chaconne . . .'. Who did Dmitry Shostakovich 'call forth'? Bach and Mozart, Musorgsky and Mahler. The latter two had already given Shostakovich a great deal of food for thought in the 1920s when he was searching for a 'tragic style'. And although Shostakovich's interest in Mahler is extensively documented, it is not well known, however, that Shostakovich at some point started arranging the first movement of Mahler's Tenth Symphony for two pianos. Neither of the two manuscript versions he began are dated,[9] but the transcription was probably something Shostakovich worked on in the late 1920s.

Art produced under tyrannical regimes has long employed coded language. Osip Mandelstam used it in 1937, as Leonid Katsis has shown in his analysis of the poet's Stalin 'ode' in his article 'The Poet and the Executioner'.[10] Many people now know that there is also a double meaning in the musical semantics of the finale of Shostakovich's Fifth Symphony.

The semantics of the 'heroic procession'[11] and its subsequent apotheosis are what make up the first plane of the finale of Shostakovich's Fifth Symphony, and which determine how the music will be perceived from the second bar. The timbre of the trumpets and the progression of fourths on the kettledrums produce an unambiguous effect. For the apotheosis in the coda it was especially important for the composer to be able to rely on worthy models, rather than various Soviet examples. The apotheoses in Mahler's First and Third Symphonies became these models. But there definitely exists a second semantic plane in the finale of the Fifth Symphony, which completely negates the triumphant meaning of the first plane. This second plane consists of the semantics of, so to speak, the 'last journey'. And so that his quotations and allusions would not be recognized by the wrong people, Shostakovich used contextual links—to the reproduction of orchestral texture and details of orchestral writing.

The musical content of the finale is fairly complex. As well as the cruel forces which rage in this music, there are also lyrical ideas which radiate with light. But it is the historically established cultural and musical symbols of the 'final journey', hidden in the coded reminiscences of scores by various composers, which really dominate the finale. The most important of these symbols are the

---

[9] RMMK (Russian Museum of Musical Culture), op. 32, ed. khr. 280. The arrangement has 94 bars of the first movement. According to M. Yakubov, among the scores that D. Shostakovich owned is a facsimile of Mahler's Tenth Symphony, without the title-page, printed in Vienna in 1924. Shostakovich could have brought it back from Berlin in 1927, or received it from one of the musicians he knew.

[10] L. Katsis, 'Poet i palach: Opyt prochteniya "Stalinskikh stikhov"', *Literaturnoe obozrenie*, 1 (1991), 46–54. M. Gasparov does not agree with L. Katsis's and other scholars' view that the ode is written in Aesopian language (see M. Gasparov, 'Metricheskoe sosedstvo odi Stalinu O. Mandelshtama', *Zdes' i teper'*, 1 (1992), 63– 73). His strictly philological analysis is aimed at revealing the metrical similarities in the ode and poems surrounding it, where the poet was looking for a natural means of establishing contact with the reality of the 1930s.

[11] M. Sabinina, *Shostakovich-simfonist: Dramaturgiya, estetika, stil'* (Moscow, 1976), 137.

funeral procession, the romantic theme of departure and parting, the journey to execution, and the apocalyptic procession.

The D minor triad which begins the fourth movement, *fortissimo* with timpani roll, can hardly be the beginning of a heroic finale. The association is with something quite different: the ominous and desolate first chord of the overture to Mozart's *Don Giovanni* and the Dies Irae from the *Requiem*.[12] The first four notes of the main theme in the trumpets and trombones (A–D–E–F), divested of the traditional 'golden progression' (sixth–fifth–third), are a commonplace pattern for many melodies (Ex. 6.1). Nevertheless a line of meaning is set up here which is based on the 'step-pattern', and reinforced by the progression of fourths on the kettledrums. The same construction can be found in the fourth song in Mahler's *Lieder eines fahrenden Gesellen*, whose text begins 'I have departed into the peaceful night' (Ex. 6.2). The theme of the march 'in the manner of Callot' in Mahler's First Symphony is also constructed in this way, as is the beginning of the 'Procession to the Execution' in Berlioz's *Symphonie Fantastique*, and the 'Procession' theme in B flat major which follows it (Ex. 6.3). In Shostakovich's fifth bar we see an almost identical reproduction of the descending figure of catabasis from Berlioz's sixth and seventh bars: F, E flat, D, C, B flat, A, G, F. It is also interesting that Berlioz's dominant cadence in bar 8, which is transferred from the winds to the strings, as if cutting through the theme, is reproduced by Shostakovich by means of the unexpected tutti in bar 6.

Later on, the beginning of the reprise in Shostakovich's symphony (fig. 121 in the score), marked by an abrupt deceleration of tempo (100–108), acquires the features of a gloomy military procession with the tiratas of the snare drum. The statements of the theme (figs. 123 to 126, D minor, F minor, shown in Ex. 6.4) are especially interesting as they have associations with the image of the Final Judgement from the finale of Mahler's Second Symphony Ex. 6.4). It is at this point in Mahler's Second Symphony that the brass chorale appears for the first time (fig. 10, in F minor), which in the reprise (fig. 42) is accompanied by the words 'That which has arisen, must disappear'. Shostakovich reproduces the texture of this image with its characteristic break in the register between the low chorus in the winds and the high tremolo of the violins, but uses oboes and clarinets (see fig. 123). The archaic character of the harmony is also preserved, as the chords are without the third (see Exx. 6.4 and 6.5). Even the rhythmic pattern is preserved, although not to the end (Ex. 6.5).

---

[12] In her article 'Mahler und Schostakowitsch' the German scholar Dorothea Redepenning points out a number of quotations and allusions to the music of Mahler's Fifth Symphony, including a parallel between the apotheoses of Shostakovich's Fifth and Mahler's Third. In the finale of the Fifth she also sees a certain similarity with the culminating point of the Scherzo in the third movement of Mahler's Second Symphony. See D. Redepenning, 'Mahler und Schostakowitsch', *Das Gustav-Mahler-Fest Hamburg 1989: Bericht über Internationalen Gustav-Mahler-Kongress*, ed. Matthias Theodor Vogt (Kassel, 1991), 355–62. See also the commentary in the Russian-language publication of her article: D. Redepenning, 'Maler i Shostakovich', *Muzykal'naya akademiya*, 1 (1994).

Ex. 6.1

Ex. 6.2

The execution theme is revealed in Shostakovich's later works, most clearly in his 1942 setting of Burns's poem 'Macpherson's Farewell'. The melody to which are sung the words 'Sae rantingly, sae wantonly, sae dauntingly gaed he [to the gallows]' clearly follows the same pattern as the principal part of the finale in the Fifth Symphony (Ex. 6.6).

In the apotheosis of the finale of Shostakovich's Fifth, there is a contextual link with the culminating fragment of Strauss's *Till Eulenspiegel*, which precedes the theme of the sentencing to death (Ex. 6.7). Shostakovich reproduces the orchestral texture by using the same key as Strauss (D major), and by preserving all three sound planes: the brass chorus with its 'golden progression', the 'nagging' repetition of the note A by the strings and woodwinds, and the tremolo in the timpani (Ex. 6.8). Shostakovich risks revealing the quotation here, as he follows Strauss in his use of seconds. In figure 133 he intensifies it with a minor harmony, turning it into a lament (C, B, A). Genrikh Orlov appears to have been the only Soviet scholar to have noticed this expressive feature in the apotheosis of the Fifth Symphony.[13] The sound of the final chords of the apotheosis (the multiple repetition of a major triad by the winds in the

---

[13] See G. Orlov, *Simfonii Shostakovicha* (Leningrad, 1961), 101.

Ex. 6.3

Ex. 6.3 (*cont*)

Ex. 6.4

melodic position of a fifth) directs us to the conclusion of Berlioz's 'Procession to the Execution'. Finally, Shostakovich's sudden 'stripping down' to the kettle-drums striking fourths in the third bar from the end, when the massive chords stop, creates the sinister effect of the lid of a coffin being nailed down. Mahler never allowed the kettledrums to sound alone in his apotheoses. He did write a

Ex. 6.5

Ex. 6.6

solo for the bass drum, however, at the beginning of the finale of his Tenth
Symphony, and Shostakovich was familiar with the facsimile of this score.

  In the odd hybrid of two diametrically opposed semantic complexes is thus
concealed the brutal truth of Soviet reality in the 1930s, when the *auto-da-fé* of
an entire nation was carried out to the accompaniment of hymns and marches.
Did Shostakovich want people to comprehend the second plane of meaning in
the finale? It would appear that he intended the finale to be understood in two
ways, which is in fact what happened. Not everyone believed the optimism of
the finale to be genuine. Some people noticed that there was something missing
in the piece, but ascribed it not to ideological flaws but to technical errors. Even
such a serious musician as Nikolay Myaskovsky found that the 'end of the finale
was completely flat' and 'empty'.[14] The Leningrad audience at the première

[14] N. Myaskovsky, letter to S. Prokofiev, 5 Feb. 1938, in *S. S. Prokofiev i N. Y. Myaskovsky.
Perepiska*, ed. M. G. Kozlov and N. R. Yatsenko (Moscow, 1977). 455.

Ex. 6.7

Ex. 6.8

Ex. 6.8 (*cont.*)

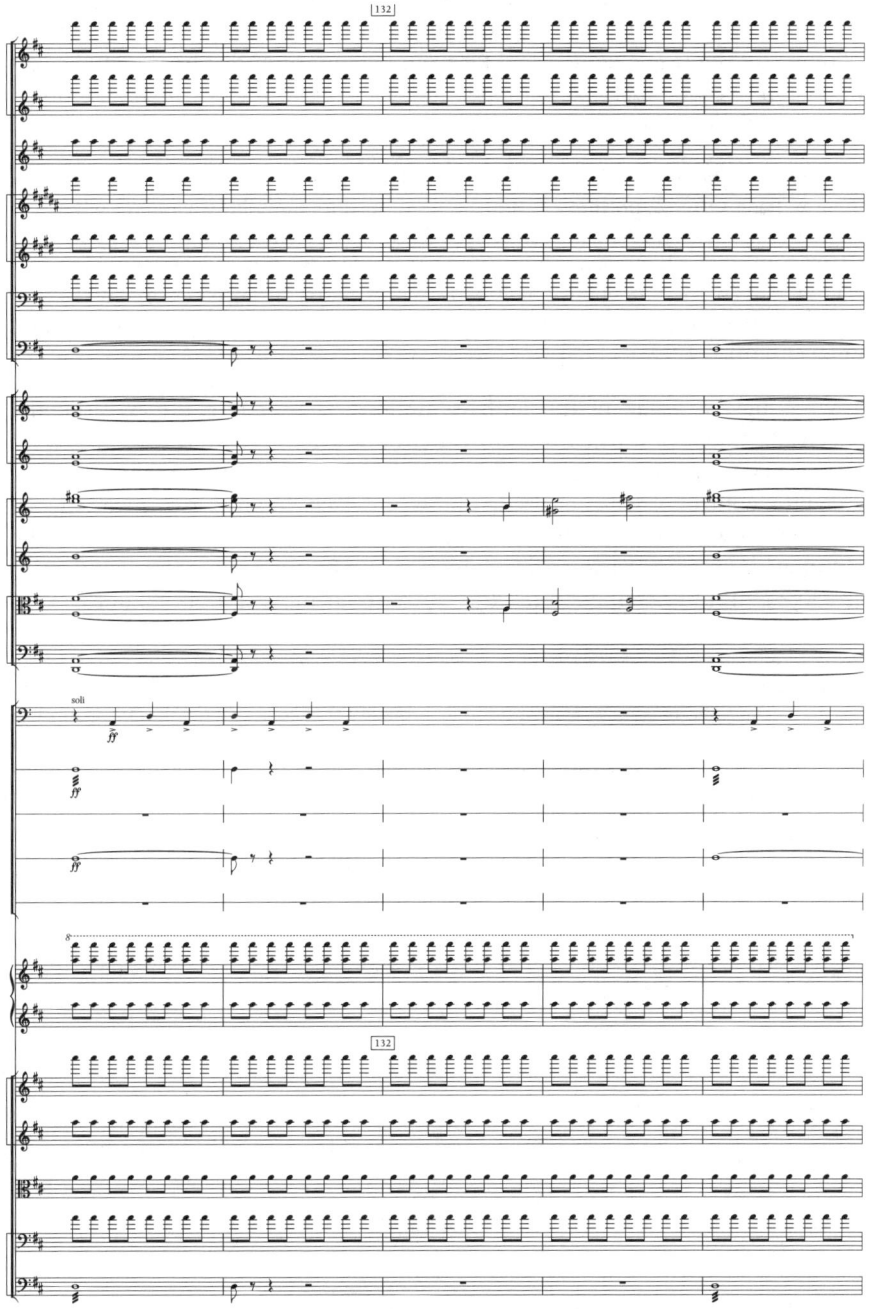

could clearly hear something else in the music, however. The words 'answered and answered well' referred to the tremendous impression the symphony made on them, in which they could distinguish (emotionally and not analytically) the hallmarks of the tragic genre. And far from being dismantled by the finale, this impression was in fact strengthened by it. According to Alfred Schnittke, Shostakovich was the sort of composer

who seemed to be weak-willed to judge from all the external signs . . . no matter how much he tried to work on himself, and he tried hard to show he was doing what was required of him, he still remained his own self. Shostakovich could not destroy himself, and did not want to, but when this was attempted under pressure, it did not work . . . He could not force himself to change, neither could he master his own personality. He was driven by some stronger impulse that came not of his own will but was already instilled in him at birth.[15]

At work in the finale of the Fifth Symphony is therefore not a rationally conceived system of musical reminiscences but an active imagination, whose subconscious released a wealth of associations. It is as if the finale somehow eluded the control of self-censorship and wrote itself. In any case, it was the art of music, in which even the tiniest material elements 'are devoid of finite meanings',[16] in contrast to words, which gave Shostakovich secret freedom in the 1930s, and the chance to tell the truth about himself and his times.

---

[15] D. I. Shulgin, *Godi neizvestnosti Alfreda Shnitke: besedi s kompozitorom* (Moscow, 1993), 87.

[16] Merab Mamardashvili writes: words 'in their common, non-phenomenological senses . . . are finite . . . have finite meanings. Only music has a quality that is nearly infinite. In contrast to language, literature, or painting, it uses such material elements that cannot be imparted with finite meanings' (M. Mamardashvili, 'Zakon Inakomysliya: zapis' odnogo iz vystuplenii pered studentami, sdelannaya osen'yu 1988 g', *Zdes' i teper'*, 1 (1992), 89).

7

Shostakovich and Kruchonykh

OLGA KOMOK

It is not easy to find in the life of Dmitry Shostakovich any calm period when there was nothing to interfere with the composer's thought processes. Each year, each decade, had its full share of the dramas, stresses, and complicated situations that are meat and drink to biographers. Yet even so, the decade of the 1940s was so filled with high drama, and with such highs and lows of fortune, as to seem positively theatrical. Among the events of those years were the blockade of Leningrad, evacuation, the death of Shostakovich's closest friend Ivan Sollertinsky, the world-wide triumph of the 'Leningrad' Symphony, the composition of the Eighth and Ninth Symphonies, the Trio, Op. 67, and the Second Piano Sonata, the devastating 1948 Decree from the Communist Party Central Committee, which was followed by Shostakovich having to join an official delegation to the USA. Against this turbulent background there is one aspect of Shostakovich's life during this period which has never been noticed by commentators, and it forms the subject of the present article.

At the beginning of March 1943, Shostakovich left Kuibyshev in the hope of settling in Moscow. As is well known, he had wished to do this even before the war started, and during evacuation this desire intensified, but it only now became practicable. To begin with, Shostakovich spent several weeks at the Arkhangels-koye sanatorium just outside Moscow where he recuperated from a serious illness (he had contracted typhoid in Kuibyshev). He then moved to the Hotel Moskva, where he settled down to work and began sorting out the details of his future living arrangements. Early in April, through the good offices of his friend Vissarion Shebalin, at that time Rector of the Moscow Conservatoire, he was appointed Professor of Composition at the Conservatoire, and by the end of the month (a considerably short period of time in wartime Moscow) he moved into a new apartment. For a time he lived here alone, his family having stayed behind in Kuibyshev. As he told Isaak Glikman in a letter dated 21 April 1943: 'I am now getting on with moving into my new apartment. Make a note of the address: Moscow, Central District, Ulitsa Kirova 21, Apartment 48. There is no telephone

I would like to take the opportunity of expressing my thanks to Lyudmila Kovnatskaya for directing me towards archive materials, and also to Laurel Fay for a most helpful and productive discussion of my work.

as yet. None of my things are here either. Nothing but walls.'[1] The meagreness of this description paints an all too vivid picture of what circumstances—or rather lack of them—surrounded Shostakovich at this time: a bleak, four-roomed flat on the fifth[2] floor of a nine-storey tenement building with windows overlooking a dark, poky courtyard, whose only attraction was presumably its location right in the centre of town: the building was opposite the Central Post Office. Some time later Nina Vasilievna Shostakovich arrived and, as Flora Litvinova has recalled,[3] there soon appeared a grand piano, a table, and a few packing cases. The children arrived during the summer. According to S. M. Khentova,[4] Shostakovich was not normally much concerned with his surroundings; however in these years the sheer difficulties of daily life stretched even his patience, and the frustration he experienced at the regular interruptions—which continued for many years—of such basic services as water and light finds expression in a bitter letter to Isaak Glikman dated 2 January 1945:

I have no clear plans for 1945. I am not writing anything, as my living conditions are awful. Between 6 a.m. and 6 p.m. I am deprived of two basic necessities: water and light. These inconveniences are hardest of all to bear between 3 o'clock and 6 o'clock in the evening, by which time it is already dark. You don't get much light from a kerosene lamp, and my eyesight is not up to much, so I cannot write. The darkness reduces me to a state of nervous exhaustion . . . At 6 o'clock, on come the lights. But by the time this joyous moment arrives I am so wound up I cannot calm myself . . .[5]

So far as we can judge, the not very open atmosphere in the Shostakovich household was in marked contrast to the noisy company that gathered at his neighbour's apartment. After a time, Shostakovich himself joined the extensive circle of friends and acquaintances attaching themselves to this decidedly unusual person. For Shostakovich's close neighbour, occupying Apartment No. 51, was Alexey Yeliseyevich Kruchonykh (1886–1968)—a notable if somewhat mysterious figure. A Futurist by calling, and dubbed the 'bogeyman of Russian literature',[6] he was as early as 1912 collaborating on an equal footing with Khlebnikov and Mayakovsky in the organization of Futurist organizations such as 'Gileya',[7] 'Syndicate of the Futurists', and '41 Degrees' with I. Zdanevich and I. Terentiev in Tbilisi, rather than LEF and New LEF in Moscow. He also co-authored various Futurist[8] editions, including *A Game in Hell* (*Igra v adu*) with Khlebnikov, and the collections *A Slap in the Face of Public*

---

[1] *Pis'ma k drugu: Pis'ma D.D. Shostakovicha k I.D. Glikmanu*, ed. I. D. Glikman (St Petersburg and Moscow, 1993), 56.

[2] This would be the 4th floor in an English building. (Translator's note)

[3] See E. Wilson, *Shostakovich: A Life Remembered* (London, 1994), 168.

[4] S. M. Khentova, *Shostakovich v Moskve* (Moscow, 1986), 112.   [5] *Pis'ma k drugu*, 69–70.

[6] This was the title of an article by S. Tretyakov used also as the title of a collection of articles about Kruchonykh (*Buka russkoi literatury*, Moscow, 1923).

[7] The word is close to the Russian 'gil'', meaning nonsense.

[8] The word used here is 'Budetlyanskii', a neologism used by the Futurists to denote themselves, derived from the first person singular form of the verb 'to be'.

Taste (*Poshchechina obshchestvennomu vkusu*), *A Trap for Judges—2* (*Sadok Sudei—2*), *The Sickly Moon* (*Dokhlaya luna*) and *Roaring Parnassus* (*Rykayushchii Parnas*). For musicians it is especially interesting that Kruchonykh was the librettist of M. V. Matyushin's opera *Pobeda nad Solntsem* (*Victory over the Sun*), produced in 1913 with settings designed by Malevich in 'the world's first Futurist theatre', established in St Petersburg's Luna Park.

In 1914 Kruchonykh published together with Khlebnikov *A Declaration of the Word as Such* (*Deklaratsiya slova kak takovogo*), in which he coined the expression 'trans-sense language' ('zaumnyi yazyk')[9] which subsequently became an accepted term in literary criticism. He was, according to J.-F. Jacquard, 'the most radical of the "zaumniki". To him can be attributed the most extreme and provocative utterances, which in the highly politicized atmosphere of the 1920s earned him a reputation as a "destructive nihilist" and resulted in the epithet "antisocial" being attached to his works.'[10] Kruchonykh created some of the classic models of trans-sense poetry, such as this famous and untranslatable poem written in 1914:

Dyr bul shchyl
ubeshshchur
skum
vy so bu
r l ez[11]

The same year Kruchonykh published a monograph, *The Poetry of V. Mayakovsky*. It was the first analytical study of this poet, and earned his high approval. But later on, during the 1920s, Kruchonykh spent less and less time on his own creative work, while devoting increasing attention to the theory of 'trans-sense language' and the battle with the 'outdated' language resorted to by poets of past and and present epochs.[12] Literary critics still

[9] With his 'Zaumnyi yazyk'—trans-rational or trans-sense language, which was made up of meaningless but expressive sounds, Kruchonykh wanted to destroy meaning in poetry and so convey the chaos of modern life.

[10] See J.-F. Jacquard, *Daniil Kharms i konets russkogo avangarda* (St Petersburg, 1995), 17.

[11] See p. 118 for original Russian. All nonsense writing, by such as Lewis Carroll or Edith Sitwell, as distinct from absurd or purely comic verse, has in common a deliberate shrouding of educible meaning, the veil being drawn over by devices such as inappropriate syntax, invented words or syllables. Kruchonykh's 'zaum' assembles strings of invented words and syllables which, by invoking aural relationships to words in common usage can suggest a variety of (generally) unsettling images which nevertheless resist conscious analysis. Thus 'dyr' could suggest 'dyra' = a hole, 'bull' could suggest 'bulka' or 'bulochka' = a loaf of bread (this word also turns up in all sorts of popular expressions to mean practically anything at all), 'shchyl' suggests 'shchel'' = a crack or fissure. The phrases and images which make up the language do therefore suggest meaning of a sort, but while there may be an implicitly shared perception among readers or listeners of what this meaning might be, it cannot be explicitly defined. (Translator's note)

[12] Among Kruchonykh's works devoted to this subject are *Tainye poroki akademikov* (Moscow, 1916), *Apokalipsis v russkoi literature* (Moscow, 1923) and others. For a complete Kruchonykh bibliography see *Russkie sovetskie pisateli i poeti: Bibliograficheskii ukazatel'* (Moscow, 1998), vol. xi.

consider that 'the school founded by Kruchonykh was a focal point for all the movements of the avant-garde, from Suprematism to Formalism.'[13] For all that, Kruchonykh's hour of glory evaporated with frightening speed. The fate of the poet echoed that of so many writers of the time: his name began gradually to disappear from the pages of the national literary publications in the first half of the 1930s, undoubtedly as a result of external circumstances. Confirmation of this is provided by the large number of his manuscripts from the 1930s, 1940s, and 1950s which are preserved in the Russian State Archive of Literature and Art (RGALI)[14] and remain unpublished. Until the beginning of the 1940s Kruchonykh was still allowed to appear in print, but not as an author in his own right, only as an editor. This was not, in fact, a new activity for him; his first collection was *Original Stories and Drawings of Children* (*Sobstvennye rasskazy i risunki detei*), which was published in Moscow in 1914. Subsequently Kruchonykh produced collections of *Unpublished Khlebnikov* (*Neizdannyi Khlebnikov*) (Moscow, 1928–33) and *The Living Mayakovsky* (*Zhivoi Mayakovsky*) (Moscow, 1930) which became tributes to the memory of his late 'comrades-in-arms'. The source material for these publications consisted of Khlebnikov's manuscripts and Kruchonykh's own notes of Mayakovsky's utterances and private conversations with him, which he had begun systematically collecting throughout the 1920s. As time went by he added to these collections (originally devoted to two friends from his youth) material from other writers, the most distinguished of whom were Pasternak and Tsvetaeva. Kruchonykh also began to interest himself in bibliography, compiling the reference guides *Twenty years of Pasternak's books* (*Knigi Pasternaka za 20 let*, Moscow, 1933), *Twenty years of N. Aseyev's books* (*Knigi N. Aseyeva za 20 let*, Moscow, 1934), and then *Twenty five years of N. Aseyev's books* (*Knigi N. Aseyeva za 25 let*, *Literaturnyi kritik*, 1939, No. 4).

Little by little this new role of collector and bibliographer took hold of Kruchonykh and became his main activity, his livelihood, and eventually his entire way of life. Thus the poet, the 'fabricator of language',[15] gave way to the guardian of other's archives. Evidence of this comes from the jocular certificate presented to him in 1931 by Mikhail Svetlov, Yuri Olesha, Vera Inber, and Konstantin Zelinsky:

To all writers of the USSR:
The bearer of the present document, Alexey Yeliseyevich Kruchonykh, is head of manuscripts of Writers of the USSR. It is therefore requested that all male and female writers should pass on to him all manuscripts in their possession, whether their own, or by Pushkin, Tolstoy and other classics . . .[16]

---

[13] Jacquard, *Daniil Kharms.*

[14] Russkii Gosudarstvennyi Arkhiv Literatury i Isskustva (Russian State Literature Archive).

[15] Mayakovsky's description of Kruchonykh, quoted in L. Ozerov, 'Seledka v kompote', *Smena*, 3 (1990), 54.

[16] Quoted in N. Koroleva, 'Sto al'bomov', *Vstrechi s proshlym*, 3rd rev. edn. (Moscow, 1980), 296.

Many people have recalled Kruchonykh's battered old briefcase, into which he stuffed manuscripts, drafts, galley proofs, and sometimes rare and valuable books from the authors of his acquaintance. Lev Ozerov has described him in the following typical situation:

Children of influential parents who could afford the luxury of owning something out of the usual, would beg Alexey Yeliseyevich with tears in their eyes to procure for them, let's say, a manuscript by Pasternak for a certain sum. So Kruchonykh would go off and ask Boris Leonidovich to write out some of his poems on nice paper. Knowing his old friend needed to earn a living, Pasternak would oblige with a beautiful, attractively penned, and grandiloquently signed manuscript. Goodness only knows how many such autographs found their way into the homes of distinguished people![17]

Naturally, Kruchonykh did not only collect manuscripts for resale to private individuals. When publication in any form proved impossible, he put together a unique form of manuscript album for his vast collection of unique documents. A great number of these albums have been preserved in the State archives: RGALI, the State Mayakovsky Museum, and the State Museum of Literature.

Within literary circles, attitudes to Kruchonykh's unorthodox activities were decidedly mixed. As the above-cited quotation from Ozerov shows, Pasternak, for instance, who had engaged in fierce polemical exchanges with him in the mid-1920s,[18] nevertheless retained warm feelings towards him, in spite of the manifest differences between them in almost everything—life-style, attitude towards art, and general *Weltanschauung*. That Pasternak truly felt an affinity with Kruchonykh can be judged from the verses he wrote for Alexey Yeliseyevich's birthday:

To Alexey Kruchonykh, in lieu of congratulations

While I grow old from day to day,
You simply grow more handsome.
O God, how different from mine is
The mask of courage you've assumed.
But I'm not right in everything,
There's no reproach to you in this:
Like me, you've been indulged by fate,
You've not been spoilt by destiny.

[17] Ozerov, 'Seledka v kompote', 55–6.

[18] As for example in the introductory essay to the collection of articles by adherents of the poet entitled *Zhiv Kruchonykh!* (*Kruchonykh Lives!*), where Pasternak takes strong exception to his views on Pushkin and Bryusov. Nevertheless, in the course of the same short paragraph he also writes: 'Whenever one comes across wishy-washy lyricism, always unconvincing and never more so than now in our age of the Fruits of Enlightenment, one is reminded how right Kruchonykh was and how readily he must be forgiven for the disdain he probably felt not just for oneself and for one's colleagues, but for those poets who enjoy one's honour and respect' (*Zhiv Kruchonykh!*, Moscow, 1932, p. 1).

For sticking close to my precepts,
That's all there is, in point of fact . . .
We'll institute a Noble Order[19]
For living right in a bad world!
Congratulations from the heart
And let me wish you as reward
Long years to flourish, dream and write
And in so doing bring us joy.
21st February 1946[20]

This little poem may be found in one of Kruchonykh's birthday albums for 1946. Another album contains examples of quite different and more sceptical addresses, such as N. Aseyev's dedicatory inscription on the title-page of his book *The Glow of Victories* (*Zarevo pobed*, 1945):

Kruchonykh
Alexey
Doesn't reap
Or sow
And doesn't grow bald—

or S. Mikhalkov's epigram from May 1943:

Kruchonykh! I am fond of you.
And when one day I'm very rich
I'll buy my archive off you
And give it to an honest man[21]

The unusual passions of Lisey Liseyich—as he was known among his circle of friends—were all of a piece with his no less remarkable appearance and manners, which were sometimes the occasion of barbed caricature (the Kukryniksy),[22] and sometimes reverential awe (see N. Starshinov's reminiscences of Kruchonykh

---

[19] Possibly a reference to the 'Order of Zaumniki' ('Order of Trans-sense Writers'), established in the mid-1920s (not in fact by Kruchonykh but by Tufanov).

[20] See p. 118 for original Russian. RGALI, f. 1334, A. E. Kruchonykh, op. 1 (hereafter referred to as FK), No. 308: Album 'Den' Rozhdeniya Kruchonykh', ed. E. Lunev. 22 Feb. 1946, sheet 8. First published by N. G. Korolyeva, 'Sto al'bomov', 296. (Translator's note: Kruchonykh's continuing personal closeness to Pasternak and his immediate circle may be judged from the fact that Kruchonykh was visiting Olga Ivinskaya, Pasternak's lover and constant companion for the last fourteen years of his life, at the very moment in October 1949 when she was arrested and taken to the Lubyanka prior to being sentenced to the first of two spells of imprisonment in a forced labour camp. Ivinskaya's daughter, Irina, later described him sitting on a small sofa, 'clearly frightened to death', especially when he was not allowed to leave. Olga Ivinskaya, *A Captive of Time*, trans. M. Hayward (London, 1978), 91–4.

[21] See p. 118 for original Russian. FK No. 292: A. Kruchonykh Album, ed. A. E. Kruchonykh from materials, 1912–1968, l. 67.

[22] FK No. 292, l. 61, No. 321. (The Kukryniksy were a well-known group of political cartoonists who always published under this acronym derived from their several names. Translator's note.)

reading his own poetry).[23] Among the range of impressions, perhaps the most objective is the description by Lev Ozerov:

He reminded one of both Gogol and of Gogol's characters at the same time. A stooping figure in a long greatcoat, a bulging file of papers under his arm, tufts of hair flying all over the place, a bouncing gait (cutting-through, he called it), head sunk into his shoulders and his shoulders proudly raised . . . He was perpetually distracted yet at the same time completely focused . . . He never played the fool, and yet there was always something mischievous in him, something of the child. He was a boy, a prankster, until late in life.[24]

It is possible that this is how he appeared to Shostakovich in 1943. It must be added that both Alexey Yeliseyevich and Dmitry Dmitrievich were both extraordinarily young-looking. Shostakovich himself drew attention to this in Kruchonykh's Birthday Album of 1944, where he adds a footnote to a telegram of congratulations sent by Vsevolod Ivanov:

My dear, most precious A. Kruchonykh! At 58 years of age* you are only 18, so at 100 you will be 30. With envy and a touch of 'flu I send you greetings and friendship. V. Ivanov.

*Are you really 58? I thought you were 30. For that, my felicitations. D. Shostakovich.[25]

Shostakovich and Kruchonykh thus became neighbours. What did this encounter bring to each of them? Clearly, Kruchonykh was delighted at the splendid opportunity to add to his collection. Indeed his archive contains several autograph manuscripts by Shostakovich. But nowhere, so far as is known, does the composer make any reference to his acquaintance with the bizarre poet. So was the meeting in 1943 their first, or had they known one another previously? A careful study of the biographies of both men reveals that their paths must have crossed during the 1920s and 1930s, moreover in so intimate a fashion that it seems impossible for them not to have got to know one another personally.

In the second half of the 1920s Shostakovich was drawn into the world of avant-garde (so-called 'left-wing') theatre and cinema, where many of the future habitués of Kruchonykh's circle worked. Although he was involved with the Left Front of the Arts (LEF), it is true that Kruchonykh did nevertheless stay on the periphery of its activities, and yet there are any number of LEFtists whom one could expect to have been intermediaries between Shostakovich and Kruchonykh. These include Mayakovsky, Vsevolod Meyerhold, Sergey Tretyakov, Vsevolod Ivanov, Semyon Kirsanov, Alexander Rodchenko, the Kukryniksy, and Viktor Shklovsky.

Naturally the closest contact between Shostakovich and the LEFtists occurred

---

[23] N. Starshinov, 'What was, so it was', *Literaturnaya Rossiya*, 3 July 1987.
[24] Ozerov, 'Seledka v kompote', 53–4.
[25] FK, op. 1, No. 304, l. 2.

during the period of the production of *The Bedbug* in Meyerhold's theatre, when he made the acquaintance of Mayakovsky, Rodchenko, and the Kukryniksy. Other LEF affiliates would have been present at rehearsals and performances of *The Bedbug*, Kruchonykh among them, however, and his archive contains a programme of the performance of this work on 18 February 1929 which has been signed by the composer: 'This is one of the first I wrote for the stage. D. Shostakovich.'[26] Since this note is not dated and the addressee unidentified, it cannot be established for certain whether it was written in 1929 or later, or for whom it was written; it is quite possible that Kruchonykh acquired it for his archive only in the 1940s.

It may be worth mentioning some less significant connections that Shostakovich had at this time with other people whom he may well have come into contact with via Kruchonykh almost two decades later. In the finale of the 'May Day' Symphony (1929), Shostakovich used verses by the poet Semyon Kirsanov. Then in 1932, along with Vsevolod Ivanov, he paid a visit to V. N. Nemirovich-Danchenko to discuss the possibility of writing an opera on Gorky's novel *Mother*, for which the librettist was to have been Mikhail Bulgakov.[27] Returning to Leningrad, it should be remembered that Shostakovich acquired valuable experience and contacts in the world of cinema by working from 1929 to 1931 in the Sovkino studio on music for the films *The New Babylon*, *Alone*, *The Golden Hills*, and *Encounter*. As well as meeting the film directors Grigory Kozintsev and Lev Trauberg, with whom he was later to become friends, he met the LEF member Viktor Shklovsky. In 1932 Shostakovich attended a poetry evening at which Shklovsky, Vera Inber, and Eduard Bagritsky gave readings of their own works.[28] We may also note some names from the projected repertoire planned for the Maly Opera Theatre from 1932 to 1935. Among the writers 'provisionally' listed are several whom he could well have later come across at Kruchonykh's: Yury Libedinsky, Mikhail Svetlov, Vsevolod Ivanov, Yury Olesha, Nikolay Aseyev, Sergey Tretyakov and Viktor Shklovsky; among the names of the composers is that of Dmitry Shostakovich.[29] Of course, mere contiguity in a list of names (moreover for a plan that was not carried out) in no way guarantees personal acquaintance, but at least it offers the possibility.

Such names and encounters provide us with evidence not only of the possibility of personal contact between Shostakovich and Kruchonykh, but of parallels between their creative worlds, bound up as they both were with the whole direction of Soviet art of the period (which flowered with as explosive a burst of energy as it was to be quickly extinguished) including Constructivism, synthetic theatre, and cinematography. Despite the fact that (with a single exception, which will be discussed later) nowhere in any of the sources extant

[26] FK, op. 1, No. 1058.

[27] See S. Khentova, *Molodye gody Shostakovicha*, ii (Leningrad, 1980), 95.

[28] See ibid. 31.   [29] See ibid. 25.

today do the names of the composer and the poet stand alongside one another, they undoubtedly shared a field of common activity at least during the 1920s and early 1930s. At this time Shostakovich was writing music for film and theatre productions by the Constructivists, while Kruchonykh published two works specifically devoted to the theatre and the cinema: *Phonetics of the Theatre* (1932), in which he demonstrates the close affinity between 'trans-sense' language and the spoken delivery of the actor, and *The Talking Cinema* (1928). This, 'the first book of verse to be written about the cinema', which the author himself describes as an 'attempt to bring together the Great Mute with the Great Talker with poetry', inescapably calls to mind Shostakovich, to whom it fell to bring together the Great Mute and Music. In the preface to the second of these publications, Kruchonykh writes: 'In this book I have written mainly of the movie-pictures which I saw between the autumn of 1926 and the autumn of 1927.' An interesting poem among the many to be found in *The Talking Cinema* is the following, which I reproduce here in its entirety:

Katerina Izmailova
(Lady Macbeth of the Mtsensk District)
after Leskov

At Shrovetide fair
In barkers' booths
They scream and wail:
Roll up, ladies and gents!
No extra charge,
Only 5 kopecks from under your nose,
But if you've a long nose
Then fifteen kopecks from it!
Tram, tram, tram tram,
Screaming, scrapping,
Vanka gets a smack in the face
Wailing at the Fair.
There on the troika
A clutch of girls
And underneath it
A bearded fellow
Turning somersaults
Snowball chucked in face,
Grinning, fancies
Katerina the fleshy modiste.
One for the matchmaker—
Two for the matchmaker—
The merchant's wife's
Under his spell,
Ready for anything!
Now see here

Zinovy's wife
Katerina
Lady Macbeth,
Spud-nosed,
Ripping off their clothes,
Squealing like sucking-pigs!
In his white blouse
Sergey,
The curly-headed bull,
Puts horns on the flour merchant
Makes a farinaceous martyr of him.
Now grandpa's mushrooms
Laced with rat poison
Taste a wee bit sour;
His mouth contorted
In black disgust,
Worms track his face.
All the kitchen in a fright,
Rushes like a mob
From pillar to post.
Katerina with a face of doom
Crosses herself and overdoes
The sighs of grief for the departed.
(While her husband
   Over at the mill
   Entertains with vodka—
   As much as they can drink—
   Tomorrow's drowned men.)
Sergey the horny bull
Sipping tea from a dish
Drinks away the flogging
He got from grandpa,
Ogles Katerina,
As she, plump and stupid, blushes.
   (While her husband
   At the building of the dam
   Bargains with the muzhiks:
   You'll get your milling free
   If you help me get the mill going.)
Oh, Seryozha the steward,
Blackhearted cuckolder,
Has snared himself a wife
Snared himself a wife
But not his own—another's!—
And now her lawful wedded husband
Hurries home from the mill

To the feather soft pillows
Of the downy double bed.
Katerina goes to meet her ever-loving,
And with her fancy-man in tow
Takes the heavy candlestick,
Neatly bashes in his skull.
   (The muzhiks took up
   The promised free milling
   And won a spell of treadmill
   For their rebellious act)
Now hard labour 'stead of home
And the ringing clink of chains
Bewitching Sonka dances round
To the ringing clink of chains.
For the murder of two masters
And the heir to the estate,
You're to be in manacles
Curly-headed devil,
Sergey.
   Three deaths
   To your name
   And fashionable
   Stockings to your bosom.
Katerina
And her partner in crime
Are off to the labour camp,
Katerina
Lady Macbeth,
Nose like a spud,
Clothes burst off with rage—
Drow-ow-owned
Her unexpected rival
Bewitching Sonyetka
In the raging Volga.
Gurg–gurg–gurgle
Three circles on the water—
That's all there is to see . . .[30]

There is no need to discuss the artistic merits of this work: the reader may judge for himself. The point is that the occasion for its composition was the production of a film by the 'Sovkino' studio of Leskov's story in Leningrad in 1926, released on 8 February 1927. (The screenplay was by B. Leonidov, the director was C. Sabinsky, the cameraman was N. Aptekman, the subtitles were by B. Eikhenbaum; leading roles were taken by E. Yegorova—Katerina, N. Simonov—Sergey, A Nelidov—Zinovy.) This film, like all Soviet movies of

[30] See p. 118–21 for original Russian. A. Kruchonykh, *Govoryashchee kino* (Moscow, 1928), 11.

those years, aroused considerable interest in the Moscow and Leningrad press. Critical reaction was varied. For example, the camera work aroused completely opposite opinions. Vladimir Nedobrovo considered that 'Naum Aptekman's photography . . . is the only aspect of the film which deserves high and unequivocal praise',[31] while the unidentified reviewer of *Soviet Cinema* insisted: 'its montage [photography] is inept, so the audience does not understand what is happening on the screen or else laughs at moments of tragedy . . .'.[32] Only on one point did all the critics concur: despite the fact that 'some incidents have been added illustrating the merchant Izmailov's lack of punishment for his exploitation of the peasants',[33] 'a critical approach to the scenario is lacking, as is a proper class-based approach to the fundamentally ethical side of the events with which it deals'.[34] All in all the film had a reasonably long run in metropolitan cinemas—the latest review (in *Zhizn' iskusstva*, 1927, No. 9) appearing seven months (!) after the première. Since in the mid- and late 1920s it was mostly old American and European films which were shown, each of the few Soviet films that were released aroused the keenest interest amongst the denizens of the artistic world. Shostakovich is very likely to have seen the film or at least to have heard it discussed (during 1927 he was away from Leningrad only for short periods: he was in Warsaw and Berlin for the Chopin Competition, and also in Moscow). It would be strange indeed if an event like this had passed him by completely. As an experienced cinema pianist he was soon invited to collaborate with those same movie directors who were to be the glory of the early Soviet cinema, and he later himself became one of the nation's leading composers for the movies. Whatever the truth is, within three years he had started work on an opera whose titles for both of its separate productions reflect both those of Sabinsky's film and Kruchonykh's poem: *Lady Macbeth of the Mtsensk District, Katerina Izmailova*.

Following the production of *Lady Macbeth*, Shostakovich's contacts with the theatre of Meyerhold and the whole 'Constructivist' group dried up. Nor is there any documentation of possible contact between him and Kruchonykh, and therefore we now turn our attention once again to the 1940s and to the material linking the poet with Shostakovich which is now preserved in RGALI.

By all appearances the two neighbours were amicably disposed to one another, which would account for the friendly lack of inhibition seen in several of the documents. This is more evident from Kruchonykh's side, although it also finds expression in the restraint and correctness of Shostakovich's language. Take, for example, the telegram from Vsevolod Ivanov quoted earlier, with its

[31] V. Nedobrovo, 'Katerina Izmailova', *Zhizn' isskustva*, 9 (1927), 12.

[32] See *Sovetskoe kino*, 2 (1927), 30.

[33] S. Yermolinsky, 'Katerina Izmailova', *Pravda*, 24 Feb. 1927.

[34] *Zhizn' iskusstva*, 9 (1927).

humorous postscript from Shostakovich. In the same birthday album from 1944 we find the following curious document:

> Provisional Page
> As it would have been composed by D. Shostakovich
>   if only poetry could be written in notes:
>   I congratulate the verse-consumer
>   of the celebrated constellation—
>   my neighbour at Entrance No. 3
> (Kirov Street No. 21, Entrance No. 3, Apartments 48 & 51)
>   P.S. Poets write in prose,
>   But we in verse,
>   Pegasuses crawl,
>   But we ride a horse.
>   Through forest and vine,
>   Through thunder and tears
>   With Kruchonykh.
>   The Composer D. Shostakovich
>   The short story writer Vodichka-Khersonka[35]

When we remember that Kruchonykh was born in the town of Kherson, we can see that this is one of the many playful pseudonyms he used at various times to conceal his true identity. In the album, the 'Provisional Page' appears as a typewritten copy, but an authenticated one: 'Certified a true copy of the original—E. Lunev'. (E. Lunev was another of Kruchonykh's noms de plume.)[36]

In the verse felicitation quoted above the voice of Shostakovich remains somewhat outside the frame, although there is no doubt that he knew of the joke and probably played his part in it. And then in 1946, also for Kruchonykh's birthday celebrations, the composer himself added his piece to the favoured form of written communication: the next album contains his response to his neighbour's handwritten little poem:

> Despite what everybody thought
> Suvorov fabulously fought.
> On the ice you drink and eat,
> Alexey, you can't be beat!
> Such is your gigantic luck
> Evil sprites will harm you not—
> They'll just disappear in smoke!
>   Lyuten, 1946. E. Lunev
> I share the vigour of these lines and join in wishing you Happy Birthday.
>   D. Shostakovich 2.02.1946[37]

---

[35] See p. 121 for original Russian. Fk No. 304, fo. 3.
[36] See *Russkie sovetskie pisateli, poeti*, xi. 379.
[37] See p. 121 for original Russian. FK No. 292, fo. 89.

At the same time Shostakovich sent—or more probably handed—Kruchonykh a short letter of congratulation:

Dear Alexey Yeliseyevich, congratulations on your sixtieth birthday. I wish you health, happiness and success. Yours, Shostakovich.
P.S. I am very glad that fate made me your neighbour. D. Shostakovich.[38]

Although the letter is written in characteristically 'impersonal' style, the postscript is highly revealing. It seems that this letter evoked 'gifts in return' (it was probably Kruchonykh himself who coined a term for these, 'otdarki'), in the shape of verses written by the subject of the celebrations and by Semyon Kirsanov. There are typewritten copies in the 1946 'Kruchonykh Birthday Album':

> Shostakovich from his mother's knee
> Was king of orchestra and key-
> Board. Symphonies all nine,
> Unheard-of marvel of the time!
> > A. Kruchonykh

> On hearing works of Shostakovich
> The audience is in a roar,
> Even critic What's-this-ovich
> Is lost for words, except 'encore!'
> > S. Kirsanov[39]

But even more than by these congratulatory effusions and epigrams, the intimacy of the relations between the two men is attested to by the number of Shostakovich's requests and proxy documents for obtaining books and photographs from libraries, 'to be given to Kruchonykh', and which Kruchonykh carefully preserved.[40] From these proxy documents we know that between 1944 and the winter of 1947, the composer several times asked Kruchonykh to get for him children's books, photographs, and books by Gogol and Wilde. (It is known that both Pasternak and Kirsanov also made several similar requests to Kruchonykh.) An interesting detail: on 22 April 1946 Shostakovich made through Kruchonykh the following application to the Political Books Publishing House: 'I would like to start a subscription to receive the Complete Works of J. V. Stalin. At the time when subscriptions were opened I was not in Moscow and am therefore late in applying. D. Shostakovich.'[41] Knowing Shostakovich's exceptional punctiliousness and

---

[38] FK No. 225.

[39] See p. 122 for original Russian. FK No. 308. Kirsanov's 'otdarok' was published by V. Dmitriev under the title 'Chernoviki-Kirsanoviki' ('Kirsanoviki —i.e Kirsanov's—Sketches'), except that in this version 'chto-zh-takovich' (literally 'what's-this?-ovich') is changed to 'bestolkovich' (literally 'dimwit-ovich' in 'Vstrechi druzei' ('Meetings between friends') in *Literaturnaya Rossiya*, 18 Jan. 1964, p. 24.

[40] FK No. 240, 1060.   [41] FK No. 1060, fo. 6.

1. Caricatures of Shostakovich by Nikolay Radlov, 1920s, 1933

2. Shostakovich at his desk, Leningrad, 1930s

3. Shostakovich with friends at a soccer match, Leningrad, mid-1930s

4. Shostakovich with students at the Leningrad Conservatoire, late 1930s

6. Shostakovich with the Borodin String Quartet (Rostislav Dubinsky, Valentin Berlinsky, Nina Barshai, and Rudolf Barshai), *c.*1946

5. Caricatures of Shostakovich by the Kukryniksy, 1942 and 1944

8. Pencil drawing of Shostakovich by Alexey Kruchonykh (from a photograph), 1945

7. Shostakovich at the piano with his wife, Nina Vasilievna, 1940s

9. Shostakovich with the popular music composer Matvey Blanter at a soccer match, Moscow, c.1950

10. Elmira Nazirova and autographed title-page of Shostakovich's Tenth Symphony, with dedication to her, 1954

11. Shostakovich in the sound studio of Mosfilm during the recording of his orchestration of Musorgsky's *Khovanshchina*, Moscow, 1959

12. Shostakovich with Mstislav Rostropovich and Svyatoslav Richter, early 1960s

13. Shostakovich at the 'Pavlov House' in Volgograd (formerly Stalingrad), 1960s.

14. Shostakovich on the island of Kizhi, Karelia, 1960s

15. Shostakovich playing cards in hospital, 1960s

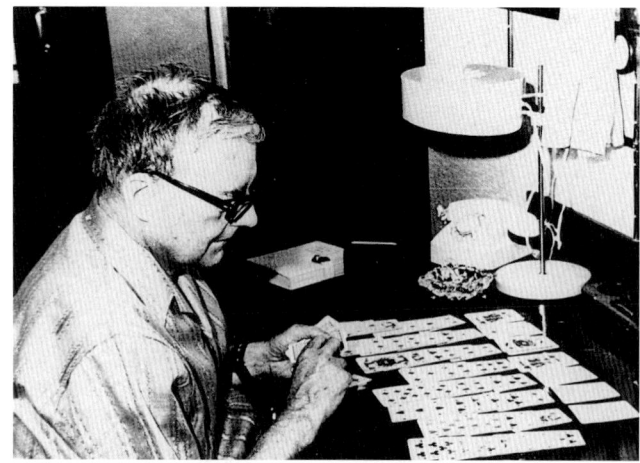

16. Shostakovich with his son Maxim, Moscow, 1960s

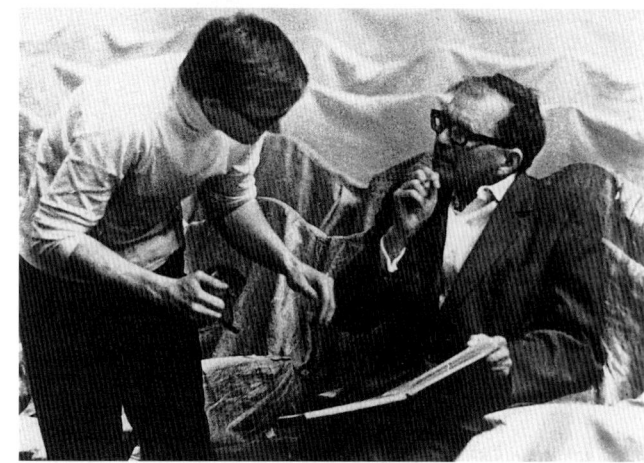

17. Shostakovich with his daughter Galina and the composer Aram Khachaturian at a sanatorium in the Caucasus, late 1960s

18. Shostakovich in conversation with Yvgeny Svetlanov, photographed unawares, late 1960s

19. Official photograph of Shostakovich, *c.*1970

20. Shostakovich putting his coat on with the help of his wife Irina Antonovna, *c.*1972

delicacy of manner, it is hard to imagine him entrusting such a request to anybody to whom he was alien or unsympathetic.

On the reverse of one of the proxy letters there is the following signed note: 'I give these books to Kruch[42] and with the books [illegible word]. Everything he has belongs to him. D. Shostakovich, 2 May 194[7?]'[43] Unfortunately it has not yet proved possible to establish which of Shostakovich's books ended up in Kruchonykh's library, but it is known that in Shostakovich's library there is at least one book that had belonged to Kruchonykh. Today this copy is the sole tangible evidence of personal contact between Shostakovich and Kruchonykh prior to their becoming neighbours, since it was presented to the composer in 1942. The book is entitled *The Second Tournament of Poets*[44] and consists of a compilation by Kruchonykh of, as he explains in the Preface, 'verbal tricks, games and poetic puns' stemming from the search for rhymes for the names of different composers, from Bach to Chemberdzhi.[45] Contributors included Nikolay Aseyev, Semyon Kirsanov, E. Lunev (i.e. Kruchonykh himself), P. Neznamov, Yury Olesha, I. Selvinsky, Mikhail Svetlov, and T. Tolstaya. In the Preface, to which he gives the title 'A musical assault', Kruchonykh tries to justify this 'juggling with words' and describes the history of its composition, which, according to him, had its origins in the 'Herzen House'. This little book was published in a cyclostyled edition of 100 copies in 1932, and the first page carries a handwritten inscription: 'To dear D.D. Shostakovich, looking ahead 10 years (see page 10). 1932–1942. A. Kruchonykh. Moscow 16/4/42.' If we follow the instructions and indeed turn to page 10, we see there two epigrams by P. Neznamov on the name of Shostakovich, both of them relatively respectful (which is by no means the case with some of the other impromptu squibs):

> Why is sea-spume foul to drink?
> Why do walruses taste so bad?
> Why is Berlin worse than Chamberlain?
> Why is a sexton worse than Chemberdzhi?
>   Enough of fibs and trivialities:
>   Shostakovich runs rings round them all!

And another about Shostakovich:

> A composer—what's that, please?
> Verkhotursky once enquired.
> Shostakovich thought then said:
> It is me and Debussy.[46]

---

[42] This was how the poet's name, which peculiarly resists declension in the standard Russian way, was usually shortened among the poet's friends and acquaintances.

[43] FK No. 240, reverse of fo. 17.

[44] RGALI, f. 2048, Shostakovich, op. 3, No. 323.

[45] Nikolay Karpovich Chemberdzhi (1903–48), composer of Bashkir origin known for his incorporation of folk material from the countries of the Caucasus into his symphonic works. (Translator's note)   [46] See p. 122 for original Russian.

It is worth noting that in the cyclostyled copy, the word 'voprosil' ('enquired') in the second epigram has the initial letter 'v' written over the original 'd'. Thus the published version has, instead of 'doprosil' ('interrogated'), a milder, less threatening, ring to it. Alongside the second epigram Kruchonykh has added a note: 'Sic! A. Kruchonykh. 1932–42.' The subtext is clear: in April 1942 Shostakovich came to Moscow for the première there of his Seventh Symphony (it was heard four times, on 29 and 30 March, 5 and 6 April). Kruchonykh must inevitably have known of the performances and of the award to the composer of the Stalin Prize First Class, which was announced on 11 April, and evidently judged that a copy of *The Second Tournament of Poets* would be a fitting present, with its foreseeing by ten years one of its subject's future triumphs in 1942. Unfortunately, the circumstances in which the book was presented to Shostakovich on 16 April are not known, nor is it known what the composer thought of the publication.

Reverting to Kruchonykh's archive, in addition to the documents already cited, there are several more 'official' ones: conventional spoils of the professional collector. The most obvious example of this is the statement written on a separate page: 'The State Literary Archive is a treasure-house of artistic creativity. D. Shostakovich. 14.10.1943.'[47] On the face of it this is no more than an autographed statement by a famous person, but knowing as we do the pride of place that archives in general and the Central State Archive of Literary Art (TsGALI—now RGALI) in particular occupied for Kruchonykh (see, for instance, the photograph of the poet in front of the TsGALI building, published in the collection *Vstrechi s proshlym* (*Encounters with the past*)—third edition), it is quite possible to imagine that the inscription was made at Kruchonykh's request. The page is oblique testimony to the possibility of discussions having taken place between the two men about the composer's donating papers from his private archive to TsGALI, which did in fact subsequently come about.

To this category of document can be ascribed Shostakovich's article on Rimsky-Korsakov with a dedicatory inscription to the poet (1944),[48] the autographed copy of the *Bedbug* programme mentioned above, programmes of and invitations to performances of his works (1940–5),[49] articles about and references to Shostakovich,[50] and cuttings from newspapers and magazines of the following articles by the composer:

> 'Thoughts on Tchaikovsky'—*Shchit i mech*, 7 November 1943;
> 'Shostakovich Speaks about his Work'—*Smena*, 1943, No. 20;
> 'Rafael Kubelik's Concerts'—*Pravda*, 1 October 1946;
> 'Let us Create Worthy Works of Art'—*Na strazhe Zapolyar'ya*, 6 November 1947; this cutting is autographed by Shostakovich;

---

[47] FK No. 1005. [48] FK No. 1057.
[49] FK No. 1059. [50] FK No. 1061.

'On some Essential Questions about the Art of Music'—*Pravda*, 17 June 1956; this one with marginal annotations by Shostakovich.[51]

The fact that this material contains one document dated as late as 1956 shows that personal contact continued, however episodically, after Shostakovich moved to Mozhaiskoye Shosse in 1947. Much the most valuable of all the material relating to Shostakovich in Kruchonykh's possession is without doubt the sketches for the Second Piano Sonata [52] and the Ninth Symphony.[53] (So far the author of this article has been able to study only photocopies of these documents; the originals cannot be accessed owing to their fragile state.)

The autograph of the Second Sonata sketches consists of two sheets of manuscript paper, on which the music is clearly written in ink, in a kind of shorthand, that is to say with no key signatures, rests, dynamic or agogic markings, and without crossings-out. It accords in everything but a few minor exceptions with the final version of the Sonata. These sheets contain the whole of the second movement and a large part of the third movement, up to bar 217. The first of the two pages is headed by an explanatory note: 'Draft manuscript of my Second Piano Sonata. 1943. D. Shostakovich. 23.v.1944.'

In contrast to the manuscript of the sonata, the sketches of the Ninth Symphony are exactly that—sketches in the true sense of the word. These also consist of two sheets of paper, signed by the composer: '9th Symphony. 1945. D. Shostakovich.' The following fragments appear in piano score form, with no indication of instrumentation: on page 1 sketches for the fourth movement, in which the layout of the material and some specific notes differ from the final version of the symphony; later on the same page the opening of the fifth movement, which likewise, although written in shorthand, is somewhat different from the printed score. At the bottom of the page the material breaks off at bar 141 of the final version. At the top of the reverse of the first page there is the figure III in Roman numerals, below which appears material which did not find its way into the finished work, and is covered with crossings-out and abbreviations of various kinds. On page 2 this material is continued, and then, below Roman figure II, it is possible to discern the contours of the opening material of the finished version of the second movement, written out however in 3/4 time rather than in 6/8. On the back of page 2, in the top right hand corner, there is an inscription: '1945. 9th Symphony. D. Shostakovich.' The whole sheet is in poor condition, such that one can barely make out the first theme of the second movement of the symphony, which is written out at the top of the page; further down the text disintegrates in a welter of corrections and crossings-out. It is clear that the Kruchonykh archive contains one of the earliest sketches of the symphony, testifying to the fact that the process of

---

[51] FK No. 1056.   [52] FK No. 1053.   [53] FK No. 1054.

composition was far from straightforward: the second movement became the third, first thoughts on the material for the third movement were abandoned altogether; the whole opus was recomposed.

The archive contains more than a dozen photographs of Shostakovich, from 1936 to 1946,[54] many of them with signed inscriptions to the composer's neighbour. Because of its personal overtones it is worth citing one of these: 'I present this bad photograph to the good collection of A. E. Kruchonykh. D. Shostakovich. 10.03.1946, the eve of the equinox.'[55] Kruchonykh, who was an excellent draughtsman (he had trained as an artist in his home town of Kherson) made pencil drawings from three of the photographs given to him by Shostakovich, which evidently pleased the composer. The first of these portraits,[56] taken from a photograph of 1941,[57] was made over a period of two days: Kruchonykh got the photograph on 7 March and it was ready on 9 March. Shostakovich wrote on the portrait: 'I like this portrait very much; it is a good likeness of me. D. Shostakovich.' The second portrait was also executed in March of 1945,[58] and is taken from a 1943 snapshot of Shostakovich at the piano in the village of Ivanovo, where there was a collective farm, which is now the Union of Composers' Home of Creative Retreat.[59] Shostakovich approved of this one too: 'A very good portrait. I like it very much. D. Shostakovich.' The last portrait appeared half a year later; it is dated 27th April 1946.[60] It was based upon a 1936 photograph of the young composer.[61] 'I recognize myself' wrote Shostakovich on the page opposite Kruchonykh's work. It is noteworthy that none of these inscriptions suffer from the stiff, official style of most of Shostakovich's written language.

The sheer act of listing and describing the materials to be found in Kruchonykh's collection reveals a kind of consistent thread: the varied nature of the documents, and the presence of material which sheds light on the composer's actual creative process (the sketches for the sonata and the symphony), testify to the trust which Shostakovich placed in Kruchonykh. And in turn, Kruchonykh's three portraits of his neighbour return the compliment.

Was Shostakovich aware of Kruchonykh's experiments in poetry? Undoubtedly he was. But to what extent? The precise answer to this question may only be known after a study of the composer's library and exhaustive publication of his complete correspondence. But it is hardly likely that

---

[54] FK, Nos. 1062, 1063.   [55] FK, No. 1062, fo. 12.

[56] FK, No. 107. The inscription on this portrait is quoted by V. Lavrov in his note 'From the archive of Kruchonykh' *(Literaturnaya Rossiya,* 1 (1979), 19 Jan.).

[57] FK, No. 1062, fo. 3.

[58] FK, No. 714/26, fo. 2. In the catalogue of the exhibition 'Dmitri Schostakowitsch und seine Zeit. Mensch und Werk' (Niederrheinisches Museum der Stadt Duisburg, 16 September–28 October 1984) this portrait is listed as exhibit No. 338 (p. 105).

[59] FK, No. 1062. fo. 4.

[60] FK, No. 714/26, fo. 1. This portrait was published in Khentova, *Shostakovich v Moskve.* See pp. 96–7.   [61] FK, No. 1062, fo. 1.

Shostakovich would have had much sympathy with Kruchonykh's aesthetic preoccupations—a 'waggish' attitude to art, an immersion in children's verse, and a predilection for children's speech and drawing. To judge from the texts and librettos of Shostakovich's works and his letter-writing style, he had little interest in phonological games and inventions, or the poetry of the absurd. In this sense he would have had more affinity with the *Katerina Izmailova* poem than with the *zaum* of 'dyr-bul-shchyl'. Clearly the language which would have and did bring them closest together was the language of Gogol, to whose works the composer often turned. As S. Rassadin has noted, 'And Kruchonykh was no mere dyr-bul-shchylster—who, better than he, wrote of Gogol: "He surpassed all his contemporaries, and revealed the nether regions of Russia"?'[62] Shosta-kovich's interest in avant-garde tendencies in the theatre and painting, in the literary polemics of LEF about Constructivism and the 'Neue Sachlichkeit', was short-lived, while his collaboration with Meyerhold, Kozintsev, and Trauberg was just one episode in his biography.

It is possible that the jolly evenings at Kruchonykh's brought back to mind the family entertainments of Shostakovich's youth. According to G. Yudin, 'at that time of his life Shostakovich was an extremely lively, direct, and witty person. He made a constant stream of pungent remarks that never seemed contrived, but always somehow natural; endless nicknames and pet names for people, all sorts of improvisations. All this changed after the sadly infamous articles "Muddle instead of Music" and "Ballet Falsehood": Shostakovich became noticeably more reserved and less talkative.'[63]

In the 1940s the fates of these two people sharply diverged. After the Seventh Symphony Shostakovich's genius was at its zenith, and even in his native land he was regarded as the 'state' composer. Kruchonykh, on the other hand, only too aware that his hour had passed, was in semi-disgrace. Not only did he not appear in print at all, but from 1940 onwards it was practically impossible even to make reference to him or to his contributions. We may nevertheless state with confidence that Shostakovich and Kruchonykh were brought together not in any forced way, but by warm and more than good neighbourly relations, and by their shared past. Such is the conclusion to be drawn from the materials in the Kruchonykh archive, in which the names of the two neighbours stand side by side.

[62] S. Rassadin, 'Poeziya—delo veseloe', *Liternaturnaya gazeta*, 6 Sept. 1995, p. 5. Evidently the reference is to the typewritten collection of poems of 1944, *Slovo o podvigakh Gogolya*. This may be found in FK No. 20; it does not appear to have been published and is not listed in any of the bibliographical indices.

[63] G. Yudin, 'Yavis', vozlyublennaya ten' . . .', *Pro Musica*, 2–3 (1995), 15.

Russian Texts

Дыр бул щыл
                                              убешщур
                                                  скум
                                             вы со бу
                                              р л эз.

Алексею Крученых. Вместо поздравления.
                        Я превращаюсь в старика,
                        А ты день от дня все краше.
                        О, Боже, как мне далека
                        Наигранная бодрость ваша!
                          Но я не прав со всех сторон,
                          Упрек тебе не обоснован:
                          Как я, ты роком пощажен,
                          Тем, что судьбой не избалован.
                        И близкий правилам моим,
                        Как все, что есть на самом деле . . .
                        Давай-ка орден учредим
                        Правдивой жизни в черном теле!
                          Позволь поздравить от души
                          Тебя и пожелать в награду
                          И впредь цвести. Мечтай, пиши
                          И нас своим примером радуй.

Крученыху
                                Алексеищу
                                не жнущу
                                не сеющу
                                и не лысеющу —

Крученых! Я тебя люблю.
                                Когда-нибудь богат я буду —
                                Архив свой у тебя куплю
                                И сдам в архив честному дюду.

На Масленой
                                у балаганов
                                визг, вой:
                                заходи, народ честной.
                                Вход без запроса —
                                пятак с носа,
                                а у кого нос длинный —
                                с того пятиалтынный!
                                Трам, трам, трам, гам,
                                визг, бой

Ваньку бьют по мордам
на ярмарке вой.
А на тройке —
куча девок,
а под тройкой —
бородач
кувырком
в лоб снежком,
улыбается
и влюбляется
в многопудовую
модистку Катерину.
Сваха — раз
сваха — два
и купчиха подневольная
готова-а!
Вот теперь
Зиновия жена —
Катерина
леди Макбет
нос картошкой
кофты бесятся от жира,
рвутся визгом белых поросят!
В белой косоворотке
бык завитой
Сергей
рога наставляет купцу
мучнистому
мученику.
А крысий мышь як
уступили дедушке
в грибочки
кисленькие.
Рот искривился
брезгом черным
по лицу — червячки.
И вся кухня всполошилась
побежала косяком
дверь — в дверь — дверь.
Катерина грозно крестится
привираючи со вздохом
поминальною слезой.
   (А муж ее
   на мельнице
   поит
   завтрашних утопленников

водкой до согласу)
Блудливым бык Сергей
чаем с блюдечка
в прикуску
запивает
дедушкину порку
за Катерину
дебелую
дубовыю
краску.

   (А муж ее
   на стройке у плотины
   помол бесплатный обещает
   мужикам:
   подсобите только мельницу
   пустить)
— Эх, Сережка-ключник
злой разлучник
залучил к себе жену,
залучил к себе жену,
да чужую, не свою! —
А муж ее
от мельницы
домой спешит
в пуховые подушки
на двоих.
Встречает мужа Катерина
Да с полюбовником —
подсвечником
и в темя
благоверное.

   (А мужики
   Из-за того бесплатного помола
   бредут на каторгу
   за бунтовство)
Мимо дома — каторжане,
звон цепей
Сонька Вьюн
звон цепей.
За убийство двух хозяев
и наследничка
быть тебе в наручниках
курчавый черт
Сергей.

   Три смерти
   за душой

и модные
чулки за пазухой.
Уходит Катерина
с подсобником
на каторгу.
Катерина
леди Макбет
нос картошкой
кофта бесится от злобы —
в лютой Волге
утопи-и-ла
свою нежданную
соперницу
Сонетку Вьюн.
   Бульк, бульк, бульк
   три круга на воде —
   и больше ничего не видно . . .

page 111
         Условная страница.
Как написал бы Д.Шостакович, если бы стихи
   можно было начертать нотами:
      Поздравляю стихоеда
         громкого созвездия —
      моего соседа
         третьего подъезда
/Улица Кирова, д.21, 3-и подъезд, кв. 48 и 51/

P.S.   Поэты — прозою,
   а мы стихом,
пегасы — ползают,
   а мы верхом.
      Сквозь лес и лозы,
      сквозь гром и слезы
      с Крученыхом.
         Композитор Д.Шостакович
         Новеллист Водичка — Херсонка[30]

page 111
         Куцой логике на зло
Суворов воевал зело.
Алексей, пируй на льдине,
Ты — непобедимый!
Тут твое счастье — дыбом,
(всякая) нечисть
уносится дымом!

page 112

Дмитрий Шостакович с детства
Король роялей и оркестров.
Симфоний девять —
Чудовинная невидь!
   А.Крученых

Композитор Шостакович
Зал в волненье погрузил,
Даже критик Что-ж-такович
Ничего не возразил.

page 113

Чем не напиток — морская пена?
Чем не лакомство — моржи?
Чем Берлин хуже Чемберлена?
Чем дьячок хуже Чемберджи?
   Довольно врать и пустяковить:
   Их всех обскачет Шостакович!

page 113

Еще о Шостаковиче . .
— Композитор — что такое?
Верхотурский вопросил.
И ответил Шостакович:
— Это я и Дебюсси.

8

Shostakovich's Eighth

C minor Symphony against the Grain

DAVID HAAS

The best and the worst interpreters of Shostakovich's Eighth Symphony are agreed on at least one point: This symphony, begun in July 1943, two days before the Battle of Kursk, has something to do with war. Too often, however, speculation as to Shostakovich's precise inspiration, whether personal or collective experience, Fascist invaders or Stalinist terror, Second World War or war in general—so occupies the commentators that they neglect basic description of the music. Thus in their reviews of the New York première on 2 April, 1944, neither Olin Downes nor Virgil Thomson bothers to mention that this is a symphony in C minor, a striking omission in Downes's case, since he proudly informs the readership that he had been granted special access to the score.[1] This is unfortunate, since key is our first, and not insignificant link back to Beethoven's Fifth Symphony. There are other shared traits as well: Shostakovich's Eighth Symphony—like Beethoven's Fifth—is unmistakably tragic, occasionally lyrical, memorably ferocious. It is also a powerful emotional experience—or journey—meant to provide the same range of highs and lows that a nineteenth-century audience once heard in Beethoven. Most intriguing of all, Shostakovich's Eighth—like Beethoven's Fifth—is a symphony without subtitles, without Red and Black army markers for its themes. And the many passages of apparent expressive intent—the multiple onslaughts of searing violence, the straining lyrical lines, the chaotic textures that clear away into soft, shimmering azure skies—depend for their coherence on abstract musical schemas traceable to the nineteenth century.

Three assumptions underlying most specialist writing on nineteenth- and twentieth-century Russian symphonies are: (1) that form and content, however defined, condition one another during the process of composition and must be examined together in any substantial critical, interpretive, or analytical project; (2) that the employment of the broad categorizations 'absolute' or 'programmatic' routinely used to distinguish Brahms from the *Zukunftmusiker* (and Beethoven's Seventh from his Sixth) is inconsistent with late nineteenth-century

---

[1] Olin Downes, 'Critique of the [Eighth] Symphony', *New York Times*, 3 Ap. 1944; Virgil Thomson, 'More of Same', *New York Herald-Tribune*, 3 Ap. 1944.

and twentieth-century Russian symphonic thought; (3) that individual canonized symphonies of Russia and the West in whatever form they are known, remembered, distorted, or misread exert as strong an influence on the composition of a new symphony as any formal scheme, modulation plan, or period fashions of scoring, genre, or melody. Tchaikovsky is usually cited as the authority for all three of these: from him the aesthetic passed on to Boris Asafiev, Vladimir Shcherbachev, Ivan Sollertinsky, and other musicians in Shostakovich's circle, as well as countless commentators since. There is time only to comment on the third assumption: that canonized symphonies play a crucial role in the shaping of new works. Assimilation of the tradition rests largely on score study and Balakirev, Rubinstein, Rimsky-Korsakov, Taneyev, Glazunov, Myaskovsky, Steinberg, Shcherbachev, in fact all of the famous Russian teachers of composition, insisted upon deep knowledge of scores. Critics, too, study scores and use their knowledge of them to reckon the stylistic debts incurred by composers. At its most simplistic, the exercise is limited to surface affinities as, for example, when Downes faulted Shostakovich for quoting in rapid succession César Franck, Richard Strauss, Sibelius, Bruckner, Mahler, and Prokofiev.[2] These surface affinities do exist for the music reviewer to detect even on first hearing, but beneath the surface lie other more significant affinities requiring deeper knowledge and longer acquaintance or else a very lucky tip-off from the composer himself. With characteristic lucidity and self-effacing modesty, Tchaikovsky gave the vital clue to his Fourth Symphony when he revealed in a letter to Sergey Taneyev:

Fundamentally, my [Fourth] Symphony is an imitation of Beethoven's Fifth; that's to say that I imitated the basic conception and not the musical ideas. Do you think that the Fifth Symphony has a programme? Not only does it have a programme but there can be no argument what it is trying to express. Much the same thing forms the basis of my symphony and if you have not understood it, all it means is that I am not Beethoven, about which fact I have never been in any doubt.[3]

Shostakovich preached the canon throughout his career and urged promising young composers to assimilate the great symphonies one by one through concentrated score study at the piano. In May 1955 he elaborated his position in an informal talk with such a group at the Composer's Union. Here is a translation made from the anthology of recorded speeches released by Melodiya:

My best advice—my desire—for those studying at the Conservatoire is that they be required to master the piano completely and thus be able to learn their scores by playing through them with ease and not with four, but two hands, as many as possible, especially those works unknown to them. Learning does not mean playing through one

---

[2] Downes, 'Critique'.

[3] Tchaikovsky to Sergey Taneyev, 27 Mar./8 Apr. 1878, P. I. Tchaikovsky, *Polnoe sobranie sochinenii; Literaturnye proizvedeniya i perepiska*, 17 vols. (Moscow: Gos. Muz. Izdatel'stvo, 1953–81), vii. 200–1. English trans. in Alexandra Orlova, ed., *Tchaikovsky: A Self-Portrait*, trans. R. M. Davison (Oxford, 1990), 120–1.

and going on to the next. I mean really practising the pieces that interest you for several days, thus gaining insights into the secrets of the art of our great predecessors, both Russian and foreign. . . . It may sound like a paradox, but I feel that the more music a composer knows, the more original is his own music. . . . When I speak about originality, I mean something more serious than just acquiring the devices and secrets from the classics—from the great composers—or even taking bars or entire pages of music from well-known works. One needs to contemplate them deeply for several days and let them enter into one's own viewpoint and thoughts. That is how one learns music.[4]

In reviewing programme notes, essays, and criticism on Shostakovich one asks: Have we made it yet to the secrets? What do we gain if we follow Downes in tagging the musical references? And once we have caught Shostakovich stealing, do we know the 'criminal' motive? Serious analysts, when confronted with the greatest of eclectics Shostakovich, must look beyond the Mahlerian funeral marches and Ländler, the Wagnerian leitmotiv, the tunes from *Carmen* and *Tell*, the self-quotations, the ubiquitous galop, Boston waltz, *chastushka* and the sentimental songs of Soviet saloons to the deeper intertextual parallels that may have little to do with pitch content and much to do with strategies of development, thematic transformation, affect, topos, dramaturgy, cyclic unity. It is these issues that provide a framework for the various component tunes and to them we must turn if we mean to comprehend Shostakovich's knowingly derivative style.

Since the Eighth Symphony is long and I intend to examine it in reference to two somewhat separate traditions, let me give my conclusions first as a working hypothesis: the Eighth Symphony in C minor was composed and is best heard in full consciousness of the canon of C minor tragedy-to-triumph symphonies that begins with Beethoven's Fifth. But Shostakovich's Eighth, with its quiet close and preponderance of lyrical interludes, breaks with tradition far more drastically than the more conventional C minor symphonies of Brahms, Bruckner, Mahler, Taneyev, and Scriabin. Absence of the bombastic, choral or collective triumph has been criticized not only by Soviet critics of the Zhdanov years but also by writers in the West, Boris Schwarz among them.[5] Instead of bombast, the Eighth closes with a thoroughly atypical chamber scoring registrally centred around a soprano flute playing its lowest pitch, 'middle C'. I read the passage as the final manifestation of a symphonic lyricism traceable to a prominent trait in Tchaikovsky's last three symphonies, especially the Sixth. The cumulative effect of successive incursions of a lyrical element— and a lyrical persona—is to deviate from and ultimately discard the Beethoven-ian tradition in preparation for Shostakovich's innovative late works. In the vastly overcrowded world of Beethovenian symphonies, Shostakovich wrote a new song, and in Beethoven's own key.

[4] Talk at the Union of Composers, May 1955, *Govorit Dmitry Shostakovich*, sound recording, Melodiya M 40—41705.

[5] '[Most likely it is the lack of a completely satisfying final movement—a miscalculation of mood and weightiness. . . . [The finale] disperses the tension rather than resolves it.' Boris Schwarz, *Music and Musical Life in Soviet Russia: 1917–1970* (London, 1972), 195.

In retraversing the musical terrain of Shostakovich's Eighth I will concentrate on the 'way-stations' that are crucial to the dramaturgy, taking these opportunities to compare Shostakovich's particular moves and devices to those of previous composers in their tragedy-to-triumph symphonies. Most significant among the predecessors is Beethoven, whose Fifth established many guidelines that later composers chose to follow. Mapping Shostakovich's Eighth against Beethoven's Fifth indeed reveals both similarities and differences. At crucial moments in the unfolding drama, both are significant. In the ensuing discussion, reference will be made not only to Beethoven's Fifth but to other minor-key symphonies bearing a significant number of marked affinities with it. All of these can be considered to be a family or subgenre of the Romantic symphony, all but one of them sharing the same tonality. The conventions that characterize this family have more to do with process, thematic type, and dramatic effect than with architectonic details. Certainly, sonata form, ternary form, and key choices within and between movements can be used to establish common ground; unfortunately they do not sufficiently narrow the field and, when dissimilar, can hide us from affinities, for example, between Tchaikovsky's Fourth (of the exceptional F-minor tonality) and Beethoven's Fifth.

If the similarities are necessary to justify the comparison with Beethoven, it is the deviations—or swerves (to use a term of Harold Bloom)—that give the Eighth its individuality. Pursuing the terrain metaphor, I find it useful to approach each new symphony as a new traversal of a wide field of common ground. When symphonies bear significant similarities, the field is narrowed and one is justified in seeking out those points where two composers have trod the same path. In the Eighth, Shostakovich at times is clearly in Beethoven's path, at other times he digresses from it. Careful study of Shostakovich's swerves enables the student of scores to document the appropriation and creative modification of borrowed devices. When all of the swerves in the Eighth Symphony are viewed collectively, one arrives at the end with a rationale for the enigmatic final bars, which convey neither tragedy nor triumph.

On Table 8.1, the charting of Shostakovich's route has been limited to ten crucial moments or 'way-stations' in the dramaturgy, most of them occurring in the first and fifth movements. The table is not intended to be a comprehensive reduction of the work, only a means of summarizing affinities between his Eighth and Beethoven's Fifth, which is charted on the left. As noted earlier, each of Shostakovich's moves has a precedent in nineteenth-century music, but not all are to be found in the main tradition of C-minor symphonies indebted to Beethoven. The right-hand column provides likely precedents from mainstream symphonic works for the moves that deviate from Beethovenian conventions. Since architectonic form and dramaturgy do condition one another, I have included traditional nineteenth-century form terminology, still used in Shostakovich's time.

At the outset of his Fifth Symphony, Beethoven bequeathed to the world a

TABLE 8.1. Shostakovich's adherence to and departures from Beethovenian conventions

Beethoven's Symphony No. 5	Shostakovich's Symphony No. 8	Possible sources of the alternatives
1. *Sonata Movement*	1. *Sonata Movement*	
Introductory fate motif	Introductory fate theme	
Agitato first theme //	Lyrical first theme	Schubert's Eighth
Relaxed second theme //	Lyrical second theme	Schubert, Tchaikovsky, etc.
Intensification in development //	'Brutalization' of 2nd theme	Tchaikovsky's Sixth
Dynamic/textural buildup as retransition	Dynamic/textural buildup	
Recapitulation: fate motif	Recapitulation: fate theme	
Lyrical interruption (brief)	Lyrical interruption (extended)	
2. *Lyrical Second Movement* //	2. *March-Scherzo*	Tchaikovsky's Sixth
3. *Scherzo* (w/fate motif)	3. *Mechanized Toccata*	
	4. *Passacaglia* (over fate theme)	
Intermovement transition	Intermovement transition	Beethoven's Sixth
4. *Sonata Finale*	5. *Rondo Finale*	Beethoven's Sixth, Mahler's Fifth
Victory hymn //	Pastoral rondo theme	Beethoven, Mahler
Reappearance of fate motif	Reappearance of fate theme	
Bombastic coda //	Hushed coda	Mahler's Second

suitable musical symbol for Fate in the form of a four-stroke rhythmic motif, played in octaves at *fortissimo*. While only Brahms risked stealing the motif itself,[6] other composers, for example, Bruckner, Mahler, Taneyev, in their C minor symphonies kept the octave scoring but found motivic or thematic alternatives, which would convey the same sense of fateful provocation, of Fate's knocking. Shostakovich began his Eighth with a more expansive theme yet akin to Beethoven's motive in its stark octave scoring, *fortissimo* dynamic, range, mode, and rhythmic incisiveness. These same traits are found in Shostakovich's own Fifth (a fact noted by most writers) and in most other post-Beethovenian C minor symphonies. A likely bridge from Beethoven to Shostakovich's Eighth by way of his Fifth is Bruckner's Eighth Symphony whose opening resembles Shostakovich's in its dotted rhythms, range, slow *de facto* tempo and vaulting minor sixth (see Ex. 8.1).

Ex. 8.1a

(a) Bruckner, Symphony No. 8, I

Ex. 8.1b

(b) Shostakovich, Symphony No. 8, I

The first theme (bars 10–35) of the exposition proper in Shostakovich's Eighth is lyrical, an obvious break with Beethoven but consistent with late nineteenth-century lyrical dramatic symphonies. If we accept Tchaikovsky's contention that his Fourth Symphony, a work that Russian commentators hold to be paradigmatic of the lyrical symphony,[7] is also modelled on Beethoven's

---

[6] The 'three-shorts-and-a long' motif dominates much of the first movement in Brahms's First Symphony. The association with Beethoven registers the strongest in the extended retransition (bars 262–338), when the brass and timpani take up the rhythm and hammer it out with repeated pitches, just as they do in Beethoven.

[7] Asafiev develops his idea of a 'lyrico-dramatic romantic symphony' in reference to the first movement of Tchaikovsky's Fourth, declaring that here 'the "excitement" of the first allegro is carried to the extreme limit of tension, so that the lyric contemplation becomes dramatic experience'. Boris Asafiev, *Russian Music from the Beginning of the Nineteenth Century*, trans. Alfred Swan (Ann Arbor, 1953), 149. Tchaikovsky himself made his famous pronouncement that the symphony is 'the most lyrical of all musical forms' in reference to his Fourth. Both the Fourth and Sixth Symphonies are used by Boleslav Yavorsky to illustrate 'psychological symphonism', a category of composition whose main line of succession he traces from the Lisztian tone poem to the symphonies of Borodin, Tchaikovsky, Taneyev, Rachmaninov, and Scriabin. See Boleslav Leopoldovich Yavorsky, 'Zametki o tvorcheskom myshlenii russkikh kompozitorov ot Glinki do Skryabina', in *Izbrannye trudy*, ii (Moscow, 1987), 189–92.

Fifth, then Shostakovich's lyrical theme is atypical but not precedent-setting. Comparing the character of the lyrical themes we find that Shostakovich did not look to Tchaikovsky. His theme is cast as an arioso, non-periodic in its phrasing and rigorously developmental. There is no espressivo marking here, but the graceful arch and texture of soli violins with accompaniment all suggest the appearance of a lyrical persona, or hero [*geroi*] of the symphony.

I will pass over the exposition's second theme—also lyrical, also scored for strings, but more regular in phrasing as is typical of second themes—and proceed to the development. As in the First, Second, Fourth, Fifth, and Seventh Symphonies, Shostakovich uses this time-span to transform his themes into jagged grotesque caricatures. For example, the exposition's second theme (bars 69–143), originally scored for violins playing *legato* at a *piano* dynamic, is rescored for trumpets and trombones in canon with most of the remaining orchestra accompanying. The technique—called 'brutalization' by Hugh Ottaway[8]—has ample precedent in the nineteenth century but not in the tragedy-to-triumph symphonies. For an art image to be perceived as grotesque, it must possess attributes that convey humanness or naturalness. Thus the precursors for brutalization are found in lyric/dramatic symphonies and works with literary programmes in which lyrical themes proliferate. An obvious precedent to Shostakovich's technique is Tchaikovsky's Sixth Symphony, wherein the lyrical theme of movement I given first to violins is similarly rescored for brass at an *fff* dynamic (cf. Tchaikovsky, Symphony No. 6, I, bars 93–5 and 190–7). The greater intensity of Shostakovich's Eighth results from the more dissonant cross-relations and greater textural density. Eventually march rhythms will dominate its development, providing evidence for numerous commentators that the Eighth is indeed a war symphony.

At the end of a traditional development must come a retransition to that crucial point at which the initial key is restored: the recapitulation. In Beethoven a swelling of dynamic and thickening of texture prepares a climactic return of the Fate motif for tutti winds and strings in octaves. Similar effects are found in later symphonies of the type, for example in Brahms's First and Mahler's Second. Shostakovich follows in their footsteps but with an important discrepancy in the harmony: his Fate theme returns at the original pitch level of C minor but with accompanying sonorities (G and A flat doubled in several octaves, then seventh chords) that are dissonant with it (see bars 285–300). Thus the recapitulation does not resolve the development's nearly unbearable tensions but pushes them even further. Right at this point Shostakovich takes an inspiration from Beethoven, a passage of only local consequence in the Fifth, to break with Beethovenian tradition and set the Eighth Symphony on a different course. Twenty bars into his recapitulation, Beethoven inserts a brief bit of oboe recitative, eleven notes in all, to interrupt the relentless drive

---

[8] Hugh Ottaway, *Shostakovich Symphonies* (Seattle, 1978), 38.

forward. Heard against the Beethoven model, Shostakovich's recitative for cor anglais (bars 301–38) is similar in placement and scoring but in its astonishing length of 21 phrases and 38 bars, does more than check the momentum: it inhibits all sense of progress towards a goal. In short, it wanders, tonally and thematically. Beethoven's oboe recitative and the beginning of Shostakovich's recitative for cor anglais are given in Ex. 8.2.

Ex. 8.2a

(a) Beethoven, Symphony No. 5

Ex. 8.2b

(b) Shostakovich, Symphony No. 8

In reaction to this passage an earlier generation of critics was moved to talk about the composer's sincerity.[9] These days one is justified, perhaps, in applying Bakhtinian dialogic theory.[10] For indeed the juxtaposition of tutti Fate motif and wind recitative presents the listener with two irreconcilable and unmergeable modes of expression. On the one hand: massive doubling, clarity of thematic statement and closure; on the other, another language, a distinctive single voice nervously fidgeting over musical ideas in a lengthy, open-ended improvisation over the barest of accompaniments. When the passage finally connects to a recognizable restatement of the second lyrical theme from the exposition, we realize that this strange solo passage has taken over much of the recapitulation, and therefore has formal as well as dramatic consequences not found in Beethoven.

[9] Downes considered this passage to be the finest in the movement, 'notable for its color and feeling'. Thomson makes Shostakovich's 'sincerity' of expression a main issue in his review of the entire work.

[10] Specifically, the two juxtaposed passages may constitute a musical counterpart to Bakhtin's concepts of 'polyphony' and 'heteroglossia' in a literary work, wherein a character, having achieved selfhood and partial autonomy from author and milieu by speaking a distinctive language, enters inevitably into dialogue and conflict with the world. The nuances of the terms are discussed in Gary Saul Morson and Caryl Emerson, *Mikhail Bakhtin: Creation of a Prosaics* (Stanford, 1990), 130–45; 231–56.

Having already invoked Bakhtin, I will also suggest that this recitative and others like it invite comparison to Dostoevsky's celebrated monologues, which are as much real-time event as structural element—where the orderly unfolding of a novel's plot is temporarily suspended, surrendered to the whims of an all-too-human Raskolnikov, Ivan Karamazov, or underground man. From this point on, we must be prepared for more unconventionality. The Eighth Symphony's three [!] interior movements are traditionally labelled Scherzo, Toccata, and Passacaglia. The nearly unanimous critical interpretation of the Scherzo and Toccata as evocations of the war experience[11] is based on the evidence of brisk tempi, mechanized motion, and extreme ranges and dynamics. Significant, too, is the lack of lyrical writing; neither lyrical themes nor arioso connecting passage-work appear in movements II or III. As for symphonic precedents, the Toccata is rather anomalous: a distant cousin perhaps to the parodistic metronomic Allegretto in Beethoven's Eighth, but more importantly a direct descendent of Shostakovich's linearism of the 1920s, for example, the Etude from the set of *Aphorisms*, Op. 13. The Scherzo (movement II) is a scherzo, however, with ample precedent in first-period Beethoven, for example, the Second Symphony and the Piano Sonata in C Major, Op. 2 No.3. The key of D flat major, Neapolitan to the tonic C, is used for interior movements in both Bruckner's Eighth and Mahler's Second. Shostakovich's originality lies in the synthesis of conflicting precedents to give us a major key movement, motivically and developmentally echoing Beethoven, yet disturbing in a way that Beethoven generally is not, until we start to read the present-day world back into him, say after a recitation of Adrienne Rich's poem about the Ninth.

We come now to decisions about the finale. In the first bar of his, Beethoven transformed dark chaos into light in a gesture derived from (or at least recalling) a passage in Haydn's *Creation*. More technically, at the point where movement III, Beethoven's Scherzo, should have reached a cadence, he inserted a transition in which a mode change to C major is prepared. Movement IV proper begins on a C major triad with a resplendent hymn of victory that would inspire later choral hymns and marches from Brahms, Bruckner, and Shostakovich (in his Fifth). Curiously, the linking gesture itself is not adapted by later composers; their third movements do cadence. Therefore I surmise that Shostakovich's use of it in his Eighth harks back to Beethoven himself. However, for the movement as a whole, it is not Beethoven's Fifth but his Sixth, which is also a case of triple-movement concatenation, that seems the more pertinent precursor. For instead of triumph, Shostakovich gives us a rondo pastorale, complete with gentle rolling themes and much use of woodwind. Again we are off course; again Shostakovich has broken with the

---

[11] Ottaway, for example, described the second movement as 'an aggressive march-cum-scherzo' and the third as a 'simple and powerful embodiment of all that is meant by a war machine' (Ottaway, *Shostakovich Symphonies*, 39–40). See also Marina Sabinina, *Shostakovich: Simfonist* (Moscow, 1976), 222–5.

conventions of the C minor symphony. No oratory, no demagoguery, no chorus, no anthem. Instead the movement commences with yet another woodwind (1st bassoon) fidgeting with a motif, eventually turning it into an odd unmetred theme. Among canonic symphonies, the closest affinity is to Mahler, in whose Fifth Symphony a Rondo Finale commences with winds and fidgeting before yielding to *concertato* counterpoint in D major.

The one conventional dramatic climax in Shostakovich's finale is occasioned by a final reappearance of the Fate theme, approximately three-quarters of the way through the movement. The obvious precedent is of course Tchaikovsky's Fourth, wherein a Fate theme temporarily interferes with the passive enjoyment of furious rounds of folk music, scored in *Kamarinskaya* fashion. Shostakovich applauded Tchaikovsky's coup later in the speech cited above and employed the very same device in his Eighth Symphony. While less sudden at its appearance, the change of mood in Shostakovich is greater since his rondo has lacked the ferocity of Tchaikovsky's finale. Since Beethoven did not interrupt the rondo of his 'Pastoral' Symphony with a Fate motif, Shostakovich's move is all the more audacious for lacking a symphonic precedent.

Shostakovich's final question was: how to end a movement that began with the pastoral topic and later became tragic in an unprecedented turn of events? With respect to endings, the post-Beethovenian tradition of C minor symphonies is rather rigid: one can end with triumph as did Beethoven or with mystical transfiguration as did Mahler in his Second Symphony. The choice required of a Soviet composer in 1943 was of course triumph, another C major apotheosis as in the 'Leningrad' Symphony, thereby making of the Eighth a 'Stalingrad' or 'Kursk' Symphony. Instead, Shostakovich remained true to the Eighth's lyrical mode and chose another woodwind—solo flute—to define the timbre of his coda.

Here I would like to propose a source for this symphonic moment and for the motif itself. In the context of the Eighth Symphony it is merely an inversion of movement I's opening gesture of C–B flat–C: lower neighbour has become upper neighbour. (The appearance of this motif in later themes including the cyclic motto theme has been noted by Sabinina.[12]) However, in the wider world of C minor symphonies, we find it in Mahler: it is prominently used in movement V of his 'Resurrection' Symphony, but not at the beginning and not in C minor. It appears well into the movement, first as the incipit of a wind chorale, then in developmental passages (in original form and inversion) among the instruments, and then, most memorably, at the hushed entry of the chorus. Certainly the motif itself is not unique to Mahler (cf. the chromatic lower neighbour in Brahms's Second Symphony). What I am suggesting is that Shostakovich followed Mahler's precept in allowing a tiny three-note idea to generate so much music of contrasting character in a symphonic finale, often in lieu of

---

[12] Marina Sabinina, *Shostakovich: Simfonist*, 235–6. The permutations of the neighbour motif are in all but the third of six cases used at the outset of the themes. The motif forms in order are as follows: (1) C–B flat–C; (2) C–D–C; (3) B–C–B; (4) D flat–C–D flat; (5) G♯–F×–G♯; (6) C–D–C.

proper themes. Among the many passages developed out of it, one seems relevant to Shostakovich's coda. At bar 452, a mysterious mood has been set by dialogues of winds; following a pause the chorus enters for the first time. It is an odd and rather perilous scoring: a soprano soloist and chorus must enter a cappella on a G-flat major triad and do so quietly enough that the single soprano (reinforced by sopranos and altos, no doubt as a necessary revision) can top off the chord by singing in her lowest range the pitches D flat–E flat–D flat. The word she sings provided Mahler's Second Symphony with its subtitle: 'Aufersteh'n!' Reductions from Mahler and Shostakovich are given in Ex. 8.3.

Ex. 8.3a

(a) Mahler, Symphony No. 2, V, bars 452–3

Ex. 8.3b

(b) Shostakovich, Symphony No. 8, V, bars 562–3

I have suggested that Mahler's use of this motif to generate much music in his finale influenced Shostakovich to employ it in five movements and that the low flute timbre in Shostakovich's unorthodox quiet coda may be a transmigrated soprano. Despite these potential links between the works, it would be a mistake to impose Mahler's text on Shostakovich's symphony, making of it a crypto-mystical Russian Resurrection. For in so doing we neglect the considerable differences in detail and overlook the possibility that musical symbols, no less than poetic metaphors, can have their meaning altered in the act of appropriation. In the Eighth Symphony, Shostakovich's *geroi* never died and thus, metaphorically, is not rising from the dead but standing up from the ground. Secondly, the single flute evokes only the *geroi* himself—no comrades in arms, no heavenly host. Finally, as many music critics realized, Shostakovich's ending does not really resolve the struggle heard earlier. The hero who announced himself using the voices of cor anglais and bassoon has not clearly triumphed, merely survived. And a long tradition of tragedy-to-triumph C minor symphonies has closed with neither triumph nor tragedy, and no endorsement of the collective or the community. Now to generalize a bit: when confronted by the densely allusive art of Shostakovich, it is not enough to spot and catalogue the individual intertextual references. If a symphony does indeed take us on a journey, then we are obliged to connect the impressions we collect along the way, perhaps in this manner coming close to the composer's own route. For the composer of forgettable symphonies, it is enough to rely on the well-marked routes provided by the time-honoured forms of sonata, rondo, rounded binary and all the rest. For Shostakovich, who had on occasion denied their primacy in his music,[13] one must venture away from the paved roads to find the special, secret routes that he discovered in Beethoven, Tchaikovsky, Mahler, Bruckner, and in Dostoevsky, Chekhov, Gogol, and the poets. In the act of seeking out the actual path he followed, one learns to appreciate the crucial crossroads of the dramaturgy, the narrow paths of genre, and the risky detours off the paved roads, sometimes following in others' tracks, and sometimes entirely on his own. These, I feel, are pressing concerns to bear in mind when listening to the last of all the C minor symphonies that we are ever likely to hear.

[13] Evgeny Braudo recalled the following view voiced by Shostakovich at a February 1935 Moscow conference on the symphony: 'With regard to the composing of a symphonic work, Shostakovich indicated that for him the forms sonata allegro, rondo, etc. had no essential significance. More essential was the appearance of a basic dialectical conflict, encompassing entire sections of a symphonic work, thus making it possible to shed new light on the musical-thematic material within the developmental process.' 'Diskussiya o sovetskom simfonizme', *Sovetskaya muzyka*, 3/5 (1935), 45.

9

Shostakovich's Anti-Formalist Rayok

A History of the Work's Composition
and its Musical and Literary Sources

MANASHIR YAKUBOV

The originality of the *Anti-Formalist Rayok*[1] should be assessed not only from the point of view of its place within Shostakovich's legacy, but in the context of the broad traditions of satire in Russian culture. Russian musical satire is an organic and deeply original part of Russia's spiritual culture. It is a legacy that is a thousand years old, and one that continues to thrive today: from the crude *Skomorokhi* lampoons of the tenth to seventeenth centuries to the obscene modern-day *chastushki* about Khrushchev, Brezhnev, and Gorbachev and the political songs of Galich and Vysotsky; from Dargomyzhsky's 'The Worm', Borodin's 'Pride', Musorgsky's 'The Seminarist', 'The Classicist', and 'The Flea', Rimsky-Korsakov's *The Tale of Tsar Saltan*, *Kashchei the Immortal*, and *The Golden Cockerel* to Prokofiev's *The Buffoon*, Mosolov's *Newspaper Announcements*, Shostakovich's secret anti-Soviet works, Shchedrin's *Bureaucratiada*, and Schnittke's *Life with an Idiot*. Musorgsky's *Rayok* and Shostakovich's *Anti-Formalist Rayok*, two masterpieces of Russian musical satire, occupy a special place in this sphere of denunciatory laughter. A whole century separates them. Musorgsky wrote his *Rayok* in 1870, and Shostakovich finished the last scene of his work at the end of the 1960s. They nevertheless have much in common. The object of the satire in these works is the relationship between art and power, and therefore art itself and also ultimately the artist.

The *Rayok* was the most popular form of vaudeville music-hall-style entertainment at fairs in Russia in the eighteenth and nineteenth centuries, in which a series of colourful, usually caricatured characters and situations would be accompanied by comic or satirical vocal commentaries. The word 'rayok' means a 'theatre of pictures' or 'peepshow', and used to be a large box

---

[1] 'Rayok' is variously translated as *The Peepshow*, *The Gods*, *Little Paradise*, or *The Learner's Manual*. The word itself is a diminutive of 'ray', which means 'heaven' or 'paradise', and therefore means literally 'little heaven'. It also means, by analogy with the English 'gods' or the French 'paradis', the cheapest seats at the back of the topmost gallery in the theatre, and thus by extension describes the kind of popular entertainment that might be expected to appeal to that audience. (Translator's note)

with round holes to peep through. Inside the box there was a revolving drum to which were attached pictures, making up a ribbon. The role of the 'cinema-operator' in this ancient version of the cartoon was carried out by the *rayoshnik*, someone who turned the drum with the paper ribbon, and commented loudly on what was being shown, amusing the public and usually never being too careful about his language.

The *Anti-Formalist Rayok* occupies a special place amongst Shostakovich's works not simply on account of its genre and its content, but because of the fact that the composer worked on it over the course of two decades, from the end of the 1940s to the late 1960s. It is also notable for being the only substantial work for which Shostakovich provided a libretto entirely of his own making (there is a close analogy to be found in the piece for voice and piano, *A Preface to the Complete Collection of my Works . . .*, Op. 123, 1966). The music and the text of *The Anti-Formalist Rayok* contain not only a multiplicity of straightforward and hidden quotations, but also the concentrated reflection of a wide range of biographical, cultural, and socio-historical allusions, without knowledge of which a full understanding of the work is impossible. The following comment-ary aims therefore to shed light (I) on the history of its composition, (II) on the fundamental sources of its music, and (III) the literary sources of its text.

I

The first version of Shostakovich's *Rayok* appeared half-way through 1948, its composition having been directly triggered by the well-known events which took place in the early months of that year. First of all in January, the Communist Party Central Committee convened a conference of Soviet musical functionaries, which was preceded by a conference of the musical community and employees of the Bolshoi Theatre of the USSR, likewise organized by the Central Committee. On 10 February the Central Committee issued the decree 'On the opera *The Great Friendship* by V. Muradeli', which was published the next day. Then there were numerous assemblies, conferences, meetings, and press publications condemning the activities of representatives of 'the antisocial, formalist tendency in music'. Finally there was the First All-Union Congress of Soviet Composers, which took place from 19 to 25 April. During the last days of that month the texts of Zhdanov's 'Introductory Remarks' and 'Address' to the Central Committee's conference of Soviet musical functionaries were published, and Shostakovich drew on them for the libretto of *Rayok*.[2] A full stenographic

---

[2] In this paper for the sake of brevity the short form of the title *The Rayok* will be used interchangeably with Shostakovich's full title *The Anti-Formalist Rayok*. Other titles occurring in the literature will be discussed below. The text referred to is that of the full score: D. Shostakovich, *Antiformalisticheskii raek*, ed. M. Yakubov (Moscow, 1995).

transcript of the proceedings of the Conference was published by *Pravda*, probably towards the end of March or the beginning of April, having been authorized for publication on 8 March. The texts of both speeches by Zhdanov were also published in the journal *Sovetskaya muzyka* (*Soviet Music*), which was approved for release on 17 April, although delegates had already received copies of the magazine during the Conference itself.

It follows that Shostakovich could not have begun work on the composition earlier than May of 1948, but the composer had already played it through not long after to Isaak Glikman,[3] who describes the event as follows: 'in the summer of 1948, in great secrecy owing to the considerable risk entailed, Dmitry Dmitrievich played and sang to me a work of grotesque parody based on certain phrases he had appropriated from the 10 February Central Committee Decree and set to the tunes of *Suliko* and the *lezginka*.'[4] Glikman also recalls that Shostakovich played him the composition from a rough sketch written on a single sheet of paper. This first rough sketch on a double folded sheet of thirty-stave (full score) manuscript paper has been preserved. The four pages of the autograph score (the last page not fully written out) contain about 180 bars, concluding with a thick double barline. The lower part of the last page continues on a new line with a small later addition, which will be discussed below. The rough sketch includes the speeches by the Master of Ceremonies, Yedinitsin ('Number One') and Dvoikin ('Number Two'), with all the basic scenes in the musical and narrative order they follow in the final version of the work. However in the first draft there is no part for the chorus, while some sections of the music are not fully written out but indicated schematically: for example the number which concludes this first version, based on the *lezginka*, consists merely of a single bar in which is written the word 'Lezginka'.

The next stage of work on *Rayok* took place at the end of the 1950s. Clearly it was during this time that Shostakovich wrote the first draft of a parodic preface entitled 'From the Publisher', which throws some light on the musical plan of the work, as it then appeared to the composer: 'True innovation, | mastery, | ease of performance, | 1 bass and chorus. | Destruction of the critic. | . . . A few pieces dragged out . . . | but in none of them was discovered . . . | The sewage-disposal

---

[3] It is possible that at the start of the year 1949 Shostakovich played through *The Rayok* to the film director Grigory Kozintsev, whose diary for 17 January 1949 contains the cryptic entry: '"Nebylitsa v litsakh" (zavyvanie starinnogo raeshnika)'. See G. Kozintsev, 'Iz rabochikh tetradei: 1948–1949', in *Isskustvo kino*, 7 (1988), 86.

[4] Glikman's letter to the composer's widow Irina Antonovna Shostakovich dated 27 May 1989. The original is in the addressee's possession. Glikman is not absolutely correct in ascribing the sources of *The Rayok*'s text: as explained above Shostakovich made use of the text not of the Decree but of Zhdanov's Introductory Remarks and Speech. Glikman's testimony yields an important piece of information relating to the *Lezginka* scene, which Shostakovich sang to him *with words*, whereas in the rough sketch which has been preserved there is no text for this section of the work. Without Glikman's clarification it might have been assumed that this had originally been a purely dance scene. A detailed analysis of the sources of *The Rayok*'s text follows later in this article.

crew. | The ambulance. | Talk with the doctor. | The friends: Partertovsky, Truvorov, Tryumin.'[5]

From this sketch of the preface, as from the initial rough draft, we can see that the original idea was to have a single soloist, as Musorgsky had in his *Rayok*. Eventually the standard line-up would grow to include a quartet of soloists and a chorus, but the option of a single soloist is left as a possible alternative. An important element in this sketch, with implications for the development of both the musical and the scenographic aspects of the production, is the introduction of the chorus, absent from the 1948 draft. Later on the chorus would assume more and more significance until by the final edition it has become an indispensable ingredient of the artistic whole, with functions important for the overall meaning and dramatic structure of the work. The sketch is on one side of a sheet from a notepad, while the text of the Preface is written on the other side. Over the years, this text underwent several revisions, and the various versions have been preserved. While the basic sense, feeling, and structure of the work remained unchanged, specific phrases became harsher, more sarcastic, and more blunt. A typical example is the replacement of one of the names in the sketch, 'Partertovsky' by the abusive and scatological 'Yasrustovsky'.[6] (Partertovsky was originally formed by changing *Yarus*, the first part of the surname of one of the targeted individuals (Yarustovsky) to *Parter*, a word close in association, since both relate to seating areas in a theatre).

A new and expanded revision of *The Anti-Formalist Rayok* was completed by the end of the 1950s. The thirty-six pages of twelve-stave (piano score) manuscript paper, of which this autograph consists, contain both music and libretto and may be regarded as the preliminary draft of the second version. As well as a fully written-out fair copy of the scenes from the first rough draft, it includes the appearance of a new character, 'Comrade Troikin' ('No. Three'). Continuation of work on the piece and the composition of this scene was triggered by a specific event: the speech by D. T. Shepilov, the Secretary of the Central Committee of the Communist Party, at the Second All-Union Congress of Soviet Composers, which took place on 3 April 1957.[7] Reading from a text that had been prepared for him, Shepilov mispronounced the name of one of the classic composers of Russian music (calling him Rimsky KorsAkov instead of Rimsky-KORsakov), which caused excitement and laughter in the hall. Shostakovich clearly points to

---

[5] The sketch is written on the reverse side of the second sheet of the MS of the Preface 'From the Publisher', the first two lines in a light-coloured ink and the remainder in pencil (autograph in the Shostakovich Archive).

[6] 'Yarus' is the term for a circle in a theatre auditorium (not usually the dress circle, which is 'beletazh', after the French), while in the same manner 'parter' ('parterre') is the stalls. 'Sru' being the grammatically impeccable first person singular of the vulgar verb 'srat'', 'ya sru' means 'I shit'. (Translator's note)

[7] The full text of the speech was published under the heading 'Tvorit' dlya blaga i schast'ya naroda', *Sovetskaya muzyka*, 5 (1957), 6–23.

Shepilov as the original target of his lampoon by giving his character Troikin the initials D.T., although he actually took most of the basic material for Troikin's lines from other speakers. The composer jotted down the first sketch for this further development on empty staves on the last page of his original rough draft, which still had some space left on it. There are more than ten bars noted down here on a new line, hastily written, and some of them quite illegible, but they are identifiable as being the transition to Troikin's speech: a flourish, followed by the speech beginning with the words: 'Glinka, Tchaikovsky, Rimsky-KorsAkov'. This sketch bears throughout the most embryonic and approximate character, but in a few places text has been added to the notated music:

Ex. 9.1

First sketch of the opening of the Troikin episode

[(flourish) We thank [our] Comrade . . . for his speech . . . Glinka, Tchaikovsky, Rimsky KorsAkov

In later revisions the melodic line of this first sketch is altered, but the rhythm and certain essential intervals survived to the final version (see fig. 29, bars 3–4, and fig. 30, bars 1–3). Having finished this version, which we may now refer to as the Preliminary Version, Shostakovich began to show it to some of his colleagues. In the circumstances of Khrushchev's 'thaw', a wider circle of people were able to hear it than the two or three who could be allowed to do so in 1948. According to Irina Antonovna Shostakovich, one of the people who became acquainted with the manuscript of *Rayok* in 1962, and who transcribed it 'from memory', was the musicologist Lev Lebedinsky. He subsequently sent this incomplete and unfinished version to Mstislav Rostropovich.[8]

---

[8] As is well known, Lebedinsky claimed authorship of the literary text of *The Rayok*. These claims

The general situation at the end of the 1950s and the beginning of the 1960s offered some hope for the possibility of the public performance and publication of *Rayok*. It was this circumstance that evidently encouraged Shostakovich to prepare a fair copy of the complete work. In addition to some other changes, the role of the chorus in this version has been greatly expanded and strengthened; in particular, the chorus's rejoinders and exclamations (in the Caucasian manner) of 'Assa!' are introduced to accompany the speech of Dvoikin (No. Two) in the *lezginka* episode, and the choral passages are extended to encompass Yedinitsin's speech. Further, this version contains many clarifications of the musical text; for example, changes to some of the tempo markings, and the addition of rehearsal numbers to facilitate practical preparations for performance. In the fair copy that Shostakovich made, the outlines of the genre to which the work belongs become clearer than before, and combine elements of the dramatic cantata with those of a satirical opera. There is also a large number of directions indicating the actions of the performers. Even before this version, the preliminary autograph had included a page in which a list of performers is headed: 'Dramatis Personae'. In front of the choral lines in the music score the composer inserted the titles 'Female musical functionaries' and 'Male musical functionaries' instead of the conventional soprano, alto, etc.

Changes in the domestic political climate towards the end of the Khrushchev 'thaw', in particular the suppression of the Thirteenth Symphony immediately after its première in 1962, the case against Andrey Sinyavsky and Yuly Daniel, and the campaign against bourgeois ideology, all combined to dash the composer's hopes of publishing *Rayok*. But these same events provided a new spur to creative activity on the work. In the middle to late 1960s Shostakovich composed the final scene of Troikin with the Musical Functionaries, beginning it literally from the same note and the same interrupted word at which the previous 'unfinished' version had broken off. As in all the other autographs of *Rayok*, the autograph of this concluding scene is not dated, but the composer Venyamin Basner, to whom the composer showed this section while he was still working on it, recalls that it was written no later than 1968. The autograph of the final section is a carefully written manuscript with no significant corrections, crossings-out, or abbreviations, etc., but in contrast to the fair copy of the rest of the work, bears no rehearsal numbers, and there is no indication to suggest which character should be singing the solo part. As in the autograph of the Preliminary Version and the

are refuted by the composer's manuscripts that have been preserved, which reflect the successive stages through which not only the music but also the written text went as he worked on them. Lebedinsky's own account also casts doubt on the validity of his claim, notably where it states that Shostakovich played and sang to him the completed part of *The Rayok*; lastly he was clearly entirely ignorant of the existence of the second version of the work and its concluding scene (from 3 bars before fig. 34 to the end). In Shostakovich's own text 'From the Publisher' there are also hints that 'composer and poet are one and the same person'.

other preceding versions, the scene has been left uncompleted: the final Dance breaks off on a dominant chord, consistent with the notion of an unfinished work still in a rough state supposed to have been found in a drawer.

II

'Quotations' from folk music and from the works of various composers play an important role in the music of *The Anti-Formalist Rayok*. For example, the speeches by Yedinitsin and Dvoikin are framed by the sort of wind band fanfare that was traditionally heard from the 1920s to the 1950s whenever there was any kind of ceremonial gathering or rally, or similar event involving the masses (figs. 5, bars 12–13, 15, 16). The concluding passages of Yedinitsin's 'Introductory Remarks' are based on a free adaptation of the popular Georgian melody *Suliko*, much loved by Stalin and incorporated at his request (like the Russian tune *Kalinka*) into the repertoire of the then hugely popular Red Banner Song and Dance Ensemble of the Soviet Army (Ex. 9.2).

Ex. 9.2

Suliko. (*Urban Folksongs of Georgia* (Moscow, 1961), 87)

In bars 7–9 of fig. 20 (*general laughter*) there appears a four-note motif exactly corresponding to the composer's monogram DSCH, but in a different pitch. It is as if Shostakovich is indicating his own presence among the male and female musical functionaries who were participants in this tragi-comic spectacle. In an especially revealing touch, his 'signature' is heard right at the end of the third and final 'outburst of laughter'—he who laughs last laughs longest (Ex. 9.3). Dvoikin's final scene (fig. 23–5) makes use of the tune of the popular folk dance known as the *lezginka* or *Kabardinka* (Ex. 9.4). The rich potential for parody and satire offered by this particular tune lies in the fact that it also enjoyed wide circulation as the accompaniment to a comic song of not entirely decent content. The idea of putting a Russian text to a Caucasian dance tune, meanwhile, which the whole situation naturally gives rise to, came from the young composer's personal impressions. A favourite entertainment of the poet Nikolay Aseyev,

Ex. 9.3

[ha, ha, ha, ha, ha, ha, ha, ha]

Ex. 9.4

Lezginka (Kabardinka), transcribed by M. Yakubov

with whom Shostakovich had close personal and professional relations at the beginning of the 1930s, was to sing his poems to similar such tunes.[9]

In the first part of Dvoikin's speech we meet several melodic constructions that bear a close resemblance to passages in Shostakovich's musical comedy *Moskva, Cheryomushki*, Op. 105, written in 1958. There is an especially close correspondence between 'Boris's Serenade' (No. 5, see Shostakovich's *Collected Works*, xxv. 37–8, fig. 65) and Dvoikin's part (8 bars before fig. 18) in the autograph of the Preliminary Version, where not only the musical but the literary texts converge (Ex. 9.5a–b). There is also a clear similarity between the basic melodic material of Dvoikin's speech (fig. 17, see also fig. 21) and Lidochka and Boris's Duet from *Moskva, Cheryomushki* (No. 36, fig. 319 and bars 5–6 of fig. 311) (Ex. 9.6a–c). Troikin's speech opens with the tune of the

---

[9] 'Nikolay Aseyev sang through his poems in recitative, some to the tune of a *Lezginka* and some to other melodies from the Caucasus', Asaf Messerer has recalled (See A. Messerer, *Tanets, mysl', vremya* (Moscow, 1990), 118).

Ex. 9.5a–b

Moskva, Cheryomushki, No. 5, Boris's Song-Serenade
(a) Boris

[Boris: Lya, lya, lya, lya, lya, lya, lya, lya, | My soul is filled with you alone, |
Lya, lya, lya, lya, lya, lya, lya, lya, | With you alone, lya, lya!]

(b) Dvoikin

[Dvoikin: Lya, lya, lya, lya, lya, lya, lya, lya, | But of course, this is strange to you.
Lya, lya, lya, lya, lya, lya, lya, lya.]

Ex. 9.6*a*

(a) The Anti-Formalist Rayok

[We Comrades, demand of music beauty and elegance. |
Do you find that strange? Yes? | Well, of course you do.]

Ex. 9.6*b*

(b) *Moskva, Cheryomushki*

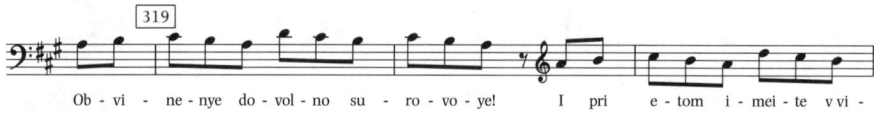

[A severe rebuke! But remember, | A friend's life is not the same . . .]

Ex. 9.6*c*

(c) Moskva, Cheryomushki

[Nina, Nina, Nina, Nina, my soul is filled with one thing alone, |
I'll give my heart for just one glance!]

Russian folk-song *Kamarinskaya* (9 bars before fig. 29), on which Glinka based his celebrated orchestral Fantasy, and it is noteworthy that from all the many various versions of this melody that exist Shostakovich chose the one closest to Glinka's. The next section of Troikin's speech (to the words 'Glinka, Tchaikovsky, Rimsky-KorsAkov') begins with a quotation from Tikhon Khrennikov's song to a text by Mikhail Matusovsky, 'We'll tell you the

Ex. 9.7*a*

(a) T. Khrennikov, *We'll Tell you the Story*

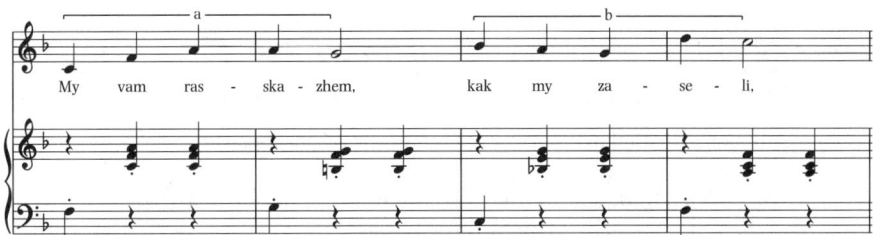

[We'll tell you the story of how we sat down . . .]

Ex. 9.7*b*

(b) Shostakovich, *The Anti-Formalist Rayok*

[Glinka, Tchaikovsky, Rimsky-Korsakov . . .]

Ex. 9.7*c*

(c) Shostakovich, *The Anti-Formalist Rayok*

[Glinka, Tchaikovsky, Rimsky-Korsakov . . .]

story' from the score he composed for the 1954 film *True Friends* (Ex. 9.7*a–b*). At figure 44, Shostakovich introduces into Troikin's part the refrain from the Russian folk song *Kalinka*, going so far as to incorporate into his text some of the actual words of the song: 'Kalinka, kalinka, malinka moya' (bars 10–13 of

Ex. 9.8

Kalinka, Russian folk-song, from *Collected Russian Folk Songs*, vol. iii (Moscow, 1937), p.270

Ka - lin - ka, ka - lin - ka, ka - lin - ka mo - ya,   vsa-du   ya - go-da ma - lin - ka, ma - lin - ka mo - ya

[Kalinka, kalinka, my kalinka, in the garden is my little raspberry bush]

fig. 33) (Ex. 9.8). Finally, in Troikin's concluding episode with the chorus of Male and Female Musical Functionaries (figs. 36–7 and 43–5), the triumphant words are sung to the unnaturally slow tune of Serpoletta's song from Planquette's operetta *Les Cloches de Corneville*, which sounds in this combination particularly mocking. The final scene of the soloist with chorus is the climax of the work, where Stalin reappears, no longer as a real person, but as a kind of eternal symbol from the other world, promising to fight for ever with bourgeois ideology and to send dissidents to the labour camps (Ex. 9.9).

It should be noted that A. M. Nevsky's translation of the original French 'look over here, look over there, don't you like what you see?' was a phrase that gained universal currency in the theatre both of Soviet and pre-Revolutionary times, generally to the accompaniment of the body movements of the cancan danced by young female would-be servants hoping to attract their future masters.

The entire final scene of *Rayok*, with its use of the tune and the last words from Serpoletta's song and the culminating dance of all the participants, clearly has its antecedents in Yevgeny Shvarts's 'comic entertainment' *The Festive Gathering*. This parody of a gathering of authors was written for a New Year's puppet show and performed on the night of 1 January 1935, to mark the opening of the new Leningrad House of Writers.[10] Many of the characters in the play were famous literary figures of the day. In one scene the writer Mikhail Kozakov bursts on to the stage dressed in a skirt, dances and sings: 'For my voice to ring out well and stir you to feel, I'll be a young maiden, although Mikhail. I think it's a great thing to fly like a bird, to flutter and sing so my voice will be heard. Look over here, look over there, don't you like what you see there?'[11] At the end of *The Festive Gathering*, all present dance until the curtain falls. While the clear impetus for Shostakovich's *The Anti-Formalist Rayok* lay in the specific events of 1948, it is also true that as the idea gradually took shape and the subject-matter developed in the course of further work, parallels with Shvarts's play multiplied and may have suggested to the composer the dénouement of the final scene.

---

[10] *Zhitie skazochnika: Evgeny Shvarts. Iz avtobiograficheskoi prozy. Pis'ma. Vospominaniya o pisatele* (Moscow, 1991), 296–302.

[11] Ibid. 298.

Ex. 9.9

R. Planquette, *Les Cloches de Corneville* (Bessel & Co., n.d.), trans. A. Nevsky

[Serpoletta: look over here, look over there, don't you like what you see?]

III

In its final edition *The Anti-Formalist Rayok* emerges as a one-act satirical opera or dramatic cantata with vividly characterized personae and actions indicated by the author in stage directions such as 'applause', 'typical gestures', 'final dance', and a highly original treatment of the subject-matter. The original *Rayok* was conceived as a chamber vocal composition, however, a genre that undoubtedly owes allegiance to Musorgsky's analogous work. The huge inner differences between the two compositions reflect the principal differences of two historical epochs, two centuries of Russian social lawlessness and Russian free-thinking. Musorgsky's work appeared at the time of the sharpest divergence of the two musical factions in the middle of the nineteenth century in Russia. One of them represented a small group of radical young talents known as the 'Mighty Handful' or the 'New Russian School'. The other, more conservative and academic group brought together musicians who enjoyed the favour and patronage of the highest court circles. The New Russian School were inspired by the idea of creating an indigenous Russian musical tradition, rooted in native folklore. Their idols were contemporary innovators like Liszt, Berlioz, and Schumann. The Conservative composers preached the classical tradition, which was a mostly German one, and the German system of musical education. They were deeply hostile to the music of their contemporaries, especially those from Russia. In a word, these were people, who, according to Dargomyzhsky, 'worshipped the works of the dead, in order not to have to give their contemporaries their due'.

Among those who were against the New Russian School were several people who are now completely forgotten. The director of the Petersburg Conservatoire, Nikolay Zaremba, for example, who was famous for his pedantry and love of scholastic theorizing, was one of them. Another was the musical critic Feofil Tolstoy, who wrote under the pseudonym of Rostislav. Rostislav was a typical music-lover, who was horrified by the slightest dissonance. He even accused Cui, the most moderate of the New Russian School composers, of dissonance and 'harmonicide'. Another was the musicologist Alexander Famintsyn, who regarded Musorgsky's romances as the 'crudest naturalism, leading to cynicism'. He also was highly dissatisfied with the New Russian School's attraction to folklore ('Surely national colour in art does not have to mean that trivial dance songs which remind one of scenes from a pub, have to be the motives of compositions?'). The composer Alexander Serov was also a furious critic of the New Russian School in the 1860s. Serov referred to the first symphonic works of Borodin and Rimsky-Korsakov as primitive and immature, and defined Cui's best opera *William Ratcliff* as a row of scenes from a madhouse with 'a clumsy heap of syncopation and dissonance'. The above-mentioned criticisms appeared in the twentieth century, too, of course.

The detractors of the New Russian School received moral and financial support from the highest spheres, principally the Grand Duchess Elena Pavlovna, patron of the Petersburg Conservatoire and president of the Imperial Russian Musical Society (the RMS). The 'German' faction, which had a lot of power in the RMS, and in Russian musical life as a whole, feared most of all that 'musical activities would be transferred into the hands of these new Russian composers, and that the uneducated, untamed flood of Russian barbarism would drown the tender shoots of German musical civilization'. The New Russian School, however, had neither influence at court, nor the possibility of entering into polemics in the press. Satire has always been the most extreme form of artistic protest, and it was precisely to satire that Musorgsky turned, having been given the idea of composing his *Rayok* by Stasov, who suggested that he should caricature all the enemies of the New Russian School. For an artist gifted with a sense of humour, and keen to explore genuinely popular manifestations of national culture, this was a felicitous suggestion.

Fully in the tradition of the 'theatre of pictures', Musorgsky constructed his *Rayok* as a series of caricatures of Zaremba, Rostislav, Famintsyn, Serov, and the Grand Duchess Elena Pavlovna. And in the introduction, he brought himself in as the *rayoshnik*, who was showing the people 'the great personages from the musical leadership'. Musorgsky must have been the first Russian musician in his *Rayok* to quote works by various composers in parodic form. For Zaremba, he took a theme from Handel's *Judas Maccabeus*, the musical portrait of Rostislav is given as a salon waltz, Famintsyn appears to the music of his own musical play, and Serov is depicted with the help of themes from his operas *Rogneda* and *Judith*. Finally, the 'great Euterpe' appears in the finale. In the figure of the daughter of Zeus and Mnemosyne, the muse and protector of lyrical poetry, Musorgsky's contemporaries correctly discerned the Grand Duchess Elena Pavlovna. The heroes of *Rayok* sing a hymn to her at the top of their voices to the theme of the song of the fools in Serov's *Rogneda*. It is important to bear in mind that Serov used the melody of the Russian folk-song 'From under the oak tree, from under the elm' here. Later we will see that Shostakovich also turned to genuine folk material for creating parody, as well as themes from the music of various composers.

Musorgsky wrote the text of his *Rayok* himself, as is customary for a *rayoshnik*, putting into it much humour and venom, but the sources of his libretto were genuine utterances of his heroes: Zaremba's lectures, Rostislav's *feuilletons* and Serov's articles, etc. He finished the score of his 'musical joke' on 15 June 1870. The censor saw nothing reprehensible in it and in 1871 it was published by Bessel. Reviewing the publication, Cui wrote that in this musical lampoon a 'new, unprecedented and original form of polemic' had been invented, and that in it Musorgsky had begun a completely new form of art. And there really were new elements in this work by Musorgsky. Organically woven into score, these musical quotations are now perceived as precursors of collage technique and 'polystylistics'. But the daring novelty of *Rayok* is not only to be found in the music. In the 'subject' itself, the composer took the liberty of laughing not only at his talentless colleagues and at the musical bureaucrats, but also at a representative of the highest power: the aunt of the tsar. A hundred years later Shostakovich began at precisely the point at which Musorgsky left off. The first hero of his musical satire was the 'great leader of all nations of the Soviet Union and all-progressive humanity'. In contrast to Musorgsky's polemical lampoon, then, Shostakovich's *Anti-Formalist Rayok* is a work with more universal artistic meaning. Musorgsky's *Rayok* is the provocative and insouciant prank of a young genius flexing his muscles. In it is the laughter of an artistic school gathering strength and confidence. Shostakovich's *Anti-Formalist Rayok* is the satire of a master driven underground, living out his fate painfully, but finding in himself the strength to rise above his persecutors in laughter in order secretly to cleanse himself morally and save himself, while 'repenting' in public. This is of course the secret freedom about which Alexander Blok spoke in his last poems. He who possesses such a freedom is no longer a slave, or rather is not *just* a slave, but is divided into two personas. His external existence is tragically complex; he is often forced to wear a mask and submit to crude force, but he has not resigned himself to his fate completely. He lives his life and bides his time, but all the while he is working away to bring it nearer, by composing the *Anti-Formalist Rayok*! Musorgsky's satire was directed primarily at his colleagues—the musicians from the opposite camp. Shostakovich's *Rayok* is a political satire, a conscious politicization of art in the battle with those who were trying to make art political. In these differences are reflected two epochs of Russian bondage, from the despotic autocracy of the Romanovs to the bloody totalitarianism of the Bolsheviks led by Lenin and Stalin.

Shostakovich's interest in the 'Rayok' began in his early youth, and perhaps long before he came across Musorgsky's work. It is very possible that he would have seen and heard the last few remaining active *rayoshniki* in Petrograd at the beginning of the 1920s. By the middle of the decade the young composer had become seriously interested in the history of this popular folk genre, and in the specific kind of doggerel verse, larded with diminutives, that the *rayoshniki* employed. In one of the letters he wrote at this time we read: 'How are your delishki (little affairs)? What are Shebalishki [the composer, Vissarion Shebalin—trans.] and Mishki (Misha) up to? Forgive me for the two last phrases—I have recently begun to study the history of *rayoshnyi* language, and so sometimes express myself in it.'[12]

The title *Anti-formalisticheskii Rayok* (*The Anti-Formalist Rayok*) was not thought up at the beginning. The first rough draft is untitled. The preliminary score is the first to include a title-page, which in its content and layout of the written text, parodies various educational publications aimed at those desirous of instructing themselves in socio-political disciplines, with titles such as *An Aid to the Study of a Short Course in the History of the VKP(b)*,[13] or *An Aid to the Study*

---

[12] Letter to L. N. Oborin dated 26 Sept. 1925 in RGALI, f. 2954, op. 1, ed. khr. 17.

[13] The initials stand for Vsesoyuznaya Kommunisticheskaya Partiya (Bolsheviki)—All-Union Communist Party (Bolsheviks). (Translator's note)

of Marxist-Leninist Aesthetics. The title *Anti-formalisticheskii Rayok* evidently arose during work on the second revision of the piece. It has survived on the title-page of the libretto, in the composer's own typescript. Alternative titles which crop up in some of the literature, such as *Zhdanovshchina* (by analogy with *Khovanshchina*) or *The Year 1948* are not to be found in the materials in the Shostakovich Archive.

Apart from their obvious meanings (the hierarchy of the First, Second, and Third levels of management in an organization), the names given to the characters have more negative connotations. There is a reference, for example, to the grading system in Soviet schools, according to which 'Yedinitsa' (1) = 'very bad', 'dvoika' (2) = 'bad' or 'unsatisfactory', and 'troika' (3) = 'satisfactory' or 'moderate'. These are the lowest marks that can be awarded. These sobriquets may well have carried for Shostakovich an added emotional and allusive significance, moreover: Yedinitsin was the nom de plume of Alexander Chekhov, brother of Anton, often encountered in the the writer's letters, which Shostakovich was particularly fond of reading. Then two of the characters in Mayakovsky's play *The Bathhouse* are 'Comrade Dvoikin' and 'Comrade Troikin'—both of whom, according to Isaak Glikman, were sources of great amusement to the young Shostakovich and often found their way in humorous contexts into his conversation at that time. Finally, one must recall the sinister connotations the word 'troika' ('tribunal') acquired during the years of mass repression which began in 1918. A single terse phrase in Ilya Zemtsov's well known handbook *Perestroika: Its Reality and its Limits* defines it uncompromisingly: 'Troika—Soviet organ of extra-judicial punishment'.[14]

The initials attributed to Dvoikin (A.A.) correspond to those of Andrey Alexandrovich Zhdanov, while Troikin's (D.T.) match those of Dmitry Trofimovich Shepilov. As for Yedinitsin's initials (J.S., rather than J.V. for Joseph Vissarionovich), they may be explained by the fact that Stalin did not as a rule use his second initial when signing his name, to the extent that the two initials J.S. (for Joseph Stalin) acquired during his lifetime the status of a universally understood monogram (there was, for example, even a locomotive named the J.S.). Introducing Yedinitsin, the Master of Ceremonies announces: 'Our Chief *Consultant*'. This title may have derived from one of the heroes of Mikhail Bulgakov's novel *The Master and Margarita*, whose original draft title was *The Cloven-hoofed Consultant*.[15]

In their final form, the literary texts of *The Anti-Formalist Rayok* (i.e. the libretto and the Preface 'From the Publisher') were the result of assiduous work, the individual stages of which may be clearly traced in the surviving autographs. The greater part of the final text is already to be found in the earliest autograph, the rough draft of 1948, but it is written very illegibly. This is probably due not only to haste but to the sense of conspiracy that surrounded

---

[14] I. Zemtsov, *Perestroika: Its Reality and its Limits: A Handbook* (London, 1989), 409.

[15] See Lidiya Yanovskaya, *Tvorcheskyi put' Mikhaila Bulgakova* (Moscow, 1983), 231.

its content. It is for instance significant that in the opening scene of the work, in which the Master of Ceremonies announces the theme of the 'Conference' (bar 7 of fig. 2 in the printed edition), the music, i.e. the vocal line, has no text: the words 'realism and formalism' are nowhere to be seen. In 1948 they could have provided too unambiguous and damaging a piece of evidence. In the course of further work on the composition, Shostakovich not only meticulously refined the text of the vocal parts but also paid more attention to both scenographic and musical markings. The *lezginka* scene (from fig. 14) was subject to the most revisions and reworkings; some lines were rewritten twice or even three times by the composer.

The basic ideas underlying the work's literary text—the stylization of actual texts, either quoted directly or reworked—were already worked out in some detail in the original rough draft. Thus, in the text of J. S. Yedinitsin's 'Introductory Remarks' Shostakovich reproduces the catechism-like question and answer construction that can typically be found in Stalin's speeches, with the wording of the question inevitably repeated in the answer, and the beloved use of the double negative: 'cannot not be'. 'Communists, as committed internationalists', Stalin wrote, for example, 'cannot not be implacable enemies of anti-Semitism.'[16] Shostakovich caricatures the 'Great Leader's' style by emphasizing this idiosyncrasy, deliberately repeating 'cannot, cannot, cannot' and turning the double negative into a triple: 'Antisocial composers, being constitutionally formalist, cannot, cannot not write formalist music.'

All the key points of 'Comrade Dvoikin's' speech bear a direct relation to Zhdanov's peroration at the previously mentioned Conference of Musical Functionaries at the Central Committee of the Communist Party. A simple juxtaposition with Shostakovich's libretto obviates the need for any commentary.[17]

Zhdanov: 'I do not intend to include dissonance or "atonality" in this analysis, although "atonality" is very fashionable just now. (*laughter and commotion in the hall)'*. (132)

Dvoikin: 'I do not intend in my address to include dissonance (*laughter*) or atonality (*laughter*) in the considerations we have heard here.' (figs. 15–16)

Zhdanov: 'You are perhaps surprised to hear that in the Bolshevik Central Committee we demand in music beauty and elegance? What a frightful thought?! But this is indeed no slip of the tongue. We really are declaring that we insist on beautiful, elegant music . . .' (143). 'Is this not so?' (144)

Dvoikin: 'Comrades, we demand of music beauty and elegance. Do you find this strange? Yes? Well, of course you do. It does seem strange to you . . . as if something was wrong here. Well, it is as I have said, I have made no slip of the tongue. We do insist on beautiful, elegant music.' (figs. 17–18)

[16] I. V. Stalin, *Sochineniya*, xiii (Moscow, 1951), 28.

[17] All Zhdanov's pronouncements are cited in *Soveshchanie deyatelei sovetskoi muzyki v TsK VKP (b)* (Moscow, 1948). Figures in parentheses following quotations indicate the page on which they are to be found in this edition.

Zhdanov: 'It must be said, straight out, that there are a great number of works by composers of today . . . that often remind one, pardon the crudity of the expression, of a dentist's drill, or sometimes of a mobile gas chamber. We simply cannot stand it, believe you me! (*laughter, applause*).' (143)

Dvoikin: 'This music is not harmonious, it is not elegant, it is, it is—like a dentist's drill! Or, or, like a musical mobile gas chamber. (*general laughter*). (5 bars before fig. 20 and the start of fig. 20)

Zhdanov: 'The music of the opera is far removed from, and alien to, the folk art of the people of the Northern Caucasus . . . If during the course of the action there is a *lezginka*, the music provided for it bears no relation to the *lezginka* we know and love. In his pursuit of novelty at all costs the composer has made up some *lezginka* music of his own, music that is illogical, boring, has much less to it and is far less beautiful than the normal folk music of the *lezginka*' (6)

Dvoikin: 'Moreover, Comrades, I have to say to you that in Caucasian operas there should be a genuine *lezginka*. . . . In Caucasian operas the *lezginka* must be simple, and it must be well known; it must be spirited, plain and popular. And it must be Caucasian. It must be authentic, it's got to be authentic . . . (figs. 22–6)

There are not one but several sources for Troikin's address. In fact, despite the obvious hint of the character's initials, not much is taken from Shepilov's speech at the Second Congress of Composers. The greater part of this passage in the libretto has been taken from speeches by Zhdanov, such as, for example, Troikin's opening words: 'We must be classical. We must write music just like the classics did' (fig. 23, bars 6–12). This is associated with the following pronouncement by Zhdanov: 'It would be no bad thing if we had a few more compositions that were like the classics in form, in elegance, in beauty and musicality. If you think this is just imitation, well, there's nothing to be ashamed of in such imitation' (142).

The next part of Troikin's role, with its enumeration of the names of the classic composers of Russian music complete with mispronunciation, is certainly connected with the speech by Shepilov, who said: 'The task of Soviet music . . . is to cherish and actively further the traditions of Glinka and Tchaikovsky, Musorgsky and Rimsky-KorsAkov.'[18] The remainder of his text comes from Zhdanov's 1948 pronouncements:

Troikin: 'Glinka, Tchaikovsky, Rimsky-KorsAkov, you are musical, elegant, harmonious. Glinka, Tchaikovsky, Rimsky-KorsAkov, you are melodious, beautiful, sonorous. Glinka, Tchaikovsky, Rimsky-KorsAkov, you touch several strings. How right this is, how true this is. Our Soviet man is a very complex organism' . . . (figs. 28–31)

Zhdanov: 'How well, how rightly, and how forcefully this is said!' (138). 'Is this not true, is this not right. . . .' (142). 'The greater a work of music is, the more strings of the human heart it causes to resonate in response. From the perspective of his response to music, man is a wonderful, boundlessly rich membrane or radio receiver, functioning on

---

[18] *Sovetskaya muzyka*, 5 (1957), 8.

thousands of wavelengths, or probably there is a better comparison—for him the sound of one note, one string, one emotion, is not enough. If a composer is able to evoke a response from just one, or several strings in the human heart, this is not enough, for the man of today, especially our Soviet man, is a very complex organism in his powers of understanding. Glinka, Tchaikovsky and Serov themselves wrote of the high musical development of the Russian people.'(144)

Troikin's opening words (from fig. 31 and the beginning of the scene, sung to the tune *Kalinka*) are taken directly from D. T. Shepilov's speech:

Troikin: 'Therefore, Comrades, we need symphonies, poems, quartets, sonatas, suites.' (fig. 32)
Shepilov: 'We need good quartets and oratorios, songs and cantatas.'[19]

At the beginning of the last quatrain in Troikin's text, to the tune of *Kalinka*, (bars 17–22 of fig. 33), Shostakovich makes good use of the words 'Glinka—Dzerzhinka—Tishinka'. They recall a comic canon written in honour of Glinka in 1836 by V. F. Odoyevsky to words by Vielgorsky, Vyazemsky, Zhukovsky, and Pushkin, which he puns on the composers's name with 'ne-Glinka' [i.e. not-Glinka—trans.] and 'Neglinka':

Sing in rapture, Russian choirs,
Here's a star that's new aflame,
Rejoice, Rossiya! For our Glinka
Now is not Glinka, but porcelain![20]

Rumour celebrates this wonder,
Running wildfire through the land,
From Neglinnaya to Neva
Glinka's name's on every hand.[21]

Shostakovich takes this already elaborate play on words a stage further and lends it an extra, maliciously satirical sense. 'Neglinka' is the popular colloquial name for Neglinnaya Street, a thoroughfare in the centre of Moscow, so Shostakovich takes this as the starting-point for a multi-layered musical-topological pun suggesting a complex trail of semantic and allusive associations, both musical and extra-musical. 'Dzerzhinka' is the nickname for Felix Dzerzhinsky Square (today Lubyanka Square), headquarters of the NKVD, later

---

[19] *Sovetskaya muzyka*, 5 (1957), 8. Profound directives of this kind were in fact not new to Shostakovich. Long before this speech by Shepilov, as early as 1936 in the *Pravda* article 'Muddle instead of Music', readers were informed that 'the mass of the people' expect from composers not only good songs, but also 'good instrumental compositions and good operas', *Pravda*, 28 Jan. 1936.

[20] Unfortunately for the translator, there is yet another double meaning here: 'glina' is the Russian for 'china clay', so 'glinka' could be the diminutive of it. (Translator's note)

[21] «Пой в восторге, русский хор, | Вышла новая новинка, | Веселися Русь! Г л и н к а — уж не г л и н к а, а фарфор! | За прекрасную новинку | Славить будет глас молвы | Нашего Орфея — Г л и н к у | От Н е г л и н н о й — до Невы».

KGB. 'Tishinka' is also the nickname for another Moscow square, but it has another association as well—with the infamous Moscow transit prison known as the 'Matrosskaya Tishina' ('Silence of the Sailors'). Moving to another dimension altogether, the play on words takes its cue from 'Ne-glinka'—i.e. someone so manifestly *not* Glinka as to be diametrically opposed to him. 'Dzerzhinka' and 'Tishinka raskhrenovaya' can be clearly understood as obvious pseudonyms for certain composers. 'Dzerzhinka' is Ivan Dzerzhinsky, for whom Shostakovich made no attempt to conceal his hostility from the second half of the 1930s onwards. The second reference can similarly be decoded: 'Tishinka Ras-KHREN-ovaya' is a clear allusion to Tikhon Khrenni-kov.[22] In view of this association, we might recall a famous anecdote about Stalin, who, when asked: 'What street should we choose to rename in honour of Khrennikov?', is said to have replied: 'What for? We already have a Ne-glinka Street!'

The literary, historical, and ideological sources of this scene are not only contemporary. Certain images, as well as the metre and vocabulary of the comic hymn to Glinka, which gave Shostakovich the idea of the pun, were inspired by the Russian national anthem sung in the time of Catherine the Great, composed by Osip Kozlovsky to words by the poet Derzhavin. Its first lines: 'Resound the sound of victory | Rejoice, O Russia brave as steel | Give acclamation to your glory | Mahomet's underneath your heel!' quite clearly resonate with Zhukovsky's text ('Rejoice, Rossiya . . . Rumour celebrates . . .'). As well as the contemporary references to Khrennikov and Dzerzhinsky, Shostakovich's field of reference thus extends from Glinka and the national anthem of the Russian Empire to the KGB and the 'Matrosskaya' gaol (founded, as a matter of fact, by Catherine II). A further layer of national and historical associations is also produced, whose meanings encompass not only the high (Glinka) and the low (the not-Glinkas of today), but the joyous and trium-phantly celebratory and the tragically dark and frightening.

The text of the Shostakovich's libretto for the final scene of *The Anti-Formalist Rayok* is deliberately reminiscent of many ideological Party statements and press items of the late 1950s and later decades. In particular, one can find parallels with articles and pronouncements by Nikita Khrushchev on his encounters with the artistic intelligentsia. In the well-known article 'For the creation of a close relationship between literature and art and the life of the people', for example, we read: 'We call you to a battle of ideological principle. Today we are witnessing a bitter fight between two ideologies, socialist and bourgeois, and in this fight there can be no neutrality. Literature and art must evolve under conditions of ideological warfare, and against the influence of bourgeois culture, which is alien to us.'[23] The reality of these warnings and

---

[22] 'Khren' (literally 'horseradish') is also a colloquial term for a boring old person, an old fogey. 'Khrenovyi' is the adjective derived from it. 'Khren' is also commonly used as a politer version of the obscene 'khui' = 'prick'. (Translator's note)   [23] *Pravda*, 28 Aug. 1957.

effectiveness of the calls to action became quite clear towards the middle of the 1960s, when the persecution of dissidents intensified, and culminated in the anti-dissident trials.

Clearly the individuals who feature in the Preface 'From the Publisher' have their prototypes in certain highly placed Party bosses in the fields of literature and the arts at the end of the 1940s and later. The model for the Candidate of Fine Arts P. I. Opostilov was evidently Pavel Ivanovich Apostolov (1905–69), a conductor of military bands, who in 1948 went to work in the chief political administration of the Soviet Army, and in 1949 became a Central Committee apparatchik. Shostakovich puns on the root of his name ('Apostol', meaning apostle, Christ's disciple) by replacing it with the emotionally and semantically negative verb 'opostilet'', to become repellent. B. S. Sryurikov, the official from the Ministry of Ideological Purity, is probably Boris Sergeyevich Ryurikov (1909–69), literary critic and publicist who from 1946 to 1949 and from 1955 to 1956 served in the Central Committee's Department of Agitation and Propaganda, and later the department of culture. According to a Soviet literary encylopaedia of 1971, Ryurikov 'battled with great energy to put into practice the principles of the Party's policies in the spheres of literature and art . . . The speeches of Ryurikov were imbued with the pathos of the fight for Communist Party values, and with the spirit of uncompromising resistance to bourgeois art and bourgeois morality.'[24] The pun Shostakovich makes on Ryurikov's surname (which comes from Ryurik, founder of the oldest dynasty of Russian leaders) when he relegates it to the scatological Sryurikov is fairly obvious, especially in the context of all the other names and the Transformation of Opostilov into seven pieces of excrement. B. M. Yasrustovsky, the official from the Department of Musical Security is certainly the musicologist Boris Mik-hailovich Yarustovsky (1911–78), head of the department of culture at the Central Committee from 1946 to 1958. He played a direct role in the preparation of the texts of the Party's statements on music in 1948, and in particular the address presented to the First Congress of the Union of Soviet Composers.[25] P. I. Sryumin is presumably Pavel Ivanovich Ryumin, musico-logist and Central Committee official. 'Doctor Ubiitsev' ('Dr Assassin'), who appears following the tragic fate that befalls the unfortunate P. I. Opostilov, is likewise a symbolic figure, whose name recalls the so-called 'Kremlin Doctors' Plot' (1953) and the consequent press witch-hunt to unmask the 'assassins in white coats' and 'doctor-murderers'. Finally, it can be seen that in naming the institutions mentioned in the 'From the Publisher' text as the 'Ministry of Ideological Purity' and the 'Department of Musical Security', Shostakovich was following the traditions of twentieth-century anti-Utopian satire, from the novel

[24] *Kratkaya literaturnaya entsiklopediya*, vi (Moscow, 1971), cols. 571–2.

[25] See Yarustovsky's own testimony on this subject, in his book *Vospominaniya B. V. Aseyeve* (Moscow, 1974), 296–7.

We by Yevgeny Zamyatin, with whom he collaborated on the libretto for his opera *The Nose*, to George Orwell's *1984*.

   The first complete performance of *The Anti-Formalist Rayok* in the composer's final version took place on 25 September 1989 in the Great Hall of the Moscow Conservatoire, as part of a concert honouring the eighty-third anniversary of Shostakovich's birth. The performers were the State Chamber Choir of the USSR Ministry of Culture directed by Valery Polyansky; the soloists were Yury Vishnyakov (Master of Ceremonies), Yevgeny Chepikov (Yedinitsin), Anatoly Obraztsov (Dvoikin), and Nikolay Konovalov (Troikin); the pianist was Igor Khudolyei. The text of the Preface 'From the Publisher' was read by the Malaya Bronnaya Theatre actor Dmitry Dorlyak. This première was preceded by a performance of the Preliminary Version, without the final chorus scene, in Washington DC, on 12 January 1989, conducted by Mstislav Rostropovich, and also by a performance on 13 May 1989 in Moscow of the final version but also without the final scene, conducted by Valery Polyansky with stage direction by Mikhail Kozakov, who also read the 'From the Publisher' text. On 5 October the same year Vladimir Pankratov (bass) and Boris Tishchenko (piano) gave a performance in Leningrad of the solo version of *Rayok*, as envisaged by the composer.

10

A New Insight into the Tenth Symphony of Dmitry Shostakovich

NELLY KRAVETZ

'In this work I wanted to express human passions and feelings'[1]

Forty years after the première of the Tenth Symphony, it is hard to believe that there could be something which might change our approach to a work which has been so thoroughly analysed and which has had such an unusually fine performance history. New evidence enables us to gain a new insight into this symphony, however, and the present article is based on eight letters written by Shostakovich in 1953, which have until now have been unknown to the musical world.[2] The letters were addressed to Elmira Nazirova, who studied in Shostakovich's class in 1947. In the interview with Elmira Nazirova which follows this article, she explains that her correspondence with Shostakovich began after they met during his visit to Baku, although she does not remember precisely when this was. According to Sofya Khentova, Shostakovich was in Baku from 1 to 12 March 1952.[3] During his visit Shostakovich performed at a recital his Six Preludes and Fugues from Op. 87. Elmira Nazirova remembers attending this concert.[4]

The correspondence lasted for almost three and a half years, from April 1953 to September 1956. During this period Elmira Nazirova received thirty-four letters from Shostakovich. She permitted me to read only eight of them (from 10, 12, 18, and 29 August, 17 and 19 September, 15 and 23 November 1953). All these letters were written in 1953 and according to Elmira Nazirova are the most significant ones of the correspondence, because they contain sensational new details about the Tenth Symphony, especially the letters of 29 August and

---

[1] 'Znachitel'noe yavlenie sovetskoi muzyki', *Sovetskaya muzyka*, 6 (1954), 120.

[2] Grateful acknowledgement is due to Professor Joachim Braun (Bar-Ilan University, Israel) for letting me have copies of the original letters, and for his invaluable comments. Special thanks are due to Elmira Nazirova for her kind permission for me to analyse these letters and for her invaluable interview. The letters are now in the private collection of Maxim Shostakovich.

[3] S. Khentova, *Shostakovich: zhizn' i tvorchestvo*, ii (Leningrad, 1986), 604.

[4] Most probably their first meeting took place on 16 May 1953 at the Plenary Session of the Union of Composers, where the *24 Preludes and Fugues* were discussed.

17 September. Five letters were written on an official sheet of the Vienna Peace Congress, which Shostakovich was invited to in 1952.[5]

At the beginning, in 1953, the correspondence was very intense. Shostako-vich wrote to Nazirova very often. It was precisely at this period of time that he was working on the Tenth Symphony. In the manuscript of the symphony, the first movement is dated 5 August, the second 27 August, the third 8 October and the fourth 25 October 1953. Most of Shostakovich's letters to Nazirova were written in August and in September of 1953, when Shostakovich was working on the second and the third movements of the symphony.[6] It is quite noticeable that the intensity of the correspondence dropped after the completion of the symphony and then the correspondence itself stops rather sharply. In 1954 Elmira Nazirova received five letters from Shostakovich and only one letter in the years 1955 and 1956. Elmira Nazirova admitted in my interview with her that after the première of the Tenth Symphony on 17 December 1953, she had a feeling that her mission had come to an end. The facts of the correspondence are not brought up here merely for information, but to provide concrete evidence for the assertion that during the period Shostakovich was working on his Tenth Symphony, he was engrossed in a correspondence with Elmira Nazirova which had a direct effect on his work.

During my interview with her, Nazirova told me that she did not answer Shostakovich's letters regularly. Shostakovich, however, continued to write without waiting for an answer. He obviously had a great need to be in touch with her. His letters are of a very personal nature. He was deeply grieved when he did not hear from her for a long while. He wanted to read her letters, and wanted to see her even more. He thought a lot about her and persistently asked her to send him a photograph of herself. This request is mentioned twice in the same letter of 18 August 1953. After receiving her photograph, Shostakovich expressed his happiness and gratitude, again twice in the same letter—at the beginning and at the end (see Plate 10). Shostakovich was possessed by the need to communicate with a woman he knew practically very little about and whom he saw only occasionally. It seems he had something of an *idée fixe*, which is reflected in his music.

Many commentators have tried to guess the meaning of the horn theme from the third movement of the Tenth Symphony (Ex. 10.1). Lev Danilevich has written about its pastoral nature.[7] Marina Sabinina has associated it with the symbolic calls of nature in Mahler's Second Symphony. She has also claimed that the horn is connected to the idea of landscapes, and that the interval of the fourth is connected with old Russian ritual songs.[8] Vladimir Karbuzitsky has

---

[5] At the top of the paper, in the right-hand corner, is the inscription 'Congrès des Peuples. Pour La Paix. Vienne 1952'.

[6] D. Shostakovich, *Sobranie sochinenii v 42 tomakh*, v (Moscow, 1979).

[7] Lev Danilevich, *D. D. Shostakovich* (Moscow, 1958), 134.

[8] Marina Sabinina, *Shostakovich—simfonist: dramaturgiya, estetika, stil'* (Moscow, 1976), 302.

Ex. 10.1

also interpreted the horn theme as a pastoral 'echo' and has related it to the 'calls' from Berlioz's *Symphonie fantastique* (Scène aux champs).[9] Lev Mazel has come closest to discovering the mystery of the theme, defining it as 'remote reminiscences, some kind of inner summons coming from the depths of the human heart'.[10] But the only person who has penetrated the mysterious meaning of the theme is David Fanning. His superb hypothesis is based on a very intensive analysis of the composition, in which he writes:

The horn signal which punctuates the central section [of the third movement] is the most enigmatic feature of the entire symphony. Its prominence suggests that it carries some deeply personal significance, but whether it is a cryptogram or some other kind of musical association can only be a matter for speculation.[11]

Fanning was the first person to abbreviate the horn theme to the letters EAEDA and almost guesses Shostakovich's thoughts when he writes: 'How convenient if EAEDA could be shown to be a musical signature complementing DSCH.'[12] The truth is revealed in a letter written by the composer himself on 29 August 1953. Here he tells Elmira that since he has been thinking about her all the time, he has transformed her name into notes. In the letter Shostakovich includes a musical example and explains in great detail the notes which make up the horn theme in the third movement. He shows that the first note is 'E'. The second note is the second note of the sol-fa system, 'la', which can be represented without the second letter. The third note is the same as the first, but can be called 'mi'. The fourth note is 're', from which we get 'r' if we omit the second letter. The fifth note is 'A' (the same as 'la').

There can be therefore no doubt that the third movement has an autobiographical meaning. There is clearly a 'concealed programme' which manifests itself in the linking of two monograms which are personifications for Shostakovich himself (DSCH) and for Elmira Nazirova (EAEDA). It is now easy to explain why Shostakovich's monogram appears in the third movement. It is heard as a familiar motif: the two minor seconds which go in opposite directions, and the diminished fourth between these extreme sounds are important elements in the symphony's thematic construction. The appearance of the monogram is directly prepared for, moreover, by the first theme of the

[9] Vladimir Karbuzitsky, '"Simfonizm", "Tematizm" und "Vokal'nost" kak esteticheskie kategorii v tvorchestve Shostakovicha', *Internationales Dmitri Shostakowitsch Symposion* (Köln, 1986), 173.

[10] Lev Mazel, *Simfonii D.D. Shostakovicha: Putevoditel'* (Moscow, 1960), 123.

[11] David Fanning, *The Breath of the Symphonist. Shostakovich's Tenth* (London, 1988), p. 51.

[12] Ibid.

third movement, and is repeated also in the finale. It is important to note that Lev Mazel came out strongly against attributing any autobiographical meaning to the motif. Doubting that Shostakovich had intentionally spelled out his own initials here, he writes in his study of the symphony: 'There is no confirmation that this was a deliberate intention of the composer, rather than mere coincidence.'[13] Elmira Nazirova claims, however, that she received a letter from Shostakovich (unfortunately lost) in which he specifically wrote that DSCH were his initials spelled out in musical notes. According to Nazirova's testimony, Shostakovich also told her that his monogram contained Eastern colouring. The motif EAEDA appears as a striking contrast to Shostakovich's monogram. It is not heard elsewhere in the symphony and its tonality (A minor or D minor) is not associated with any other parts of the score. The motif is repeated twelve times, like an *idée fixe*, and is performed only by the horn. I would now like to formulate some conclusions.

The pastoral idea obviously lies on the surface. The timbre of the horn and its calls in fourths evoke definite associations with images of nature. But the motif also conceals a different, highly tragic meaning which is revealed with the sound of the fateful tam-tam after EAEDA, accompanying the motif like an ominous shadow. It is the silent stroke of the tam-tam which ends the third movement like a funeral knell.

The tragic significance of Elmira's monogram is revealed in its interval structure. If the fourths performed by the horn (E–A–E) in slow tempo can actually be associated with pastoral calls (they contain a clear progression from the dominant to the tonic and back to the dominant), the descending major second (E–D) does not demand resolution and, because of the tonal ambiguity, leads the theme into a different emotional mood. There is a sense of loss of orientation, and a feeling that this road does not lead anywhere. The last rising fifth (D–A) strengthens this feeling of hollowness because of the tonal ambiguity (A minor to D minor), as if a question were hanging in the air without an answer.

The rising fifths occupy a prominent position in the finale, in that they help us to grasp the meaning of the whole conception. The slow introduction features calls in fifths which are derived from Elmira's monogram. The beginning of the exposition presents an unexpected psychological shift, however, when the sorrowful fifth turns into a cheerful version of the primary theme. Yet the obvious analogy with the horn motif gives us cause to doubt this optimism. It is actually a mask which can be discarded at any time. The disguise is revealed before the coda (4 bars before fig. 198), when the so-called 'cheerful theme' ends with an introduction of the DSCH motif, played *forte*, as if it was a symbol of fate. The theme is performed by the horn, reminding the listener of the timbre of the Elmira monogram. The DSCH motif is drummed urgently into the listener's

---

[13] Mazel, *Simfonii Shostakovicha*, 122.

consciousness as the main idea of the symphony (figs. 202–4). All this suggests that EAEDA occupies a prominent position in the symphony's conception.

Paradoxical as it may sound, the real meaning of the mysterious horn theme is revealed not in the Tenth Symphony itself but in another work. Shostakovich himself unravels it in a letter to Elmira Nazirova dated 17 September 1953. He tells her here how the day before he had played one of his favourite compositions, Mahler's *Das Lied von der Erde*, and explains the content of the first movement in the following way: there are people living in a town. Once in a while the terrible cry of a giant monkey is heard coming from the cemetery, located out of town. In China monkeys are the symbol of death, of cruel fate and of all kinds of other misfortunes. The citizens listen to the cries with fear. Shostakovich then explains his reason for retelling the story. The notes of the ominous cry of the monkey are the same ones which make up the horn theme of his Tenth Symphony. Shostakovich even includes a brief musical example in the letter, remarking that this coincidence would be an interesting topic for musicological research (Ex.10.2).

Ex. 10.2

It is remarkable that David Fanning is once again the only person who has noticed this striking resemblance, even giving the same musical example. I would like to point to an important circumstance. Shostakovich first wrote to Elmira Nazirova about his intention to make a musical monogram of her name on 29 August 1953, and only 19 days later he played one of his favourite pieces of music. This means that while he was working on the third movement, he unconsciously found himself under the influence of a familiar pattern which was preserved in his mind. An interesting and unknown fact, which Shostakovich reveals in a letter 10 August 1953, is that he had heard the third movement in a dream, had remembered some of it and intended to use it in his future work. Perhaps it is possible that the parallel with Mahler was 'worked out' in that dream. Shostakovich worked on the third movement longer than on any other part of the score (from 27 August to 8 October 1953). This is not accidental—he was looking for a theme, he badly needed to find one and eventually had to compose one.

Further proof of my hypothesis is provided by the fact that Shostakovich changed the monogram itself: twice in the third movement (figs. 118 and 119) he added an extra 'E' and the theme began to resemble the theme of Mahler's symphony even more closely (Ex. 10.3).

Only the last 'E' is needed to create an exact replica of the interval structure of the monkey's cry. It is possible that Shostakovich 'adapted' the musical image

Ex. 10.3

of the name Elmira to the beloved theme by Mahler. We should recall how he 'played' with the letters of Elmira's name: notes with Latin letters are combined with notes denoted by the syllables of the solfeggio system. He also freely discarded unnecessary letters and the last syllable of Elmira's name ('ra') is divided into the sol-fa note ray ('D') and the Latin 'A'. Consequently the monogram becomes more than an image of a woman he was corresponding with. It turns into a symbol of the tragic fate of the composer himself, because it coincides with the ominous cry of the monkey which symbolizes cruel fate in Mahler's symphony. And when Shostakovich became aware of this, he was amazed by his discovery.

The similarity is really startling. There is a resemblance in notes, in the horn's timbre and even the number of repetitions, which is almost the same (Mahler—eleven times, Shostakovich—twelve times). The similarity is indeed a deeply rooted one, as there is an organic connection which links the styles of the two composers, their devices of formal construction, their orchestration, and the very conceptions of both works. The easiest approach to understanding the Tenth Symphony is to connect it to the political events which took place during the period of its composition. Some commentators have directly associated the symphony with the death of Stalin. In my opinion, the importance of the role played by external circumstances in the composition of this work is overestimated. The real tragedy lies in the inner world of the composer himself, in his doubts and in his dissatisfaction with the results of his creative work, and in his concern for the future of his music. In the letter to Elmira Nazirova of 29 August 1953, he writes that he has finished the second movement of the symphony, is writing the third one, and is not satisfied with the results: 'My powers must be in decline, including my abilities as a composer. There is nothing to be done about it. Such is the law of life, such is fate . . .'

A composer's destiny is usually hidden from the public eye and only his music can reflect his thoughts and feelings. Shostakovich did not reveal the mystery of his symphony. Even in the seven letters addressed to his friend Isaak Glikman in 1953 he never wrote about it except to mention his dissatisfaction with the second movement.[14] It is fortunate that Shostakovich's letters to Elmira Nazirova, which contain such valuable explanations, have been safely preserved. They give us abundant food for thought and further research.

---

[14] *Pis'ma k drugu: Dmitri Shostakovich–Isaaku Glikmanu* (Moscow and St Petersburg, 1993), 104.

A List of Shostakovich's Letters to Elmira Nazirova

1953

12 April	(Moscow)	10 August	(Komarovo)	12 September	(Moscow)
30 May	(Moscow)	12 August	(Komarovo)	17 September	(Moscow)
4 June	(Moscow)	18 August	(Moscow)	19 September	(Moscow)
20 June	(Bolshevo)	21 August	(Moscow)	19 September	(Moscow)
21 June	(Bolshevo)	27 August	(Moscow)	30 October	(Moscow)
25 July	(Moscow)	29 August	(Moscow)	2 November	(Kharkov)
29 July	(Komarovo)	1 September	(Moscow)	6 November	(Bolshevo)
2 August	(Leningrad)	2 September	(Moscow)	15 November	(Moscow)
4 August	(Moscow)	8 September	(Leningrad)	23 November	(Leningrad)

1954

25 January	(Moscow)
8 April	(Moscow)
21 May	(Leningrad)
10 June	(Moscow)
24 October	(Bolshevo)

1955

26 September (Moscow)

1956

13 September (Bolshevo)

INTERVIEW WITH ELMIRA NAZIROVA*

Before me lies a unique copy of the Tenth Symphony, given by Shostakovich to Elmira Nazirova, with whose name is linked a whole period of intensive correspondence with the composer. This work turned out to be the most important and complete 'letter' from Shostakovich, in that only symbols embedded in its score are capable of synthesizing what was said with everything that was unsaid. I was anticipating my meeting with Elmira Nazirova with great curiosity and excitement as I walked up the stairs of an old building. An elderly woman of average height opened the door. After a few words of greeting she eagerly set out on a voyage into the past.

N.K.   Mrs Nazirova, you emigrated to Israel in 1990. You are a pianist and a composer. Could you tell me about your childhood? When and where was your talent first discovered?

* Sponsored by the Dr Irving and Cherna Moskowitz Fund.

E.N.   I was born in Baku, on 30 November 1928.[15] My mother Leila Muradova was an excellent pianist, who taught music to children. My mother's sisters were musicians too. I started to play the piano at the age of 4, composing little pieces of my own. When I was 6 years old I attracted the attention of the outstanding musician and composer Uzeir Gadjibekov.[16] I studied in a musical school for gifted children, taking up both piano and composition. I gave my first piano recital, of Beethoven's First Piano Concerto, when I was 10 years old, with the Philharmonic Orchestra conducted by Nikolay Anosov. By then I had already composed many musical pieces which I played myself.

I started to compose seriously when I was 12. Professor Zeidman[17] from Leningrad, the founder of the Azerbaijan school for composers, was my teacher in composition. In 1946 I joined the Baku Conservatoire and studied in two departments simultaneously. The following year I moved to Moscow and continued my studies at the Moscow Conservatoire. I got married and my elder child was born in Moscow. Circumstances made it difficult for me to remain in Moscow. I had studied for three years and then moved back to Baku in 1950, where I completed my studies in piano and composition. From 1951, until I emigrated to Israel, I worked at the Baku Conservatoire, first as an assistant, and finally as a professor and head of department. I never taught composition but I had many bright students and I taught them to improvise. Many of my students are now working in America, in Australia, and in Israel.

N.K.   How often did you go on tour, and where did you go?

E.N.   I performed a lot in various cities of the Soviet Union. I also gave several piano recitals abroad—in Poland (1958), in Czechoslovakia (1963), and in Egypt (1963). I had the honour to play with such outstanding conductors as Ginzburg, Stasevich, Svetlanov, Anosov, Rakhlin, and Satanovsky (from Poland).

N.K.   Did you compose music as well while you were teaching at the Conservatoire?

E.N.   Yes, of course. I was writing all the time, mainly pieces for the piano. It was quite natural, as I was a pianist myself.

N.K.   When did you first meet Shostakovich? How did you get acquainted?

E.N.   In 1947 I came to Moscow for the admission exams to the Conservatoire. I brought my 'Preludes for the Piano' and hoped to join the class of Shebalin who, strangely enough, was considered the best teacher at the Conservatoire. I literally had to be talked into studying composition with

---

[15]   Baku is the capital of Azerbaijan (the former USSR Republic).

[16]   Uzeir Gadjibekov (1895–1948) was the founder of Azerbaijani national music.

[17]   Boris Zeidman (1908) was a pupil of Maximilian Steinberg. He taught theoretical subjects at the Baku Conservatoire and at the Music School for gifted children.

Shostakovich. He was on tour somewhere and it was several months before I first met him. When he returned to Moscow I went to see him at home. Somehow I got confused about the address and I sat on the pavement and cried.[18] It was already late. Then he went abroad again and I attended the first lesson in his class only two months later. He didn't teach in the Conservatoire building itself but in Shebalin's office (who was then rector), located next to the Great Hall. When I first entered I was very embarrassed. I was the only woman present. Among others were the well-known musicians Boris Chaikovsky and Karen Khachaturian, with whom later I became very friendly. Shostakovich never waited for anyone to approach him. He was always the first one to go up and say hello. This also happened to me. The students were sitting quietly with their scores, and he asked all of them if they wanted to show what they had written. They were all silent; nobody had the courage. Then when he saw me, he said: 'Well, you and I are now going to sit down and play some Haydn Symphonies for four hands.' And then we ended up doing some very vigorous sightreading almost every lesson. The other students got awfully jealous, and used to smirk. They knew he liked me and respected me as a musician. My studies with Shostakovich didn't last long. Over the course of a whole year I only attended only a few lessons with him, and then after the Central Committee Resolution of February 1948 Shostakovich was made redundant, or rather he was expelled from the Conservatoire. He told me then: 'I doubt whether you will be able to pass the exam into the next class. They will try to fail you because you are my student. Maybe it would be better if I didn't come to your exam?' He advised me to transfer to the composition class of Vasilenko, which I did, but I never attended any of his lessons, of course. The students of Shostakovich were treated very badly. This was probably the main reason why I left Moscow.

N.K.   How long did you study with Shostakovich?

E.N.   All my life, I would say, since my tuition did not just consist in me going to classes and showing my compositions. You learn something from the very process of communicating, and later on you begin to look at things through the eyes of your teacher. Formally, Shostakovich was my teacher for only a year.

N.K.   What can you tell us about Shostakovich as a teacher? How did he use to work with his students?

E.N.   As I have already mentioned, the actual lessons were rather few in number. Shostakovich used to travel a lot and then he got expelled from the Conservatoire. Our lessons really couldn't be called lessons in the usual sense of the word. Students used to bring in a part of a symphony, he would make a single remark and that was all. I remember that he always used to say: 'One can

---

[18] At that time, Shostakovich's address was 37 Mozhaiskoe shosse, apt. 45 (now Kutuzovsky Prospect).

be taught how to orchestrate well but you can't ever be taught how to compose music.' As a matter of fact, Shostakovich didn't regard himself as a good teacher. Zeidman, on the other hand, was a good teacher; he actually taught you how to compose and made useful remarks. It's quite different when you are dealing with someone with such a strong personality like Shostakovich. He couldn't teach in the conventional sense, but his influence on students was immense. He used to say: 'You should borrow from the real masters—not steal from them, the way most musicians do. Then you'll become a real composer.'

No matter how many musicians approached him, whether they were from Central Asia or Russia or amateurs, he would always give them time, and never criticized anyone. I remember asking him about that and he replied: 'No one is going to become a better composer from anything I say. And what if they are suddenly inspired?' Even when he clearly disliked a piece of music he wouldn't express his opinion openly, believing that nobody had the right to judge music from a position of 'this is good and that is bad'.[19]

N.K.   While you were studying with Shostakovich, did you find that you were influenced by his music?

E.N.   No, I have got a completely different style, in fact. Other students imitated him, though, and sometimes they actually just copied bits of his works. They imitated not only his manner of composing but his manner of speech as well. Even the Baku composers who wrote in their own national style were strongly influenced by his music. That's why their music was so alike. Zeidman's students never lost their creative individuality, on the other hand, both because of his weakness as a composer and because of his talent as a teacher. Shostakovich's students were all alike because he was such an authority, but that's completely understandable.

N.K.   What can you tell us about Shostakovich's musical preferences? Which composers did he most respect?

E.N.   I think he definitely had great respect for Stravinsky, and, of course, for Prokofiev, but he talked more about Mahler than anyone else. He never expressed any admiration for Scriabin, who was quite alien to him, but he acknowledged Scriabin's role as an innovator in Russian music at the beginning of the twentieth century. Whenever I visited Shostakovich at home, he always put on a Beethoven symphony, and thought one should know all of his quartets.

N.K.   So how did your correspondence with Shostakovich begin?

---

[19] A proof of this can be found in the letter from 10 Aug. 1953 (sent from Komarovo). Shostakovich wrote that it would be very difficult for him to give Elmira any advice on her Piano Concerto, since he perceived music spontaneously and sometimes could not understand what was good and what was bad, and that he could not explain why it was good or bad. It was a great mystery to him.

E.N.   Well, I happened to find out that he was coming to Baku in March of 1952 and so I went with a group of composers to meet him at the railway station. It turned out that he was really pleased to see me amongst all those other musicians, which I found out about when he wrote to me afterwards. We then met again at one of the Plenary Sessions of the Union of Composers in Moscow. During the recess Shostakovich came downstairs and saw his *24 Preludes and Fugues* on sale. He bought a copy for me and inscribed it: 'To dear Elmira from Dmitry Shostakovich'. Then I went back to Baku, and a month later I got a letter from him addressed to the Baku Conservatoire, since he didn't know my home address. He wanted to alert me to all the misprints in the music he had given me and he had written out all the corrections. I answered his letter out of politeness. That is how our correspondence started. Unfortunately, some of his letters have been lost, but I have kept most of them.

I have to relate one sad episode during Shostakovich's visit to Baku in 1952. No one came to his concert. No one came to hear this great composer and genius of our times. He played his *24 Preludes and Fugues* in an almost empty hall. The audience consisted of soldiers who were forced to come, and they found listening to Shostakovich quite excruciating. After the notorious 1948 Central Committee Resolution, few people dared to attend his concerts. People were afraid to show any interest in his music because he was an 'enemy of the people'. That label was attached to many outstanding artists.

N.K.   You have mentioned the most difficult period in Shostakovich's life, when his music was neither played nor published, and he was constantly persecuted. What can you remember about it?

E.N.   Yes, we certainly got to know each other at a very difficult time. After being fired from both the Moscow and Leningrad Conservatoires he was entirely preoccupied by material problems, and worried about how to make ends meet. He sold his car and even started to sell his private library. People were of course eager to buy scores autographed by Shostakovich. Almost no one would say hello to him; they all gloated. I can't remember all the people who had it in for him, but they were generally very mediocre composers. I saw all these worthless composers and musicologists accuse him of 'formalism' once at a debate in the Great Hall of the Moscow Conservatoire. When I walked in, I saw him sitting pathetically all alone, in the last row, nervously pulling his hair. I went up to him and sat next to him. 'Aren't you afraid to be seen with me?' he asked. But apart from enemies, he was also surrounded by people who gave him a lot of support. One of them was the popular composer Blanter. His portrait used to hang in Shostakovich's study next to the portrait of Beethoven. He was well-off and always lent Shostakovich money. Shostakovich's closest friends were Vainberg, Levitin, and Atovmyan amongst composers, and Lev Oborin and Alexander Gauk. He often talked about Sviridov but I never met him at the private concerts Shostakovich arranged for his close friends. At that time

Shostakovich's music was almost never played. His 'rehabilitation' only began with the Tenth Symphony, and until then his music was basically banned. He only wrote music as a way of keeping himself going. The story of how he composed his 'Song of the Forests' is typical. He told me: 'I sat down late one night and within a few hours managed to scribble something down. I was surprised and horrified when I got shaken by the hand for it and even given money.' But he was too afraid to show people some of his most brilliant compositions, such as the 'Jewish' cycle, and the Fourth and Fifth Quartets.

Shostakovich never shared his anxieties with anyone. He was an unusually reserved person and gave the impression that he lived entirely inside himself. Of course he knew who Stalin was, and understood the structure of Soviet society completely, but he was very careful about what he said and always spoke little. He remembered 1937 with such horror that I think that what went on then had an even greater effect on his life than the war and all the tragedies that followed it. He guessed what was going on, and suffered horribly, but did what was expected of him, because he had the most amazing inner discipline.

Stalin himself called Shostakovich up one night and said: 'They are going to give you your dacha back, and let your pieces be performed.' That was in 1949. Shostakovich confessed to me that had been waiting all the time for them to come and arrest him, and could only begin to breathe again after Stalin's telephone call. And yet despite his awareness of the tragic regime we lived in, Shostakovich never wanted to leave the Soviet Union. He dreamed of settling down in Bolshevo (he would have liked me to be with him), where he could light the stove and fetch water from the well. He always yearned for solitude.

N.K.   What do you know about Shostakovich's parents, and about his family?

E.N.   Shostakovich had great respect for his mother, and she worshipped him. She was an aristocratic lady from a typical gentry family, whose opinion Shostakovich always adhered to. He warned me about her jealousy towards people in his circle. She could make up her mind about a person just from the telephone, and Dmitry Dmitrievich taught me to say a particular phrase when I rang him up. He never mentioned his father.

His first wife was a talented astrophysicist. She was the daughter of a friend of his mother's, born to a family of the Leningrad intelligentsia. She was always totally wrapped up in her professional life. Shortly after Nina Vasilievna's death Shostakovich remarried. His second wife was a Komsomol activist whom he had met on some committee. His third wife was Irina Antonovna, a very refined and intelligent woman. She was very fond of him and was a great help to him, even to the point of getting up while no one noticed to give him an arm to lean on when he found it difficult to walk. She never went anywhere without her husband, and never compromised herself in any way, despite the huge difference in age between them. She developed a good relationship with his children, and they respected her. As an educated person, she of course knew who she was living with, but since she wasn't a musician herself and couldn't understand the specifics of music composition, she could stay calm in his presence. His genius used to affect me so much, however, that I would already feel it after being with him for an hour. I used literally to go crazy about his music and about the things he said. I doubt that I could have lived with him, even if I hadn't had a family already, although he asked me to move in with him. It's difficult for me to say whether he was actually a human being. He was like God for me.

N.K.   Could you tell us a little more about your meetings with Shostakovich?

E.N.   Our relationship wasn't limited just to letters. We met whenever I came up to Moscow from Baku. I would go to his apartment, and go to concerts to hear performances of his latest quartets and the Tenth Symphony. Our meetings were very odd. He would write to me and be dying for me to reply, but whenever I turned up in person, after ten minutes he quite often asked me to leave. But then he would rush off down the street, write to me, or ring me up and tell me he had been looking for me. It was completely perplexing. He couldn't talk to me quietly even for a moment. He would be constantly lighting cigarettes, getting up to open the window, sitting down again, and then getting up again to walk about. After a few minutes his complex personality would start to make me feel quite strange.

I remember my visit to Leningrad on 17 December 1953 for the première of the Tenth Symphony. He met me at the door, and even helped me to change my shoes, before accompanying me to my seat. He sat in a nearby box in order to be able to see me. While the audience was applauding he kept looking at me, but no one could guess whom he was staring at. After the concert he came up to me and then took me to my hotel. But we didn't talk—there were no comments, no explanations. It was if my mission ended with my coming to Leningrad. I dropped by once to pick up some tickets for a concert, and sat down, thinking we would have a talk, but he didn't ask me a single question. The tickets after all were an excuse to see me, and I think he was dying for me to arrive, but . . . This would have been strange behaviour for an ordinary person, but for him it was quite normal. Shostakovich was very shy and never talked about his emotions. There was one letter, though, which made me laugh. Well, I was very young then. I was reading a letter from him and then I suddenly saw at the bottom that he had written out the notes from a line in Lensky's aria 'I love you'—obviously intended for me. Such was his unusual declaration of love then. Thankfully I still have this letter.

N.K.   No one has known until now that the horn theme in the third movement of the Tenth Symphony was a monogram constructed from the letters of your name. How did you learn about it?

E.N.   Shostakovich wrote to me in detail about his intentions in one of his letters, and there is a story behind it all. I was very young then and didn't appreciate then what kind of a genius I was corresponding with. I didn't answer his letters for quite a long time. The theme, composed from the letters of my name, sounds like a call; there is a note of expectancy in it. Shostakovich was very lonely and decided to express his melancholy in a very unorthodox manner. Right after the publication of the first edition of the Tenth Symphony, Shostakovich sent me a copy with a dedicatory inscription (see Plate 10).

N.K.   I've often found myself reading about Shostakovich's critical attitude to himself, and it is well known that during the discussion of the Tenth Symphony at the Union of Composers, he claimed that it was hurriedly written, that he was dissatisfied with much of it. How should we judge these statements? Is he just being modest?

E.N.   No, he wasn't being modest; he was just scared about how his music would be perceived. You have to remember that the Tenth Symphony was the first major work he composed after all the traumas he'd been put through. It proved to be a turning-point actually, because his life got significantly better afterwards: they gave him a flat, returned his dacha to him, and started publishing and performing his music again. He was very depressed though at that time. He felt completely shattered, not only from the point of view of morale, but physically, and it wasn't surprising this had an effect on his health. He didn't feel well, he was very unsure of himself, and was very uncertain about what the future had in store for him. He knew his worth as a composer, of course, though, otherwise he would not have gone on composing music. So it was fear above all, and the 'episode with the sparrow,' described in such detail in one of his letters, is also testament in some way to his psychological state of mind.[20]

N.K.   Did Shostakovich value your musical comments?

E.N.   He always listened to what I had to say, although he doubted the sincerity of those around him. He was never sure whether their evaluation of his music didn't stem from self-interest, and some desire to get something out of it. Shostakovich was always surprised that I never pestered him with phone calls, letters, and requests for autographs like everyone else, and didn't ask him for anything. Maybe that's why he trusted me so much, and would often ask me

[20] The 'episode with the sparrow' is described in a letter dated 12 Aug. 1953 (Komarovo). While Shostakovich was working on his Tenth Symphony, a sparrow flew through an open balcony window. He and his son Maxim tried to chase the bird out. In the commotion that followed, the sparrow dirtied the pages of the score which was lying on his desk. Shostakovich succeeded in saving some of the pages, the others had to be copied anew. Here is a noteworthy quotation from that letter: 'Well, if a sparrow dirties your creative work with his . . . it can't be that bad. Much worse when it is done by more significant personalities than a sparrow.' It is interesting that Shostakovich related the same episode to Isaak Glikman. Although Glikman's mother and his wife explained it as a lucky sign, 'he thoughtfully shook his head and said with a smile: "I wish you were right"' (see Glikman, *Pis'ma k drugu*, 102).

'How did you come to turn out like this?' I complained to him once that I had to finish my Piano Concerto, and couldn't come and see him because there were exams on, and I was also having problems with the orchestration. He offered to help saying: 'Send me the piano score and I will orchestrate it.' Now many years have gone by and I'm thinking how stupid I was not to accept his offer! Can you imagine how wonderfully my concerto would have been orchestrated?

Whenever Shostakovich had composed a new work he used to invite his close friends over. I was lucky enough to be present on one or two of those occasions. Once Shostakovich told me half-jokingly: 'You know, Elmira, when I am playing [he usually played four-hand versions with Vainberg—E.N.] nobody is really interested in the music. Everybody knows the table is being laid next door and they are listening to the clatter of cups and teaspoons. You watch— they will all be quick to say nice things so they can sit down at table sooner.'

N.K.   How were these private concerts organized? Which compositions did you hear?

E.N.   I heard his Tenth Symphony and the vocal cycle 'From Jewish Folk Poetry', which he sang in his hoarse voice. At the concerts he would always play first, and then everybody would sit down at table. Nobody would say anything in Dmitry Dmitrievich's presence. Despite his physical frailty he had such a powerful aura that people could barely open their mouths, let alone say something. He never talked much himself either.

N.K.   What else do you remember about Shostakovich as a person?

E.N.   I will tell you one interesting story. During the autumn of 1953 I was on vacation in Ruza. He came to spend a day there too and we travelled back together. There weren't any suburban trains going to Moscow at that time, and he couldn't get the Union of Composers chauffeur to take him back. So we got a lift to the station at Ruza to get the main line train from there. There was a crowd of people there who had had a few drinks and they were singing songs with a harmonica. I was rather apprehensive, but Shostakovich said to me: 'I'm glad we aren't going back by car. We're closer to people this way.' His human qualities are also epitomized by something that happened during our vacation in Dilijan in July 1969. One day when we were out sightseeing, a so-called 'poet' who had had far too much to drink decided to attach himself to us. When he heard he was talking to Shostakovich, he immediately started to recite his poems to us. It was incredibly hot, and we should have left. Shostakovich was very uptight, and yet he stayed and listened to the very end, because he could not bring himself to hurt the man's feelings.

One day I asked him why he never conducted his own works. To this he replied: 'You know, I feel ashamed to stand with my back to the audience.'[21] He

---

[21] Shostakovich made his début as a conductor in 1962 in Gorky during the First Festival of Modern Music.

was a very neat and tidy kind of person. There was never anything unnecessary on his desk. He smoked a lot, but he hated the smell of cigarettes and would always be getting up to open the window to let fresh air in. He used to work in the morning, from seven to nine, so as not to be disturbed, and never sat up late working, as he preferred to spend his evenings relaxing. He composed at his desk rather than at the piano and advised me to do the same. He never needed to write out drafts, and would make a fair copy of the full score right away, rather than a piano version. Once I asked him why we needed so many composers writing all this music, and he replied: 'Where there are no toadstools, there are no edible mushrooms.'

N.K.   Did you see him at all in his last years?

E.N.   The year before he died, Shostakovich came to Baku to attend a festival honouring Russian–Azerbaijan friendship.[22] They were performing his Fifteenth Symphony. I had read about his visit in the paper, but wasn't feeling well enough then to meet him at the station or go to hear his symphony on the first day either. I decided to go to the second concert. Then suddenly the telephone started ringing and it was him. He told me he had been very worried not to see me with everyone else who met him at the station, and that he was going to have to leave that day because he wasn't feeling well. That meant we would have no chance of meeting, and I deeply regretted not going to welcome him and missing the concert. I was intending to invite him over, you see, since I knew he was supposed to be in Baku for a whole week. Unfortunately things didn't turn out as I had planned. I went to see Dmitry Dmitrievich off at the station with a group of other composers. That was our last meeting. I was informed about his death the day after it happened. I was on holiday at a composers' retreat in Kiev at the time and wasn't able to go to the funeral.

[22] This is inaccurate. Shostakovich last visited Baku in 1972, when he participated in an Azerbaijan–Russian Festival of Literature and Art.

Shostakovich and Britten: Some Parallels

LYUDMILA KOVNATSKAYA

The juxtaposition of the two names in the title of this article will come as no surprise to those who know of the personal relationship that existed between these two outstanding composers, or to musicians who have performed their works. But even if nothing was known about their meetings, or about their having dedicated compositions to one another, the attentive and musically informed reader will already have realized that there exists a fruitful field of study here, and will sense how organic, serious, and potentially rich this comparison is. At the same time, it is clear that these were two individuals who came from entirely different worlds and cultural traditions, and whose works revealed the fundamental disparities between their conceptions of art, ideology, and politics, their socio-cultural attitudes towards music, and their perception of musical genres in the context of their respective national schools of composition.

The name of Shostakovich is a symbol the world over of the symphony as a living force in the twentieth century, following conceptually and socially in the line established by Beethoven and consolidated by Mahler. Symphonic writing was inherent in Shostakovich's musical thought, and in his fifteen works that bear this title he found forms sufficient to the genre. The exceptional flexibility and variety of these forms allowed the composer fully to express himself, and to summarize in sound the events of half a century of contemporary life. The string quartet was of equal importance to Shostakovich. He himself attached great significance to it and returned to it throughout his creative life, finding the less declamatory medium an ideal one in which to work out his ideas and his purely musical discoveries with maximum expressivity. One could argue that in the quartets, along with the Quintet and the Second Piano Trio, Shostakovich found the greatest freedom of expression.

Britten's world-wide reputation rests principally on his success in demonstrating the vitality of opera in the second half of the twentieth century, despite frequent assertions to the contrary. Not counting realizations of others' work, he composed sixteen musical works for the stage, in which he succeeded in

This article was originally given as a paper in December 1989 to the international conference 'Ars Britannica II: Anglo-Russian artistic links' in the House of Composers, Leningrad.

giving full rein to his expressive powers. He demonstrated to the world of music the extraordinary social power of the genre: the ability of opera to concentrate within itself social, artistic, and compositional ideas of contemporary relevance, with a plasticity of form and a wide range of dramatic techniques. The essence of Britten's musical personality lay in the various genres of music drama.

For him the song cycle was also a genre of no less importance. The Britten vocal landscape, which is filled with volumes of folk-song arrangements, Christmas carols, editions of Purcell's music, canticles, and cycles for children's choirs, amounts to a richly varied *œuvre* in which the vocal cycles parallel the operas throughout the trajectory of the composer's work. The vocal cycles trace the smallest developments of Britten's artistic preoccupations and composing style to no less an extent, perhaps even to a greater, than the operas. It is a genre to which Britten brought enormous variety and innovation; he was as attracted to it as Hugo Wolf was.

Although Britten and Shostakovich are associated with different spheres and directions in contemporary music, the heterogeneity of their legacies also offers scope for comparison on the level of their creative biographies. I shall omit a comparison of the details surrounding these composers' earliest encounters with the world of music. 'Is it not all one,' observed Vladimir Nabokov, 'whence comes that gentle nudge which moves and tears the soul, thereafter condemning it forever to an activity from which it cannot cease?'[1]

In their youthful years, both composers had avant-garde reputations, although in neither case was this essentially accurate. Britten's sister recalls how, when he was 15 years old, he was considered to be an avant-garde composer whose music was not liked by his contemporaries.[2] 'Britten was virtually untouched by the Modernism which the young Shostakovich so provocatively affirmed and of which *Lady Macbeth* was a particularly exuberant example,' writes Donald Mitchell.[3] As if to disagree with him, Mikhail Druskin has commented:

Both the *Aphorisms* for solo piano (1927) and the opening of the Second Symphony (1927) sound like the latest in aleatoric experimentation . . . as do the thirteen-voice fugue in that symphony and the kaleidoscopic changes of theme in the Third Symphony (1929), where the composer seems deliberately to eschew any thematic repetition at all, or the boldly innovatory entr'acte for percussion in the opera *The Nose* (1923–1928). All this is evidence that Shostakovich, had he wished, could have become a leader of the avant-garde. However, and not, so far as one can tell, from any external pressure but from inner conviction, he later confined such excursions to other spheres of self-expression, opting rather for a dynamic enrichment of the living national tradition, in

---

[1] V. Nabokov, 'Podvig', *Raduga*, 1 (1989), 92.

[2] Beth Britten, *My Brother Benjamin* (London, 1986), 52, 55.

[3] See Donald Mitchell, 'What Do we Know about Britten now?', *The Britten Companion*, ed. C. Palmer (London, 1984), 37.

harmony with the conditions of the new contemporary reality, as his personal path to liberation from the dead hand of the Conservatoire tradition he had inherited.[4]

It is interesting to note that neither Shostakovich nor Britten developed long-standing creative links with their official teachers in the Petrograd Conservatoire and the Royal College of Music; nor, relatively speaking, did either of them identify particularly with conservative or progressive wings. Each had his circle of intimate associates, contact and collaboration with whom stimulated and aided their development as composers. While they distanced themselves from conservative factions in their student years, however, the traditional desire of young people to overthrow authority and come into conflict with one's elder contemporaries to establish independence was also strikingly absent.

In his article 'The Early Years of D. D. Shostakovich', Y. N. Tyulin recalls how Shostakovich, being younger than his fellow students, studied in both the piano and composition faculties at the Conservatoire as well as attending classes in a conventional school at the same time. He managed to accomplish 'all that was necessary'. And the main thing was that 'in the midst of this time of crisis, when the rift between academic studies and creative practice had got to breaking-point, and major reforms in music education were imminent, Mitya Shostakovich . . . was steering a skilful course between all the Scyllas and Charybdises, neatly side-stepping all obstacles in his path, and absorbing everything that was useful to him! And all this without apparent effort, in a stubbornly systematic and strategic pursuit of the highest professional mastery.'[5] Britten's letters and diary entries for the late spring and summer of 1931 and 1932, around the time of the annual examinations, show that despite his strained relations with his professors and his dissatisfaction with his studies, the young musician continued to work unremittingly, with the utmost confidence in his powers: on the day of the examination (20 July 1932), he even looked through some of his old compositions.

In the way both composers conducted themselves in their early lives, there were pointers to their future creative psychologies. Neither proclaimed the need for a complete overhaul of any established genre, or announced a new system of ordering sounds. Their individual styles grew from works that were already classics or were on the way to assuming classical status, while their own experimentations fitted comfortably into existing contexts, and so transformed tradition from the inside.

Both Shostakovich and Britten in their early years paid their respects to jazz, which had conquered the hearts of European composers in the 1920s. Both approached jazz less in the French manner (as a symbol of a new and fresh

[4] M. Druskin, 'Shostakovich v 20-ie gody', *Ocherki. Stat'i. Zametki* (Leningrad, 1987), 47.

[5] Y. N. Tyulin, 'Yunye gody D.D. Shostakovicha', in G. Ordzhonikidze, ed., *Dmitry Shostakovich* (Moscow, 1967), 78.

dimension of popular culture) than in the German, as an ironic subtext to the everyday culture of modern urban life. For them jazz was not, as it was for Stravinsky, a stimulus to seek out new forms; they both tended to avoid it in their mature work.

The composition of incidental music played a large part in both composers' development of mastery and individual styles. This includes music for stage and radio productions, and—most importantly—for the cinema.[6] Both had a rich 'cinema life' (to use Shostakovich's phrase). I shall not list each work in an attempt to find fortuitous points of correspondence in subject-matter or quantity of opus numbers; the point lies elsewhere. It is their mutual predilection for a form so specific in its demands on compositional expertise that provides the link between their gifts. The fixed time limits, the need to convey or reinforce a mood in a short space of time, to create a musical landscape or situation, to express by purely musical means a subtext for the images on the screen—in other words to find forms of counterpoint between what is seen and heard—such are the difficult tasks of the composer of film scores. Neither Shostakovich nor Britten concealed their interest in the techniques of this kind of work. Both Britten and Shostakovich saw the writing of incidental music as an important (perhaps the most important) training for the acquisition of professional mastery, witness Britten's commentary on the first page of the manuscript score of his music for *The Sword in the Stone*, his answers to cinema historian Jay Leyda's questionnaire, in which he sets out his views on film music, Shostakovich's fiery article 'Declaration on the Duties of a Composer' (a reflection of his early experience of work in the cinema), his remarks on the music for *The New Babylon*, and finally his article 'The Cinema as a School for Composers'.

In order not to give the impression that the gifts of all composers of genius can be bent towards the writing of film music, I must give the example of Stravinsky, who steadfastly refused to have anything to do with the cinema, since he had no faith in its creative potential. His views were set out in an extensive interview in 1946, which he launches with the categorical statement: 'What is the job of film music? What are the specific problems of music for the screen? Both questions may be answered directly and succinctly: the sole, unarguable purpose of film music is to feed the composer!'[7] Shostakovich takes issue with this view: 'Work for the cinema . . . is an excellent school of composition'; 'The cinema teaches the composer valuable lessons: inner

---

[6] See P. Reed and J. Evans, 'Benjamin Britten. The Incidental Music: A Catalogue raisonné', *A Britten Source Book* (Aldeburgh, 1978), 130–65; D. Mitchell, *Britten and Auden in the Thirties: The Year 1936* (London, 1981). See also D. Shostakovich, *Sobranie sochinenii v 42 tomakh*, vols. xxvii, xxviii, xli, xlii (Moscow, 1987), and S. Yutkevich and L. Arnshtam, 'Vspominaya Shostakovicha', *Muzykal'naya zhizn'*, 2 (1995), 23–6.

[7] Quoted in *I. Stravinsky—publitsist i sobesednik* (Moscow, 1988), 147.

discipline is developed, which has a beneficial effect on the composer's musical language.'[8]

The literature on Shostakovich and Britten contains many reflections on the cinematic nature of particular dramatic devices in their works. M. Sabinina has researched an intellectual process she provisionally calls 'cinematic', and by showing the possibilities offered by film music in relation to other genres, notably the symphony, she reveals this methodology at work at various levels of the composer's consciousness and the audience's perception.[9]

As far as Britten is concerned, his skill in composing spacious and concentrated dramatic scenes, either in chamber operas (for example *The Turn of the Screw*), cantatas (*Phaedra*) or canticles (*Abraham and Isaac*), where the construction is based on a succession of such laconic scenes, suggests a type of dramaturgy one might call 'frame by frame' (M. S. Druskin's term).

Both Shostakovich and Britten loved music theatre. Both began their work in this field with comic operas: in 1928 the 23-year-old Shostakovich completed *The Nose*, and in 1941 the 28-year-old Britten produced the operetta *Paul Bunyan*. In each case (1932 and 1945 respectively) the same period of four more years was to elapse before both produced masterpieces which have found their place in the treasure-house of European opera and stand as classics of their national operatic traditions. *Lady Macbeth of the Mtsensk District*, Op. 29, and *Peter Grimes*, Op. 33, are both works which signalled a new stage in the evolution of opera and at the same time elevated the artistic maturity of their authors to a new level.

Circumstances favoured Britten's further development in this direction, and the result was an *œuvre* of fifteen operas, differentiated one from another by genre, dramatic approach and scenographic form, two versions of other composers' operas (Purcell's *Dido and Aeneas* and *The Beggar's Opera* of Gay and Pepusch), and a ballet—an impressive achievement. Britten's work in opera served to stimulate the rejuvenation of a national,[10] and undoubtedly, European opera tradition.[11]

Shostakovich also had in mind a multitude of opera projects. He had intended that *Lady Macbeth* should be the first in a tetralogy of operas on the subject of Russian women, and mentions in one of his articles a projected opera on

---

[8] 'Kino kak shkola kompozitora', *30 let sovetskoi kinematografii*, ed. D. Eremin (Moscow, 1950), 356.

[9] See M. Sabinina, *Shostakovich-simfonist: Dramaturgiya, estetika, stil'* (Moscow, 1976), 316–23, 323–32.

[10] See the testimony of Sir Michael Tippett: 'As to England, it can be said that English opera has only here and now become a living force—since the Second World War, in fact,' M. Tippett, 'Opera since 1900', *Music of Angels: Essays and Sketchbook by Michael Tippett*, ed. Meirion Bowen (London, 1980), 199. See also pp. 202 *et seq.*

[11] One of the first commentators to write of the European significance of Britten's operas was S. Borris. See S. Borris, *Der Schlüssel zur Musik von heute* (Düsseldorf, 1967), 168–87, 201, 232.

Sholokhov's novel *Quiet Flows the Don*.[12] However, as is well known, the circumstances in which Shostakovich then found himself prevented him from following a path similar to Britten's. The 'external' criticisms and political obstructions that were put in his way by the Soviet government resulted in deeply embedded 'inner' psychological motifs.[13] Over the seven years separating the première of the Third Symphony (1929) from the completion of the Fourth (1936) Shostakovich produced a total of two operas and three ballets. And that was all there was to be.

If the hierarchy and panorama of genres in Shostakovich's work were altered 'in favour of' the symphony and away from the opera house, something similar occurred with Britten, but in the opposite direction, that is to say, away from symphonic music and towards opera. The prime cause of this new direction was however a very different one: the composer's friendship with Peter Pears, whose voice became the major creative impulse in his work and subconsciously influenced the whole direction of his inspiration. Let us recall that the early period shows a line progressing through a series of orchestral works—from the *Simple Symphony*, Op. 4 (1934) to the *Russian Funeral March* (1936), with its extraordinary insight into the world of Mahler and Shostakovich, and the Violin Concerto, Op. 15 (1939), to the tragic *Sinfonia da Requiem*, Op. 20 (1940). This succession of works might have seemed to presage the birth of a symphonic composer anchored firmly to the aesthetic mould of the European tradition so dear to Shostakovich. But this did not in fact happen, and almost as if forced out of its usual dimensions, Britten's symphonic writing began venturing into other genres, permeating large-scale cantata works such as the *Spring Symphony*, the *War Requiem*, and the operas *Peter Grimes* and *Death in Venice*. In the same way, Shostakovich's natural theatrical inclinations, still very much alive, if latent, frequently show through into the symphonies in the form of references to specific events and the inherently dramatic nature of some of their developments, behind which lurk visual or theatrical, and sometimes cinematic concepts (see, for example, the First, Seventh, Eleventh, Thirteenth, and Fourteenth Symphonies).

Despite the breadth of their visions, both artists acknowledged their deep and intense association with place, which lies at the root of their styles. Britten said in 1971: 'From time to time I wonder whether I am not too interested in local colour . . . but that is the path that I myself chose.'[14] As well as self-appraisal,

---

[12] See: Preface 'From the editors' to vols. xx–xxii of the collected works of Shostakovich. See also the testimony of I. Glikman in the commentary to a letter from Shostakovich, *Pis'ma k drugu: Dmitry Shostakovich–Isaaku Glikmanu* (Moscow and St Petersburg, 1993), 288, 293.

[13] A. Klimovitsky discusses this phenomenon in his article 'Shostakovich and Beethoven' in terms of the 'crown of thorns' (Beethoven on himself as himself and as the composer of *Fidelio*), with reference to the great number of uncompleted operatic projects. See *Traditsii muzykal'noi nauki* (Leningrad, 1989), 187–8.

[14] Quoted in the journal *Za rubezhom*, 33 (1971), 30.

this judgement carries a sense of conviction that the right path had indeed been chosen. The artistic originality of Shostakovich and Britten can be felt in the presence of a distinct integrated image, which defines the atmosphere of the action in their works. Britten conveys a strong sense of the outdoors, embodying the spirit of the coastal region of East Anglia, familiar from the landscapes of English painters such as Constable. Shostakovich's music is imbued with a sense of the city: St Petersburg—Petrograd—Leningrad, experienced through the prism of the traditions of Gogol, Dostoevsky, Dobuzhinsky, and Blok. The first of these two images is associated with the myth of water, the symbol of the fluidity of life and also the deep permanence which it conceals. The second belongs to the myth of that strangely inspired city on the water, whose graphically delineated outlines sometimes appear unstable and phantasmagoric. The two images converge when they invoke dim worlds of twilit withdrawal. Both have been called into life by visual impressions (landscape, architecture), and have been filtered through their respective national cultural traditions. Both function as cultural symbols.

In their final phases of creativity, both Britten and Shostakovich produced a group of works that may be considered valedictory. There is moreover a certain congruence in the logic with which both composers signalled their 'farewell period'. For example, in the last years of their life both composers returned to the works of their youth. Between 1966 and 1969, Britten looked over the early songs he had written between 1927 and 1931, and revised them for publication. Evidently he found nothing in them to offend against the sensibilities of the later master he had become, whose great works were known all over the world. At the end of the *Suite on Verses of Michelangelo* Shostakovich introduced a theme he had composed when he was 10 years old.

Returning to one's earliest, childhood compositions is determined not only by a desire to put one's inheritance in order, but actually signifies a return to the world of childhood. On the occasion of Ingmar Bergman's seventieth birthday, Akira Kurosawa wrote to him: 'A man is born a child, becomes a boy, passes through youth and maturity and then, before ending his path through life, returns again to childhood.'[15] Kurosawa intended the 'second childhood', of course, to be understood symbolically, as the purity, transparency and wise simplicity achieved by the artist in the declining years of his life. This comes about at the moment when, seemingly before our eyes, the artist takes a step towards Immortality: such is the message of the poetry of Michaelangelo's sonnets and of Shostakovich's music. There is also a barely restrained 'mythologizing' element in the circumstances in which Shostakovich and Britten worked on some of their final works (including the mutually dedicated *Prodigal Son* and Fourteenth Symphony), and in their stylistic sources, as will be discussed below.

---

[15] 'Materialy k 70-letiyu I. Bergmana', *Sovetskii ekran*, 14 (1988), 23.

There are certain lives whose meaning lies in spiritual creation, and which conceal a myth. It is in spiritual creations that the myth is embodied and revealed, but these achievements are in essence only phases and stages of the myth's self-embodiment. Each such life has a theme, which is at first sometimes only hinted at through a single word, an expression, or a phrase . . . The phrase may then develop into a study, while a casual hint may turn into an explicit subject. This is how this mythological theme arises. It may be fleetingly glimpsed among other mythological themes . . . Sometimes it glides along with other waves, or more often slides beneath the waves as an autobiographical subtext, and at other times it is clearly outlined. Finally it is embodied in a full-length work. The mythological theme can now be developed, and can become the aim and meaning of the creator's life . . . This usually happens in the first major early work, which is the apotheosis of the romantic phase. Since the mythological theme is the revelation of the myth of the artist's actual life and soul, and a kind of presentiment of his ultimate fate, this work emerges as the primary imprint of the myth of his life. Later the mythological theme undergoes many metamorphoses, changing its image and its name.[16]

This passage from E. Y. Golosovker's autobiographical essay *The Myth of my Life* wonderfully describes the creative process of the artist, and also gives a pointer as to how it may be examined in detail. I propose to use some of its propositions for further comparative study of the creative phenomena of Shostakovich and Britten.

Extending from the first decade of the twentieth century to the middle of the 1970s, the lives of both composers were exposed to the same background of social unrest and political catastrophes: the First and Second World Wars, economic collapse, and the Spanish Civil War, for example. Europe immersed itself in the depths of tragic conflicts and became entwined in the mesh of political and ideological antagonisms, perceiving painfully, and at first only latently, the unity of its complex and difficult destiny. The period of political history lived through by both Britten and Shostakovich stimulated the civic ideas and feelings of many of their compositions. It was then that the understanding of the moral mission and purpose of their works was also formulated. Creative interaction between Britten's and Shostakovich's music occurred for the first time in the context of the civic theme (the 'mythological theme'), the scale of which in their work is commensurate, both in specific early works, and in the broader chronological perspective.

There are two thematic groups of compositions in the Shostakovich legacy: the revolutionary works and the anti-war works. The peaks of the former are the Second, Third, and the Eleventh Symphonies, and the *Ten Poems on Texts by Revolutionary Poets*. To this thematic line also belongs Britten's *Russian Funeral March*. The peaks of the second thematic group are for Shostakovich the Seventh and Eighth Symphonies. Linked with them (admittedly, in the widest

---

[16] Quoted in I. S. Braginskaya, 'Ob avtore i knige', in Y. E. Golosovker, *Logika mifa* (Moscow, 1978), 196.

sense) are many of Britten's works, from the vocal cycle *Our Hunting Fathers* and the orchestral *Variations on a Theme of Frank Bridge* to the *Ballad of Heroes* and the Violin Concerto to the *Sinfonia da Requiem*, and later the *War Requiem* and the *Children's Crusade*.

As we can see, the anti-war theme is clearly a dominant one in Britten's music. Nevertheless it received a powerful impulse at its source from the theme of revolution, which edged its way into it and took root. I refer to the *Russian Funeral March* for brass instruments and percussion. This piece was written for a concert of overtly political cast given in the Westminster Theatre on 8 March 1936 by the London Choral Union under Alan Bush. It was first analysed by Donald Mitchell in the context of Britten's life, and his intellectual and creative preoccupations during the late 1930s.[17] The thematic material of the composition is formed from two songs. The first of them, widely known in Russia as a revolutionary funeral march, *As a victim you fell* [*Vy zhertvoyu pali*] forms the basis of the outer sections of the piece, which deal with Death. For the 23-year-old English composer, working in collaboration with W. H. Auden and drawn into experiencing artistically the politics of those years by Auden's circle, who represented the left-wing faction of the artistic community, it was important that the Funeral March was a Russian song.[18] Judging by the programme of the concert, which also included Brecht's and Eisler's *Die Massnahme*, it was also essential to Britten that this Russian song was a revolutionary song. The theme of the middle section, 'War', is the Soviet Navy song *March of the Communist Fleet*, treated by Britten as a kind of reveille or fanfare of trumpet calls. Was Britten aware that he was quoting a Soviet popular song of mass appeal? He probably did so unconsciously.[19] This small opus displays the soldering together of several stylistic elements: Mahler, Shostakovich, a song from revolutionary urban folklore, a funeral march, and trumpet calls. This kind of synthesis was extremely important to Britten, and not only to him; other major composers of the twentieth century, including Shostakovich, Honegger, and Bartók, assimilated this stylistic trait. But Britten was the first to explore its expressive potential. Moreoever, 'modal transformation' (as A. Dolzhansky terms it) provides Britten with an Alexandrian pentachord precisely in the melody of the song which was later to serve as the theme for the third movement of Shostakovich's Eleventh Symphony. It is interesting to note that even the textural resolution of the climax of the central section of Britten's work closely

[17] D. Mitchell, *Britten and Auden in the Thirties: The Year 1936*, 70–6; 'What Do we Know about Britten now?', *Britten Companion*, 34.

[18] For the history of the composition, sources, and dissemination of this Funeral March see M. Druskin, *Russkaya revolutsionnaya pesnya* (Moscow, 1954), pp. 91–159; and the later edition of this book (Leningrad, 1959), 27–90.

[19] For a more detailed discussion of this work see L. Kovnatskaya, 'Russian Funeral through Russian Ears: Aural Impressions and Some Questions', *International Journal of Musicology*, 2 (1993), 321–32.

resembles the passage leading up to the climax of the second movement of that symphony. This and many other details show the extraordinary extent to which Britten at this stage anticipated features of the mature Shostakovich style.[20]

As some of his diary entries and letters show, Britten was a great admirer of Shostakovich's music. One of his earliest references to Shostakovich can be found in a passionate and dramatic letter to Marjorie Fass, dated 30 December 1935. Shaken by the death of Berg, with whom he had recently expressed a wish to study, he casts about for names among contemporary composers who could be set alongside Berg, and adds at the end: 'Shostakovitch—perhaps—possibly'.[21] This mention of Shostakovich in a letter about Berg is highly significant. Decades later, in an enthusiastic and heartfelt letter to Shostakovich written on 26 December 1963 after the English première of *Katerina Izmailova*, Britten acknowledges: 'I must say there is no one composing to-day who has had an equal influence on me.'[22]

But from the very beginning Shostakovich's name was not simply for Britten that of a composer whose music produced a powerful effect upon him. It resonated beyond the bounds of the world of music, and was also the name of a Russian composer, inheritor of a culture which had tremendous artistic force and authority in the West. It was, above all, the name of a Soviet composer. Britten, like many Western intellectuals at the time, was attracted to Communism and to Communist ideas. He numbered Communists among his friends; after all, to be a Communist in the era of the Spanish Civil War and during the rise of Fascism in Europe, was to be in the vanguard of world history.[23] In a letter to the American conductor and violinist Henri Temianka, Britten wrote: 'I envy you most terribly going to Russia.' Tired and irritated by political discussions, he noted in his diary on 18 July 1937: 'I have to stand up to the whole company to defend my (and all our set's) "Left" opinions.' He was intensely interested in politics and was alarmed by what he saw: 'I have premonitions about travelling on the Continent then, though—the tip at Lloyds is, of course, that Germany is preparing to attack U.S.S.R. in the Spring,' he wrote in a letter of 2 January 1937.[24] In other words, his interest in Soviet Russia was genuine. In those years there were many who trained their gaze on that country and placed in her their hopes, practical as well as idealistic.[25]

---

[20] Kovnatskaya, 'Russian Funeral through Russian Ears', 328–9.

[21] See: *Letters from a Life: The Selected Letters and Diaries of Benjamin Britten 1913–1976*, ed. D. Mitchell, asst. ed. P. Reed, P., assoc. eds. R. Strode, K. Mitchell, J. Young, vol. i (London, 1991), 391.   [22] Ibid. 410.

[23] Ibid. 376, 431. On Britten's intention to go to Spain, see ibid. 590, 460.

[24] Ibid. 386, 497, 464.

[25] This recalls some of Arnold Schoenberg's plans for his future during the 1930s, one variant of which was to emigrate to the USSR. See his letter to Fritz Stiedry of 12 September 1934, in which Schoenberg asks for advice about emigration and the possibility of organizing in the USSR a musical institute based on his project. A facsimile copy of this letter can be found in G. Shneerson, *Stat'i o*

Such was the context in which Britten responded to the name of Shostako-vich. Is it any wonder that the direct influence of the Russian composer's music is especially noticeable in Britten's compositions of the 1930s and 1940s, compositions in which are embodied social themes, dramatic images, and tragic experiences (the *Russian Funeral March*, the Violin Concerto, the *Sinfonia da Requiem*)? Shostakovich exerted his influence on Britten precisely at the time when the English composer's identity was being shaped and consolidated. The actual nature of the artistic influence was also important. It was not a novelty which might bring about a clash with his own creative identity, nor a temptation to master new musical territory. The influence Shostakovich had on Britten resulted in the revelation of new depths within himself, of previously unsuspected facets of what had seemed to be completely known territory. It made him want to realize and intensify his ideas, and to bring them out of the shadows and into the foreground. Britten's long interaction with Shostako-vich's music, especially his chamber works, clearly point to the truth of this.[26]

The impact Britten's music made on Shostakovich was similar in nature, beginning from the 1960s, when Shostakovich first heard it and became acquainted with the composer. 'Personally I do not like listening to a composi-tion that leaves me the same as before I heard it', Shostakovich used to say; 'it must affect me, reveal something new in the world and in me. Britten's works all affect me powerfully, from the operas and the *War Requiem* to the quartets and the Pushkin songs.'[27] In the course of the same interview Shostakovich acknowledged: 'If I were to try naming the composers I love most of all, it would turn out to be a long list. Gustav Mahler, of course . . . Then Prokofiev, Myaskovsky, Stravinsky, Bartók, Alban Berg . . . The Englishman Benjamin Britten is a very great composer.'[28] The similarity of Shostakovich's 1968 list with Britten's of 1935 is striking. Britten begins with Berg, and follows with a small list (Berg, Stravinsky, Schoenberg, Bridge), then, in a category of his own, Shostakovich.

The work of Britten that made the strongest impression on Shostakovich was the *War Requiem*. Shostakovich advertised this fact more than once, as has been stated by friends and former students.[29] Anyone who knows the music of Britten as well as the music of Shostakovich will hear many allusions and quasi-citations, and will not find it hard to draw parallels between the concepts and ideas of these two great artists, and evaluate the extent of Britten's influence on

sovremennoi muzyke. Ocherki. Vospominaniya (Moscow, 1974), 189. See also *Pamyati I. I. Sollertins-kogo: Vospominaniya, materialy, issledovaniya* (Leningrad, 1979), 169.

[26] See E. Roseberry, 'The Solo Chamber Music', D. Matthews, 'The String Quartets and Other Chamber Music', *The Britten Companion*, 375–82, 383–92.

[27] *Shostakovich o vremeni i o sebe: 1926–1975*, ed. M. Yakovlev (Moscow, 1980), 309; *Dmitry Shostakovich about Himself and his Times*, trans. A. and N. Roxburgh (Moscow, 1981); (from an interview with the journal *Yunost'*, 5 (1968)).

[28] *Shostakovich o vremeni i o sebe*, 308, 286.   [29] See: *Pis'ma k drugu*, 192–3, 217, 295.

Shostakovich's late works. For this reason there has been more detailed discussion of this aspect in England than in Russia.[30]

Writing about Shostakovich, Britten said: 'this great man took pleasure in my compositions, very different as they are from his own . . . of like mind in many of the aims of his work, as if we had sprung from the same stock of forebears'.[31] There is deep significance in this statement, which also provides the point of departure for a new angle of study. If we examine the stylistic genesis of both composers, we find the same names: Mahler and Bach, Schubert and Tchaikovsky, Prokofiev and Berg, Stravinsky and Musorgsky. However, they were interested in different aspects of their 'forebears'' work, or rather, they generally reacted differently to the same impulse. For example, what attracted the young Shostakovich to Stravinsky and Prokofiev was their eccentricity, humour, irony, grotesque, and play with laughter: humour masquerading as approval behind the veneer of mockery, and irony masquerading as mockery behind the veneer of approval. The vigour of Shostakovich's quick tempo marches and the vividly changing kaleidoscope of thematic material (First Symphony, First Piano Concerto) was in keeping with young passion as the spirit of the age. Britten was more receptive to the 'new classicism' of Prokofiev and the neo-classicism of Stravinsky as a single tendency which also manifested itself in his own compositions, from the very earliest (the *Simple Symphony*, his answer to the *Classical Symphony*), through to the *Soirées musicales* and the *Matinées musicales* (composed under the influence of *Pulcinella*, which Shostakovich also admired), and late works (the cantata *Phaedra*).[32]

It has to be recognized that creative impulses derived from the same source did on occasion lead to a similar artistic outcome. One example will serve: the operas *Katerina Izmailova* and *Peter Grimes*. In the body of literature specifically devoted to the influence exerted on Britten by Shostakovich's opera, the two works are compared from the standpoint of the subject-matter, the underlying ideas, details of dramatic construction and compositional techniques. The name of Berg is scarcely mentioned in this context.[33] But surely much greater attention deserves to be paid to the influence of *Wozzeck*, both as a primary source of inspiration and as a prism through which are refracted certain

---

[30] On the inspiration derived from Britten's *Seven Sonnets of Michelangelo* towards *Suite on Verses of Michelangelo Buonarotti* see I. Glikman, *Pis'ma k drugu*, 224.

[31] B. Britten (untitled article), *Dmitry Shostakovich*, 82.

[32] A. Tauragis. 'Britten's Opera *Peter Grimes*', *Iz istorii zarubezhnoi musïki*, ed. S. Pitina (Moscow, 1971), 202; L. Kovnatskaya, *Benjamin Britten* (Moscow, 1974), 81–4; D. Mitchell, 'Britten on "Oedipus Rex" and "Lady Macbeth"', *Tempo*, 20 (1977), 10–12.

[33] See D. Mitchell, 'What Do we Know about Britten now?', *Britten Companion*, 36; D. Matthews, 'Act II, Scene I: An Examination of the Music', *Benjamin Britten. Peter Grimes*, ed. P. Brett (Cambridge, 1983), 132, 135; P. Brett, 'Britten and Grimes, Postscript', ibid. 181, 194; A. Tauragis, 'Britten's Opera *Peter Grimes*', 202; L. Kovnatskaya, *Benjamin Britten*, 71.

Mahlerian traits.[34] It was in Berg's opera, which stunned both Shostakovich (in 1927) and Britten (in 1933), that they had their first opportunity to hear a basso ostinato used in a contemporary operatic score. As is well known, the fourth scene of Act I of *Wozzeck* is a passacaglia. This form, the choice of which was semantically predetermined by the composer, is not invested with dramaturgical qualities in the opera. It becomes the pre-climactic point of the first act, leading to the real culmination, in quasi-rondo form, in the fifth scene, which features Marie with the Drum Major.

But if Berg chooses the passacaglia to provide an uncharacteristically satirical subtext, a parody, so to say, of the inherent grandeur of its form, then for Shostakovich (in *Katerina Izmailova*) and Britten (in *Peter Grimes*, later *The Rape of Lucretia*, *The Turn of the Screw* and other operas), it assumes a philosophical form. Both the Russian and the English composer followed historical antecedents in their symphonic and chamber music by using it to convey tragedy and sorrow. The passacaglias in *Katerina Izmailova* and *Peter Grimes* embody a metaphor of life as a chain of metamorphoses taking place within the confines of a closed circle of fate. Through them the composers aim to bring another dimension into their work: they create a spiritual compass bridging the gap between the commonplace and the eternal.

It is worth pointing out that for both Britten and Shostakovich the passacaglia represented the art of polyphony, but free rather than strict polyphony, led by canonical forms. Shostakovich's passacaglias derive in the main from Bach, while Britten drew also on Purcell, in whose operas (and semi-operas) the passacaglia embodies philosophical thought and effect. Another prism through which this tradition was refracted for both Britten and Shostakovich was the Finale of the Fourth Symphony of Brahms, impressive in its heightened sense of tragedy, and a precursor of the use of the basso ostinato in the symphony of the twentieth century. The similar use of passacaglias by Britten and Shostakovich in their operas as a device of dramatic emphasis, in contrast to Berg, brought together different areas (contemporary symphonic practice and the revival of early music) and set a precedent in contemporary opera.

Clearly it would be an inadequate response to the creative interaction between Britten and Shostakovich to categorize it as a mirror image. It is, rather, a mirror-prism. The influence is not so much reflected as refracted. The various facets multiply, and the associations reverberate, while the semantics of their language are enriched. Beneath the surface layer of meanings, deeper and more substantial meanings protrude. The text acquires many inner voices, which are recognizable. Identifying them, and searching for their source and its original meaning can help one to unravel the hidden meaning of the music.

---

[34] These are discussed in detail by Donald Mitchell. See D. Mitchell, 'What Do we Know about Britten now?' 27–8.

In the third 'Lorelei' movement of the Fourteenth Symphony, dedicated to Britten, Shostakovich twice introduces in the vocal part an upward leap of a ninth (third bar after figs. 40–8). Its appearance in Grimes's signature leitmotif, heard to equally telling effect in the part of Katerina L'vovna (Act I, scene iii, figs. 153–4), is a response to the character's pressing need to give vent to a feeling which is by its very nature confessional. The interval of the ninth appears at the most intimate and extreme moment of Katerina L'vovna's confession ('Wherefore, wherefore, this fate?') and similarly in Peter Grimes's confession ('What harbour shelters peace? . . .'). In the intonation of this interval of the ninth, combining both the energy of the expansive gesture and of superhuman effort, and the delicate play on the second (the major ninth and the minor ninth), can be heard the voice of Mahler, whose melodies are characteristically distinguished by lyrical expression and exaltation.

The leap of the ninth is the root intervallic figure of Mahler's Fifth Symphony. Forged in the furnace of the Funeral March and in the motto intonation of the second movement, it is the most intense element of this symphonic drama. It is the very 'heart of the symphony, pumping life to all the other movements and nourished by the elements of the whole organism'.[35] The endless variations of Britten's leitmotif and Shostakovich's phrase are both close relations of this motif from Mahler's Fifth Symphony. Of course, in Mahler's œuvre the motif or phrase of the ascending ninth extends well beyond the bounds of the Fifth Symphony. We can hear its apotheosis in the third movement of the Fourth Symphony (at fig. 12), where its extended flowering heralds a critical moment; again in the climax of the first movement of *Das Lied von der Erde*, the major and minor ninths ('dieser Erde', 'Seh dort hinab!') prefigure the expressionist-sounding upward leap and tragic disintegration—the glissando down a major ninth on the word 'Lebens!' Many more examples could be given. For the most part the motif of the ninth in Mahler is found in passages of elevated, romantic style, and is invested with considerable ambivalence: emotionally explosive—overtly narrative, unambiguous action—hidden depths of feeling—earthly suffering and earthly joys—heavenly beauty, spiritual ecstasy. The semantics of the upward ascent, whether by a sudden leap or through sustained striving, followed by the gradual downward slide or the sharp dive, embrace a huge range of expressive possiblities. Following Mahler, Shostakovich and Britten both drew from this source.

In *Katerina Izmailova*, *Peter Grimes*, and the 'Lorelei' movement of the Fourteenth Symphony, the motif of the ninth can be seen as a dream motif. In the Fourteenth Symphony the soprano soloist's voice is answered by the celeste (at fig. 42), a timbre which finds a quintessential affirmation in *Das Lied von der Erde*, where in the final 'Abschied' the celeste responds to the word 'ewig' (in the fourth bar after fig. 61). *Das Lied*, Mahler's 'ewig' and the other-

---

[35] I. Barsova, *Simfonii Gustava Malera* (Moscow, 1975), 179.

worldly celeste, that sound-world which opens the door to the furthest reaches of the mind where, in Stefan George's words, we sense 'the air of distant planets', stayed in the minds of Shostakovich and Britten for the whole of their lives.[36]

In Act I, scene iii of *Katerina Izmailova* (fig. 160), the resolutely earthy dramatic situation still fails to still the echo, in the C minor celeste chord, of the final 'Abschied'. And of course in the Fourth Symphony, in the coda of the finale (fig. 255), the ensemble writing, the orchestral tension, the tonality, and the entry of the celeste all resonate with the concluding passages of *Das Lied*. In its accents of farewell the celeste moves us as it does in the Thirteenth Symphony (the 'Babi Yar' section): 'It seems to me that I am that same Anne Frank.'

In Britten's sound-world the celeste plays an exceptionally important role, from *Peter Grimes* through *The Turn of the Screw* and *Midsummer Night's Dream* to *Death in Venice*. The sound of the celeste dying away in the silence of *Peter Grimes* or the bewitching cajoleries of Peter Quint in *The Turn of the Screw*, whose appearance is summoned up by the celeste, are as characteristic elements of Britten's style as the motif of the ninth. In his Fourteenth Symphony, which is, like *Das Lied*, also a symphonic song, and is, especially in the final movement, filled with allusions to the earlier work, Shostakovich skilfully interweaves into his Mahlerian universe echoes of Katerina's cries of anguish, and the same exalted resonances of Grimes's frenzied visions of a better life. The spirit of Britten hovers over it. Perhaps this was Shostakovich's farewell gesture to a composer who was for him one of the closest and most dearly loved of all his contemporaries.

[36] See *Letters from a Life*, 439; K. Meyer, 'Mahler und Schostakowitsch', *Gustav Mahler; Sinfonie und Wirklichkeit*, ed. O. Kolleritsch (Graz, 1977), 118.

12

Shostakovich, Tsvetaeva, Pushkin, Musorgsky: Songs and Dances of Death and Survival

CARYL EMERSON

> The only whole gift I can give to others is my death, because only after death can the 'aestheticizing' of my personality begin.
>
> Mikhail Bakhtin

The title of this essay combines so much Russian genius in a single sentence that one hesitates to pronounce it. The issues it addresses, however, are more modest: first, how Shostakovich's penultimate song cycle, op, 143, *Shest' stikhotvorenii Mariny Tsvetaevoi* [Six Poems of Marina Tsvetaeva], represents an especially dense cluster of Russian cultural myths about the appropriate life and death for poets; and second, how this cycle differs in message and in 'aesthetic consciousness' from another intonationally-based song cycle by a composer who was dear to Shostakovich's heart, namely, Musorgsky's masterwork from the 1870s, *Pesni i pliaski smerti* [The Songs and Dances of Death]. Musorgsky was Shostakovich's constant life companion. Tsvetaeva, however, was discovered late, during the composer's final decade;[1] Shostakovich was reading her verse and the memoirs of her daughter Ariadna in July 1975, the summer of his death.[2]

Anyone familiar with those two cycles, Musorgsky's *Songs and Dances of Death* and Shostakovich's cycle of Tsvetaeva poems, would agree that as statements about mortality, their effects are quite totally opposite. Tsvetaeva, in these matters a High Romantic, had a vertical sense of time and an extensive view of tradition. She believed that true poets, while living in time, were equipped to commune with all poets on a timeless plane; in fact, death for poets (and especially for maligned and persecuted poets) is a status to be emulated, for it releases them into that blessed sphere where only other poets can be their critics.[3]

---

[1] For this information I thank Marina Katseva of Tufts University Library, currently working on a monograph on Tsvetaeva and music. According to personal correspondence in her possession, Shostakovich first became acquainted with Tsvetaeva through her prose (her essays were available clandestinely by the mid-1960s); he was also impressed with Tishchenko's settings of her verse.

[2] V. Pavlova, 'Dva dara', *Muzykal'naya zhizn'*, 7–8 (1992), 19–20.

[3] See e.g. 'The Poet on the Critic' [1926], in *Art in the Light of Conscience: Eight Essays on Poetry by Marina Tsvetaeva*, ed. and trans. Angela Livingstone (Cambridge, Mass., 1992), 39–63.

Musorgsky—in these matters an unforgiving realist—reflected a different and more unsettling aesthetic when he adjusted Golenishchev-Kutuzov's cycle of poems on death for his own *Songs and Dances*.[4] The musician peeled away the poet's reassuring story-teller's frame from each little scenario (four encounters of an innocent victim with a medieval, personified Death), thereby making certain that the death of the victim coincided absolutely with the end of the song. In each instance—a mother with her dying infant, a young girl dying of consumption, a drunken peasant freezing to death in a snowstorm, soldiers being slaughtered on the battlefield—there were no survivors to remember the deceased, no poets left alive to round out the story or bow to the audience. In so stripping the texts of second-hand poetic closure, Musorgsky emphasized above all music's immediacy, its subjugation to time, the inescapable vulnerability of all live performance, and the inevitability of human ageing and loss. In a word, he dramatized the whole marvellously cruel efficiency with which music can communicate both the infectious pulse of an ongoing life in time, and its absolute and sudden cut-off or closure, which is death. Musorgsky's *Songs and Dances of Death* are profoundly pessimistic about survival—both of the personality and of human culture in general. We see a similar world-view at work in Musorgsky's great historical operas.

Shostakovich, in contrast, created a song cycle near the end of his own rich and troubled life that raises the question of survival (personal as well as artistic) to tragic—and yet, one could argue, optimistic—heights. Let us consider the six poems that Shostakovich chose for that cycle, for the juxtapositions and dialogue among poets found there is extraordinary. After the 1973 première, one critic wrote that:

the impression of cyclicity, of wholeness, of a beginning, middle, and end, seize and conquer the listener as a finished cycle. But it's remarkable: when you read these verses in the programme notes before the concert, you're surprised: why did Shostakovich pick just these ones? What do they have in common? Where's the connection . . .[5]

At first glance it is indeed an odd compilation. The first poem, 'Moim stikham, napisannym tak rano '[To my verses, written so early], Tsvetaeva composed in 1913. The second, 'Otkuda takaya nezhnost'' dates from 1916; it recalls the summer that Tsvetaeva spent with Osip Mandelstam and is dedicated to him. The third dates from the early years of her emigration, Prague 1923, 'Dialog Gamleta s sovest'yu' [Hamlet's Dialogue with his Conscience]. Then come two poems from the 1931 cycle 'Stikhi k Pushkinu': 'Poet i tsar' and 'Net, bil

---

[4] For more on this transformation and a summary of Russian work on the cycle, see Caryl Emerson, 'Real Endings and Russian Death: Musorgskij's "Pesni i plyaski smerti" ', *Russian Language Journal*, 37/129–30 (1984), 199–216.

[5] M. S. Shaginyan, *O Shostakoviche* (Moskva, 1977), 44; see also S. Khentova, *Shostakovich, Tridtsatiletie 1945–1975* (Leningrad, 1982), 322.

baraban . . .'; and the final setting is of an early poem, dating from 1916, one of several dedicated to Anna Akhmatova.

The eminent scholar of Russian song, Vera Vasina-Grossman, has linked together the six poems as follows. The general theme, she claims, is the 'fate of a poet', in which the 'personal fate of the lyrical heroine . . . is tragically interwoven with [the themes of] love and duty, love and death, and then there is the even more generalized theme of the fate of the artist in the surrounding world, a theme personified by the image of Pushkin'.[6] Vasina-Grossman discerns finer subdivisions. At the centre of the cycle are two groups of two poems each, the first group on the dynamics of love and rage and the second on the poet versus power; these four at the core of the cycle are capped fore and aft by a poem about a specific poet—first, as opening statement, Tsvetaeva's own artistic credo and then, as epilogue, the tribute to Akhmatova. In the large, Vasina-Grossman's thematic architecture for the cycle is certainly correct. But love, death, duty, and rage are exceptionally capacious as organizing principles: almost any piece of verse more serious than a limerick would find a place. The specific binding material must be found in the play of times and perspectives that Shostakovich brought to bear in the cycle.

Tsvetaeva hanged herself in Yelabuga in 1941. She was thus released into that space where all artists have absolute access to one another. Three decades later, Shostakovich composed his cycle, drawing heavily on those poems of hers that were dedicated to poets—Mandelstam, Pushkin, Akhmatova, herself. For this task, of course, Shostakovich had the whole of Tsvetaeva's life at his disposal: he was free to set her earliest adolescent poems in the context of her later fate, and, if he chose, in a voice that had already experienced that later fate. We should note here that Shostakovich himself identified the 'personal integrity' of the cycle with the personality of the poet and with the voice of the singer who was to perform it. From the start he had in mind the Leningrad mezzo-soprano Irina Bogacheva—who had, he said, the same sort of voice he imagined for Tsvetaeva herself: thick, raspy, powerful, shrouded in the 'bitterness of homegrown tobacco', a voice that had 'smoked, smoked, and wept'.[7]

But let us speculate further. For how intriguingly incongruous some of this voice-setting appears! For example: the first poem, 'Moim stikham', was considered by Tsvetaeva herself to be a signature lyric. She wrote it in praise of her earliest verse, unsold and unread, collecting dust in bookstores but certain, 'like precious wine, to come into its own [nastanet svoi cheryod]'. When asked, eighteen years later in Paris, 'about her attitude towards her own work', in response she quoted this poem intact; it was, she said later, 'a formula

---

[6] V. Vasina-Grossman, *Muzyka i poeticheskoe slovo*, parts 1–2 (Moskva, 1978), 325–7.

[7] Khentova, *Shostakovich*, 318: 'takim predstavlyal golos samoi Tsvetaevoi—gustoi, krupnyi, okutannyi gorech'yu samosada, kotoryi kurila, kurila, kak plakala'.

for her fate as a writer and as a human being' ['Formula—naperyod—vsei moei pisatel'skoi (i chelovecheskoi) sud'by']. How appropriate, then, that Shostakovich should take this early poem, so full of youthful egoism and desperate self-confidence, and set it largo, for a deep matured voice, 'a voice that had outsmoked itself'. For the poem is musically transcribed not for a young girl's 1913 voice—pre-war, pre-Revolution, in all important respects still of the nineteenth century—but for a wiser voice that has registered every shock of the twentieth century. As Russian critics have pointed out, its opening lines set the tonality for the cycle as a whole: a twelve-tone row with Shostakovich's own, only slightly masked 'monogram motif' or melodic signature DSCH occurring precisely at the words 'moim stikham', 'my verses'.[8] Thus do the fates of all poets fuse in this cycle: Tsvetaeva, Akhmatova, Pushkin, Shostakovich. They all lived their own singularly triumphant, tortured lives, but they could continue to resurrect one another in that special 'poets' time' in which Tsvetaeva believed so stubbornly. As she insisted in her 1932 essay 'The Poet and Time': 'The genuinely contemporary is that which in time is eternal . . . [that which is] timely for ever, contemporary with everything' ['Istinno sovremennoe est' to, chto vo vremeni—vechnogo . . . [to, chto] svoevre-menno—vsegda, sovremenno—vsemu'].[9]

The first and last poems provide a sort of key to this unexpected, salvational timelessness. Shostakovich arranged the first five poems of his cycle in strict chronological order: 1913, 1916, 1923, two from 1931. The poet is born in poem No. 1, and by poem No. 5—the burial of Pushkin—the poet is dead. The circle has closed.[10] But is this linearity really the fate of poets? The final, sixth song suggests that it is not. Tsvetaeva wrote thirteen poems dedicated to Anna Akhmatova. But for the final song of his cycle, Shostakovich selected the earliest tribute, 'O muza placha' [O keening Muse], the first poem of Tsvetaeva's 1916 Akhmatova cycle. It was Akhmatova's own favourite among the many tributes Tsvetaeva paid her. It is also the most ode-like and elevated of the celebratory poems, although written long before Akhmatova's full impact on Russian culture had been felt and long before Russia had come to require the magisterial lament that we now associate with the mature Akhmatova of *Requiem*. Akhmatova was a name, an 'ogromnyi vzdokh' or 'enormous sigh': Tsvetaeva could not have known the further fate of her poetic mentor, nor her own fate, nor her country's. In Tsvetaeva's view of things, only poetry itself could provide that timelessly true perspective, and in the real world of artistic creation, only a survivor of those years—a composer such as Shostakovich, writing in 1971—could reflect such wisdom.

Poems Nos. 2 and 3 are about failed or inadequate lovers. The first poem,

---

[8] See Pavlova, 'Dva dara', 20.

[9] 'The Poet and Time', in *Art in the Light of Conscience*, 99.

[10] For the basic outline of this reading I am indebted to Pavlova's ingenuity (pp. 19–20); my departures from and expansions on her thesis are my own responsibility.

'Otkuda takaya nezhnost'' and dedicated to Mandelstam,[11] 'is set low and exhausted; in it we witness another aural illusion', the very young Tsvetaeva sounding experienced far beyond her years and the man in tow passive and virginal. Hamlet's dialogue with his conscience is a more straightforward and fatal failure: the other's voice is the Ophelia within, now resting at the bottom of the river.[12] Hamlet loved her as forty thousand brothers could not have loved her, which was still 'menshe, chem odin lyubovnik', 'less than one lover'. Since for Tsvetaeva all lovers were inadequate—as her much-battered husband Sergey Efron put the matter, 'Marina is a huge stove whose fires need wood, wood and more wood'[13]—that particular aspect of conscience is quickly appeased. (It is interesting that of all Shakespeare's women, Tsvetaeva selected for poetic reflection only Ophelia and Gertrude, the virgin and the overripely corrupt; she was not at all drawn to the virtuous yet experienced female types such as, say, Desdemona.) In her 1933 essay 'Art in the Light of Conscience', Tsvetaeva is explicit about the peculiarities of poetic conscience. 'Artistic creation', she writes, 'is in some cases a sort of atrophy of conscience—more than that: a necessary atrophy of conscience, the moral law without which art cannot exist.'[14] A more worthy confrontation would seem to occupy us in the second pair of centrally located poems, the heart of the cycle, which is a stand-off between the poet of genius and the trivial representatives of governmental authority: the two poems to Pushkin.

Tsvetaeva's passionate and possessive relationship with Russia's supreme poet has been the subject of many fine studies.[15] In her own essays 'Mother and

[11] In the context of this poem, written, as it were, from the vantage-point of the pillow and with its final lines on 'the wandering singer, with eyelashes longer than all', consider this portrait of the young Mandelstam, in Tsvetaeva's posthumously published 'History of a Dedication'': 'Mandelstam's eyes are always lowered: timidity? greatness? heavy eyelids? heavy centuries? . . . Mandelstam's wide-open eyes are stars, with the curly lashes reaching the brows.' In *Art in the Light of Conscience*, 69.

[12] Here Shostakovich, pitying Hamlet, compassionately alters one of Tsvetaeva's punctuation marks. The final line, in the poet's original, reads ironically: 'No ya ego lyubil??'; the composer changes the question marks to an ellipsis.

[13] For an eloquent account of this aspect of Tsvetaeva's hungers, see David M. Bethea's review of Viktoria Schweitzer's 1993 biography *Tsvetaeva*: 'In terms of mythical time', Bethea writes, 'Tsvetayeva's marriage belonged to an earlier plot, that of the sleeping princess who is awakened from her spell (spiritual loneliness) by the kiss of a prince. But the couple married very young and the "happily-ever-after" left the plot-hungry Tsvetayeva little to work with. "Marina is a woman of passions. . . . Plunging headfirst into her hurricanes has become essential for her, the breath of life," Efron wrote to Voloshin. Now, according to Efron, lover after lover is "invented", passed through and then mercilessly (though usually justifiably) derided when the affair does not meet expectations, when "life" fails "art".' David M. Bethea, 'Headfirst into the Hurricane', *New York Times Book Review* (4 July, 1993), 22.

[14] 'Art in the Light of Conscience', in *Art in the Light of Conscience*, 157.

[15] See especially the recent Ph.D. diss. of Peter Joseph Scotto, 'The Image of Pushkin in the Works of Marina Cvetaeva', University of California at Berkeley, 1987; and Alexandra Smith, *The Song of the Mocking Bird: Pushkin in the Work of Marina Tsvetaeva* (Frankfurt, 1994).

Music' and 'My Pushkin', Tsvetaeva assembled a cluster of images that linked
Pushkin, death, blackness, monuments, duels, poetry—and, perhaps of some
importance for Shostakovich's piano-vocal cycle on her verse—pianos. ('The
Pushkin monument was black as the piano,' Tsvetaeva remembers,[16] and in
'Mother and Music' she writes: 'The piano was my first mirror and my first
awareness of my own face was through blackness, through its translation into
blackness, as into a language dark but comprehensible. That is how it has been
my whole life: to understand the simplest thing I had to plunge it into verse, to
see it from there.')[17]

Tsvetaeva's dialogue with Pushkin, however, neither reflected nor imitated
the texture of its illustrious subject. One point always stressed in the commentary on Tsvetaeva's poems to Pushkin is—here I quote Peter Scotto—'the
aggressively anti-Pushkinian quality of the verse. Jagged, elliptical, at times
strident to the point of being offensive, they contain little or nothing to remind
the reader of Pushkin's own diction, style or technique.'[18] Tsvetaeva's themes
as well as her manners are confrontational. Little in her treatment recalls the
exquisite frivolity of the anacreontic and love lyrics, there is nothing of Pushkin
the family man or court historian, everywhere it is Pushkin the rebel: the poet
confronting Nicholas the First in 'Poet and Tsar', the great poet murdered and
ridiculed in 'No, a drum was beating . . .'. Tsvetaeva's image of Pushkin, and
Shostakovich's selection of precisely these two poems to set for black piano,
itself appears to be conditioned by a deeply engrained cultural myth.

'The poet and the tsar', Georgy Gachev writes in an essay on Andrey
Sinyavsky, 'has been since olden days the main theme in Russia and tempts
all our writers to tackle it: Lomonosov, Derzhavin, Pushkin, Lermontov, Gogol
. . . In our times too, both Bulgakov and Mandelstam (who openly provoked his
own ruin . . . he asked for trouble so that his ruin would not be so simple, but by
a higher will, in a personal duel, so that he would be worthy of Pushkin's
standing up to the tsar) were drawn to the infernal autocrat like moths to a
flame. . . . That's it: let it be mercy, let it be anger, but let it be *personally!*—that
is the ambition of the Russian writer.'[19] The question then arises: does
Shostakovich's setting belong squarely in this reverent, pathos-laden tradition?

I suggest that it does not. And here the fusion of Tsvetaeva's restless,
hyperbolic genius with that of the composer works its magic. In 'her' Pushkin,
Tsvetaeva gives us a lofty rebel, against whose profound, spiritualized figure all
else becomes mere diminished and trivialized background. Shostakovich highlights every grotesque element in Tsvetaeva's portrait of Pushkin's environ-

---

[16] See 'Moi Pushkin', in Marina Tsvetaeva, *Izbrannaya proza v dvukh tomakh 1917–1937*, ii (New
York, 1979), 253.

[17] 'Mat' i muzyka', Tsvetaeva, *Izbrannaya proza*, ii. 187–8.

[18] Scotto, 'Image of Pushkin', 52.

[19] Georgy Gachev, 'Andrei Siniavskii-Abram Tertz and his Novel Goodnight! (Confesstory)', in
Russian Studies in Literature, 28/1 (Winter 1991–2), 27.

ment; a marvellous talent for toy-box effects and the quirky Chaplinesque quality that can turn human images instantly into caricatures was in fact quite compatible, in Shostakovich, with lyrical seriousness—indeed, such juxtaposition of styles is one of Shostakovich's creative trademarks. (Think of *The Nose* and also of the grotesque, burlesque, gratuitously slapstick police-officer scene in *Lady Macbeth of Mtsensk*, so alien to Leskov and to the larger pathos of that plot.) In the two poems from Tsvetaeva's cycle to Pushkin that Shostakovich included in his own vocal cycle, travesty works because it is not only lovers who are inadequate to poetry: power is too.

According to Tsvetaeva's hierarchy of values, 'the poet and power'—"Poet i vlast'"—is a fraudulent contest; in fact, it is no real contest at all. The case could even be made that Tsvetaeva responds to the theme of 'poet versus tsar' in Russian culture not as Pushkin himself actually lived out that confrontation but rather as the early, fantastical Nikolay Gogol of the Petersburg tales would have responded to it. For the human background in Tsvetaeva's Pushkin poems are all dismembered voices and parts: police mugs and chests lined up seam to seam, without real faces, in a world run by rumour and by inexplicable violence. The real Alexander Sergeyevich Pushkin, of course, understood imperial power absolutely and valued his aristocratic prerogatives within it; the idea of regal authority intrigued Pushkin—as it did so many writers of genius—and to a certain extent he emulated it. (In his 1830 lyric 'Poetu' ['To the Poet'], to take but one example, Pushkin tells the poet: 'Ty tsar', zhivi odin . . .' ['You are a tsar, live alone']: to be a tsar is to have the right to treat the mob with indifference. There is much in Boris Godunov's embittered soliloquies, as well as in his death-bed advice to the Tsarevich Fyodor, that recalls Pushkin's own respect for the obligations and burdens of those wielding absolute power.) But neither Tsvetaeva, nor Shostakovich in his settings of her two Pushkin poems, display sympathy for tsars of any stripe. For them, the essence of secular power, *vlast'*, is comic, impotent, caricatured. And here Shostakovich's deep understanding and love of Gogol serves him exquisitely well, just as it had served his predecessor Musorgsky. If the 'important personages' in these songs are inflated Gogolian frauds, unresponsive and insensate, then the realm of the poet is precisely an acute, highly sensitized, mocking angle of vision. It is not until the final line of 'Net, bil baraban'—where Tsvetaeva quotes the famous remark of Tsar Nicholas I in 1826, after his personal interrogation of Pushkin, that he had just spoken with 'the most intelligent person in all of Russia'—that the largeness and dignity of the tsar's station is returned to these Gogolized figures, these 'zhalkie zhandarmy' [pitiable policemen] who were masquerading as a threat to poets. This change of diction and the instant sobriety of the musical setting take us out of the toy-box and into the world of the last song of the cycle, the one that resurrects all earlier casualties: Tsvetaeva's tribute to Anna Akhmatova's weeping muse.

Pushkin, Musorgsky, Tsvetaeva, Shostakovich: to various extents they were all hounded, all anxious about audience, but they differed in the degree to which they believed an accretive cultural tradition could forge the necessary life-saving links. On this score Musorgsky, judged by the ideology of his last two vocal cycles and by his historical operas, was bleak and sacrificial. There was no way that music could save one from the march of everyday time. Pushkin too, although of infinitely more buoyant temperament, must have had his moments of doubt, especially during periods of exile. But Marina Tsvetaeva, who spent a year of her childhood copying and recopying Pushkin's poem 'K moryu' [To the Sea] into her own albums so that, as she put it, 'Chtoby moei bylo, chtoby ya sama napisala' [So that it could become more mine, so that it was me who'd written it], continually proclaimed the absolute transcendence of poetry over life understood as mere lived experience.[20] As she wrote in 1925: 'I have no love for life as such, for me it begins to have significance, that is, to acquire meaning and weight, only when it is transformed, that is, only in art. If I were transported beyond the sea—into paradise—and forbidden to write, I would renounce the sea and paradise. I don't need life as a thing in itself.'[21] Tsvetaeva's own organism, as we know, lived and died on those terms. Which could have been one reason why Shostakovich considered her such a perfect twentieth-century poet to prolong in music.

[20] In 'Moi Pushkin' [*Izbrannaya proza*, 273].
[21] From a letter of Tsvetaeva's to Anna Teskova, Paris, 30 Dec. 1925.

13

Shostakovich and Chekhov

ROSAMUND BARTLETT

Thanks chiefly to the notorious events of 1936, Shostakovich was able to complete only two operas in his lifetime, and the projected Wagnerian-style tetralogy which was begun with *Lady Macbeth of Mtsensk* was to remain forever unfinished. It was as an opera composer, however, that Shostakovich had originally wished to make his name, and the fact that he never gave up the idea of writing further operas after the traumas of 1936 is testament not only to his abiding interest in the medium but also to the inescapable truth that opera composition was his true *métier*. *The Nose* and *Lady Macbeth*, the two operas which Shostakovich composed while still in his twenties, were both settings of famous short stories by nineteenth-century Russian writers, and it was Russian literature which continued to inspire the composer with ideas for operas in later years. At the beginning of the 1940s, for example, Shostakovich began work on a treatment of Gogol's play *The Gamblers*, working much as Musorgsky had done in the nineteenth century, by trying to write music to Gogol's text without changing a single word.[1] Lermontov's *A Hero of Our Time*, Gorky's *Mother*, Tolstoy's last novel *Resurrection*, Fadeyev's Socialist Realist classic *The Young Guard*, Sholokhov's epic *The Quiet Don*, and Solzhenitsyn's story 'Matryona's House'[2] were amongst other works of Russian literature Shostakovich intended to use as subjects for operas after the *Lady Macbeth* débâcle.[3] But perhaps the most intriguing work that Shostakovich ever wished to use as material for an opera was

I would like to acknowledge Laurel Fay's generous assistance with sources in the preparation of this article, and I would also like to thank Alexander Medvedev for discussing the history of his collaboration with Shostakovich with me. Parts of this article reproduce material published in my articles 'Tchaikovsky, Chekhov and the Russian elegy', in Leslie Kearney, ed., *Tchaikovsky and his World* (Princeton, 1998), 300–18, and 'Sonata Form in Chekhov's "The Black Monk"', in Andrew Wachtel, ed., *Intersections and Transpositions: Russian Music, Literature, and Society* (Evanston, Ill., 1998), 58–72.

[1] See Elizabeth Wilson, *Shostakovich: A Life Remembered* (London, 1994), 170.

[2] See ibid. 337.

[3] See Derek Hulme, *Dmitri Shostakovich: A Catalogue, Bibliography and Discography*, 2nd edn. (Oxford, 1991), 408, and Y. Dimitrin, *'Nam ne dano ugadat'*' (St Petersburg, 1997), 56, for a list of projected operas between 1930 and 1964.

Chekhov's 'The Black Monk' (1894), a morbid story of the supernatural about madness and genius which culminates in the central character's death. It was also Shostakovich's very last opera project, begun in the last few months before his own death in August 1975.

Gogol is the writer traditionally considered to be the author closest to Shostakovich's heart,[4] and not only because 'The Nose' became the subject of his first opera. Shostakovich's relationship with the works of Chekhov, which has received less attention, was also an important one, however.[5] Although in certain important respects the two writers occupy different ends of the literary spectrum (Gogol the arch-Romantic, rhetorical and emotional, Chekhov more often the sober realist—laconic and reserved), they shared a gift for sardonic humour, caricature, and irony which had an obvious appeal for Shostakovich. In these areas Chekhov actually owed much to Gogol's example, and it was a debt he readily acknowledged. And yet it was perceived musical qualities exclusive to each of these writers—in Gogol's case his distinctive language and in Chekhov's case his methods of narrative construction—that fired Shostakovich's imagination, as Gianfranco Vinay has pointed out.[6] And if the exuberant Gogol was particularly important to Shostakovich at the beginning of his career, it was the compassionate, wise Chekhov who meant more to the composer in the latter part of his life, and not just because of his technical virtuosity. Like all great literature, Chekhov's understated stories (whose lack of pretension belies the profound level on which the author probes the sort of existential questions more self-consciously taken up by Tolstoy and Dostoevsky) seem to have provided Shostakovich with the perfect medium through which he could explore his own feelings about life and death as he was forced to confront his own mortality. This article will explore three aspects of Shostakovich's relationship with Chekhov: firstly, the role of Chekhov as a writer and moral exemplar in Shostakovich's life, secondly, his creative experiments with Chekhov (the 'Rothshchild's Violin' and 'Black Monk' opera projects), and thirdly, the significance of Shostakovich's own important and original contribution as a critic to the study of narrative construction in Chekhov's writings.

I

It is important to place Shostakovich's affection for Chekhov in the context of his other literary interests. The written word was integral to the composition of much of his music, both early on when he was writing operas, and also towards

---

[4] See Wilson, *Shostakovich: A Life Remembered*, 165.

[5] See ibid. 41, 75, 164.

[6] Gianfranco Vinay, 'Šostakovič, la morte e il monaco nero', *Nuova rivista musicale italiana*, 1 (1988), (57–69), 57.

the end of his life, when his settings of poems by Pushkin and Tsvetaeva, for example, provided him with an outlet for the veiled expression of some of his innermost feelings about his life and fate as a composer in Soviet Russia. Shostakovich collaborated with many of the leading writers of his day, and read voraciously throughout his life. His knowledge of Russian and world literature was extensive, and the texts that he read often became interwoven into his daily life. Not only would he frequently cite favourite passages in conversation, speaking the words in Gogol's case, as Nikolay Malko has commented, 'with a special deep sense of enjoyment as he brought out the inner meaning of each word',[7] but he would also mimic the language of literary characters and favourite writers in his own speech. Shostakovich was an extremely fast reader,[8] with an astonishing capacity to absorb and retain what he read, and an ability to quote lengthy extracts from his favourite works from memory.[9] This was true of his knowledge of Gogol, but also of Chekhov. According to Grigory Kozintsev, Shostakovich knew Chekhov's works 'to perfection', and loved to recite 'whole tracts' from memory.[10] He was a composer, then, who took a particular interest in verbal language (as Svetlana Savenko shows in her article in this volume), and, like Chekhov, was a gifted letter writer.

Like any young boy growing up in an educated Russian family, Shostakovich would have begun reading Chekhov at an early age, along with other classics of Russian literature. His intellectual precosity can be seen, however, in the comparisons he makes between Chekhov and Tchaikovsky in a letter to Tatyana Glivenko of 1923. The conviction and ease with which the 17-year-old musician draws parallels between creative worlds of a writer and a composer who, interestingly, had great admiration for each other's work[11] is remarkable. Suggesting an unusually sophisticated understanding of literary technique, Shostakovich found that whereas with works by Tolstoy and Taneyev his admiration of their form was followed by disappointment with their contents, with Chekhov and Tchaikovsky, by contrast, everything was 'in place' with form and content.[12] It is regrettable that Shostakovich never expanded on this comparison, although he gave a clue when he returned to this topic in 1943. In an article about Tchaikovsky published in *Literatura i iskusstvo*, he draws a link between the composer's Sixth Symphony and Chekhov's story 'The Black Monk'. As well as the harmony of form and content he clearly perceived in both works, in which the theme of death is prominent, Shostakovich was also thinking about these artists' 'elegiac perception of Russian nature, their

---

[7] Wilson, *Shostakovich: A Life Remembered*, 66.

[8] Ibid. 164.   [9] Ibid. 75, 166.   [10] Ibid. 75.

[11] See *Anton Chekhov's Life and Thought: Selected Letters and Commentary*, trans. Michael Henry Heim in collaboration with Simon Karlinsky (Berkeley, 1973), 147–8.

[12] See Dmitry Shostakovich, letter to Tatyana Glivenko, 29 Nov. 1923; cited in Sotheby's, London, Catalogue: Fine Printed and Manuscript Music, including the Mannheim Collection, 6 Dec. 1991, p. 151.

tender, emotional lyricism, and, most importantly, their total lack of indifference to the world'.[13] It is interesting that Shostakovich should mention 'The Black Monk' in this article published in June 1943, as Chekhov was in his mind at this time. He was finishing *Rothschild's Violin*, an opera based on Chekhov's story which his deceased student Veniamin Fleishman had started (at his suggestion) before the war. Both stories were published in 1894, and may well have been included in the same the volume of Chekhov stories Shostakovich had with him during evacuation in Kuibyshev, where he began to think about completing Fleishman's opera (as will be discussed below). Flora Litvinova, his Kuibyshev neighbour, has recorded that Chekhov was a topic of conversation at that time, noting that Shostakovich's admiration for Chekhov emanated from his strong conviction that the personality of an artist is inseparable from his art.[14] Although Donald Rayfield's 1997 biography shows even more clearly than before that Chekhov was no saint, the writer's unpretentiousness, hatred of hypocrisy, and relative lack of prejudice have all been well documented. Condemned by his contemporaries for his apparent lack of principles, since he treated prostitutes and peasants with his same unflinching doctor's objectivity in his writing and refused to adhere to the Russian didactic tradition, Chekhov was in fact a *rara avis* among Russian writers. Not only did he choose to deal in his art with the humdrum reality of everyday life rather than its idealized or debased version, he also had no desire to preach 'the Truth'. Certain only that he would never find it, his stories and plays are nevertheless an unending quest for the answer as to how one should best live one's life. Chekhov's comment to confused readers about 'The Black Monk'—that just because he was writing about someone who was psychologically not in good health, it did not automatically follow that he himself was sick—could stand as an eloquent rejoinder to the earlier generations of readers and critics who persisted in seeing Chekhov as a gloomy writer who wrote stories about unhappy people whose lives are a failure. The clear-eyed Shostakovich was undoubtedly one of those readers who understood that, on the contrary, Chekhov's writings are a sustained invective against the complacency and moral apathy he depicts. Shostakovich was also clearly moved by the psychological and emotional depth of Chekhov's stories and plays, and by the extraordinary compassion he shows for his often unhappy characters. It is telling that in April 1948, an undeniably bleak time for persecuted Soviet artists such as himself, Shostakovich sent greetings to his friend Nikolay Smolich as he was leaving Leningrad, quoting Sonia's radiant words in the face of utter despair at the end of *Uncle Vanya*: 'We shall see the whole sky sparkling in diamonds.'[15]

---

[13] See Lev Grigoriev and Yakov Platek, eds., *Dmitry Shostakovich about Himself and his Times*, trans. A. and N. Roxburgh (Moscow, 1981), 105.

[14] Wilson, *Shostakovich: A Life Remembered*, 164–5.

[15] See G. Yudin, '. . . Vasha rabota dlya menya sobytie na vsyu zhizn'', *Sovetskaya muzyka*, 6 (1983), 93.

In 1960, Shostakovich confirmed Chekhov's importance to him with a tribute written for *Literaturnaya gazeta* in honour of the 100th anniversary of the writer's birth:

I am very fond of Chekhov. I love to read and reread not only his stories and plays, but also his notes and letters, and I am delighted that the 100th anniversary of his birth is being celebrated all over the world. Of course, I am not a specialist in literature, and am in no position to give a competent appraisal of this great Russian writer's works, which, I feel, have not yet been fully studied, and are not always properly understood. But if I were to write a dissertation about any writer, then it is Chekhov I would choose, so great is the affinity I feel for him . . .[16]

This was presumably the source for Shostakovich's thoughts about Chekhov in *Testimony*, as they begin in exactly the same way (although with some slight linguistic variation because of the translation of the manuscript of *Testimony* into English) as the 1960 article: 'I really love Chekhov, he's one of my favourite writers. I read and reread not only his stories and plays, but his notes and letters. . . .'[17] Later we learn in *Testimony* that Shostakovich liked 'everything he wrote, including the early stories', and frequently reread 'Ward Number Six'.[18] (That Shostakovich should have been drawn to this particular story, which is set in a lunatic asylum, is not surprising; many Russian readers have seen its treatment of nonconformity not only as allegorical of Russian society under Alexander III, but as prophetic of conditions in the Soviet Union.) The second half of the first sentence in the *Literaturnaya gazeta* article ('and I am delighted that the 100th anniversary of his birth is being celebrated all over the world') is missing in *Testimony*,[19] but since Volkov and Shostakovich supposedly began work on *Testimony* in the early 1970s, deliberate mention of the celebration of Chekhov's 100th anniversary would clearly have been highly inappropriate at this point. The text in *Testimony* then follows Shostakovich's *Literaturnaya gazeta* article word for word, however ('Of course, I am not a specialist in literature, and am in no position to give a competent appraisal of this great Russian writer's works, which, I feel, have not yet been fully studied . . .'). The second part of Shostakovich's *Literaturnaya gazeta* article, where he explains why he thinks Chekhov is a musical writer, and declares that the story 'The Black Monk' is composed in 'sonata form', also appears word for word at a later point in *Testimony*.[20]

The affinities Shostakovich felt with Chekhov are interesting for the insights they afford us into his own personality, for the writer was thus clearly not only

[16] D. Shostakovich, 'Samyi blizkii', *Literaturnaya gazeta*, 28 Jan. 1960; repr. in L. Ordzhonikidze, ed., *Dmitry Shostakovich* (Moscow, 1967), 34–5.

[17] Solomon Volkov, *Testimony: The Memoirs of Dmitri Shostakovich* (London, 1979), 225.

[18] Ibid. 178.

[19] This is one of the passages discussed by Laurel Fay in her review of *Testimony* (Laurel E. Fay, 'Shostakovich versus Volkov: Whose Testimony', *Russian Review*, 39 (1980), 484–93).

[20] Volkov, *Testimony*, 223.

important to him as an artist of the finest calibre, but also as a model of the kind of human being he himself aspired to be. If Shostakovich was awed by Chekhov's mastery of artistic form, he also strongly identified with the way he lived his life, something he made a particular point of stressing in his 1960 article: 'Reading his writings, I often recognize myself; I think that in many of the situations in which he found himself, I should have reacted in just the same way as he did.'[21] A conversation Shostakovich had with a group of morally compromised 'official' writers in 1955 was perhaps one of those situations. When he pointedly told them that 'a writer should never be an assistant of the police', Shostakovich was consciously echoing Chekhov's admonition to Suvorin in a letter of 1898, when the Dreyfuss affair was at its height.[22] In December 1955, he wrote to Isaak Glikman (who had first drawn his friend's attention to this letter), asking for the exact source of the quotation, in order to prove to these 'representatives of the progressive literary community' that Chekhov had really said this.[23]

Shostakovich writes in his 1960 article that 'the whole of Chekhov's life was a model of purity and modesty, and not in an ostentatious way, but inwardly'. It was for this reason, and Chekhov's 'exacting attitude towards his works, which he would never publish until they were brought to perfection' that Shostakovich objected to certain editions of his correspondence, 'much of it being so intimate that one would rather not see it in printed form'.[24] Shostakovich himself, of course, possessed the same kind of modesty, and never kept any of his correspondence for that reason. As the comments he once made to Flora Litvinova reveal, he had specific criticisms to make of Chekhov's widow Olga Knipper, who published their correspondence after his death:

Can you imagine what Chekhov's reaction would have been had he known that his wife would expose him in front of honest people? She should be ashamed of herself, publishing all the intimate details of their life together. Chekhov was right in nicknaming her the Aktrissulya [a disparaging diminutive for an actress]. What these actresses won't do to please the public! And the public doesn't want to be fed on bread alone, they want to know whether the goings on in famous people's bedrooms are the same as in everybody else's, or whether they get up to something more inventive . . .[25]

When he talked about the stories 'His Wife', 'Ariadne', and 'The Grasshopper', Litvinova recalls Shostakovich telling her that Chekhov 'didn't like women', that he 'saw straight through them', and 'hated all that was vulgar in them'.[26] One

---

[21] Shostakovich, 'Samyi blizkii'.

[22] In his letter to Suvorin of 6 Feb. 1898, Chekhov states that 'a writer's work is not to accuse or persecute . . . there's already enough policemen, accusers, procurators as it is . . .'. See Simon Karlinsky, introduction to Heim and Karlinsky, *Anton Chekhov's Life and Thought*, 317.

[23] Isaak Glikman, *Pis'ma k drugu: Pis'ma D. D. Shostakovicha k I. D. Glikmanu* (Moscow and St Petersburg, 1993), 117–18.

[24] Shostakovich, 'Samyi blizkii'.   [25] Wilson, *Shostakovich: A Life Remembered*, 165.

[26] Ibid. 164.

wonders whether these stories, with their satirical portraits of flighty, predatory females who are involved with self-effacing, rather passive men, were the sort of writings by Chekhov in which Shostakovich recognized himself, as he claimed in his commemorative tribute to the writer. Shostakovich was certainly accurate in perceiving a strong vein of misogyny in Chekhov's stories.[27]

It seems that Chekhov was particularly important to Shostakovich at acute times of his life: at the height of the purges and during Second World War, and in the last months before his death. In 1975, he began to make serious plans to write an opera based on 'The Black Monk'. In his 1943 Tchaikovsky article, Shostakovich had described this story as 'one of the most musical works in Russian literature, written almost as a sonata [*sic*]'.[28] Another work by Chekhov which Shostakovich found particularly musical was 'Gusev', a story inspired during the writer's journey home from Siberia by sea in 1890. His particular attachment to 'Gusev' and 'The Black Monk' is intriguing, for these are two of the most unusual and poetic stories of Chekhov's mature period, in which the language is particularly rhythmical. A parable about nature's indifference to humanity, the former also deals with death, in this case that of a Russian peasant soldier, Gusev, on board the ship bringing him back home from duty in the Far East. The story ends with an extraordinary (for Chekhov) lyrical flight as Gusev's corpse is attacked by a shark while descending gently to the sea bed, following burial at sea, the whole scene set against a backdrop of impartial and transcendent marine beauty. Shostakovich confided to Flora Litvinova that he thought 'Gusev' the 'most musical prose in all Russian literature', and wanted himself to write music to it.[29] It was 'Gusev' which the composer asked his wife to read to him on the night that he died.[30]

II

In 1934, following the triumph of *Lady Macbeth of Mtsensk*, Shostakovich asked Alexander Preis to write a libretto for a new opera drawn from the works of Chekhov and Saltykov-Shchedrin.[31] These plans were abandoned after the events of 1936, but it is interesting to note that while Shostakovich was unable to write operas himself subsequently, he nevertheless suggested Chekhov stories, particularly 'The Black Monk', as potential opera subjects to all his students. (Funnily enough, Chekhov himself had thought that 'The Black Monk' would make a good subject for an opera, and had suggested to

---

[27] See Donald Rayfield, *Anton Chekhov: A Life* (London, 1997), 348.

[28] D. Shostakovich, 'Mysli o Chaikovskom', *Literatura i iskusstvo*, 7 Nov. 1943.

[29] Wilson, *Shostakovich: A Life Remembered*, 170.

[30] Conversation with Irina Antonovna Shostakovich, Moscow, June 1996.

[31] Wilson, *Shostakovich: A Life Remembered*, 102.

Rachmaninov, with whom he came into close contact in 1900, that he should take it on, although the project never materialized.)[32] In 1938, while he was teaching at the Leningrad Conservatoire, Shostakovich was keen that his student Veniamin Fleishman (1913–41) should write an opera on 'The Black Monk',[33] and after he moved to Moscow in 1943 (the year his *Literatura i iskusstvo* article was published), he suggested the story to another student, Revol Bunin. He later proposed another Chekhov work, *The Seagull* (which he admired as a play with no negative characters),[34] as a possible subject to Bunin.[35]

Shostakovich's alternative suggestion to Fleishman was to write an opera based on Chekhov's story 'Rothschild's Violin', and this was a suggestion his student took up. Not only did the story have a musical theme, but it was about Russian anti-Semitism, which Fleishman, as a young Jewish man growing up in the equally anti-Semitic Soviet Russia, could certainly relate to. The story's more universal theme of man's inhumanity to man, moreover, was something both teacher and pupil must have found particularly poignant in the late 1930s, at the height of the purges. If this was a frightening time for a young Jewish-Russian composer, it was, of course, an even more terrifying time for Shostakovich, who had endured recent public castigation and the arrest of numerous relatives, friends, and colleagues. *Rothschild's Violin* thus cannot properly be understood outside the social and political context of its composition. Ironically this was to prove to be Shostakovich's only real experience working with a Chekhov text, as he decided to complete the unfinished score of the one-act opera after Fleishman's death during the Second World War.

'Rothschild's Violin', published in 1894 like 'The Black Monk', is another story about death and the waste of life, and its mixture of exquisite sadness and macabre humour must have made a powerful impression on Shostakovich, who certainly found it a very 'complex' work, according to Isaak Glikman.[36] The story's central character is Yakov Ivanov, a misanthropic and poverty-stricken coffin-maker, who occasionally plays the violin in the local Jewish band. Shortly before his death, he starts playing an exquisitely mournful song of atonement—for his recently deceased wife, whom he has mistreated for fifty years, for the hapless, poverty-stricken (and ironically named) Jew Rothschild, flautist in the band, and victim of his anti-Semitic taunts, and for his own sad life. Yakov's one act of generosity is to bequeath his violin to Rothschild, who for ever after can only play mournful melodies on it. Chekhov was one of relatively few Russian writers before the Revolution to create Jewish-Russian fictional characters and it was typical of the writer that these characters are

---

[32] Oskar von Riesemann, *Rachmaninov's Recollections* (London, 1934), 151.

[33] Conversation with Alexander Medvedev, Moscow, May 1997.

[34] See R. Bunin, 'S glubochaishchei priznatel'nost'yu', *Sovetskaya muzyka*, 9 (1976), 14–17.

[35] See Evgeny Makarov, 'Ya bezgranichno uvazhal ego . . .', *Muzykal'naya akademiya*, 1 (1993),
154.   [36] Glikman, *Pis'ma k drugu*, 16.

viewed with the same mixture of wry humour, compassion, and irony as the various Russian protagonists in his stories. The relationship between Yakov Ivanov and Rothschild is in some ways emblematic of fraught Russian-Jewish relations both before and after the Revolution, but the story addresses more generally the quintessentially Chekhovian theme of the tragedy and absurdity of the human condition. Gennady Rozhdestvensky, who conducted the first recording of *Rothschild's Violin* in 1982, also researched the history of its composition, and explored what drew both Shostakovich and Fleishman to this story:

Above all, it was the idea of the necessity of a meaningful life, one of human dignity, and free from the tyranny of money and egoism. The words of the opera's main character, the coffin maker Yakov Ivanov, 'Why do people prevent each other from living?', which could stand as an epigraph to the opera, became the philosophical starting point of the work, like the words of the old convict in Shostakovich's opera 'Katerina Izmailova': 'Why is our life so dark and awful? Is this what man was born for?'[37]

Fleishman was 26 years old when he began work on the one-act opera in 1939. In the summer of 1941, as soon as Russia entered the Second World War, Fleishman volunteered for the front, leaving behind his unfinished score. He had already completed the libretto, following Shostakovich's Musorgsky-inherited practice of regarding the original author as the best possible librettist. He had probably worked closely with his teacher, in fact, to produce the resultant stage version of Chekhov's story, which is condensed into three central scenes. Although Fleishman had also written most of the music, he had only managed to orchestrate the central section before leaving for the front. In May 1942, when it was already clear that Fleishman had been killed (after the war it was established that he had died in September 1941), Shostakovich wrote to Orest Yevlakhov, another of his Conservatoire pupils, from Kuibyshev, where he had been evacuated in October 1941. He was particularly keen to enquire about the unfinished opera, with whose composition he had clearly been closely involved:

It's a great pity that I did not bring *Rothschild's Violin* with me. I could have finished it and orchestrated it. Dear friend! If *Rothshchild's Violin* can be found at the Leningrad Union of Composers, will you keep an eye on it; even better, make a copy of it and send it to me in Kuibyshev if there is an opportunity. I love that work very much, and worry about it; I don't want it to get lost.[38]

Shostakovich eventually received the score at the end of 1943, by which time he had moved to Moscow, and it was here that he finished it, after completing his Eighth Symphony. On 5 February 1944, having rewritten Fleishman's piano score, and finished the orchestration, he recorded the details of the work's composition on the first page of the manuscript. As Laurel Fay has suggested,

[37] Gennady Rozhdestvensky, liner note to 1982 recording of *Rothschild's Violin*.
[38] Ibid.

Shostakovich seems to have been responsible for slightly more than the orchestration of the opera, and was typically modest about the role he played in its completion.[39] Isaak Glikman has recorded that Shostakovich went to great effort to have the work staged at the Bolshoi Theatre, but only succeeded in organizing a concert performance, which took place on 20 June 1960 in the members-only auditorium at the Union of Composers in Moscow.[40] The opera's essentially sad plot alone guaranteed difficulties for performance in an era when exclusively uplifting epics were called for, but its troublesome Jewish theme, and the fact that Fleishman himself was Jewish (never mind that he gave his life for his country) made Shostakovich's task even harder. Shostakovich's song cycle *From Jewish Folk Poetry*, written a few years later in 1948, but not performed until 1955, suffered similar problems. *Rothschild's Violin* was finally staged on 24 April 1968, at the end of the 'Thaw' period, in a production at the Experimental Chamber Opera Studio at the Leningrad Conservatoire, conducted by Maxim Shostakovich.[41]

In 1997 Edgardo Cozarinsky made a French-produced film about *Rothschild's Violin*, which traces the opera's composition, and includes a performance of the opera itself as its centre-piece. It is perhaps justifiable cinematic licence that the film gives the erroneous impression that Shostakovich finished the work in Leningrad during the Siege. Rather more worrying is the inexplicable casting of Yakov Ivanov as a Jew, however, and the transformation of his primitive one-room dwelling into a charming country cottage set among bucolic (Hungarian) countryside.

In the 1930s, Shostakovich had originally suggested 'The Black Monk' as a good subject for an opera to Veniamin Fleishman. None of Shostakovich's students ever did write operas based on this story, but in 1971, it is likely that Shostakovich himself was prompted to think about doing so again himself when he was sent an article about the presence of sonata form in the story by the literary scholar Nikolay Fortunatov.[42] It had been Shostakovich's comment in *Literatura i iskusstvo* in 1943 which had originally stimulated Fortunatov to write this article, and in December 1971 the critic received a cordial note of thanks from the composer for the copy he had sent him.[43] In the meantime, however, Fortunatov had acquainted himself with Abram Derman's 1959 study of Chekhov, in which the author claims (erroneously) that Shostakovich had said 'The Black Monk' was composed like a symphony.[44] By now naturally

---

[39] Laurel Fay, 'Skripka Rotshil'da', *New Grove Dictionary of Opera*, ed. Stanley Sadie (London, 1992), 410–1.

[40] Glikman, *Pis'ma k drugu*, 63.

[41] Laurel Fay, 'Skripka Rotshil'da'.

[42] N. M. Fortunatov, 'Muzykal'nost' chekhovskoi prozy (opyt analiza formy)', *Filologicheskie nauki*, 3 (1971), 14–25.

[43] See N. Fortunatov, 'Tri neizvestnykh pis'ma Shostakovicha', *Muzykal'naya zhizn'*, 14 (1988), 13.

[44] A. Derman, *O masterstve Chekhova* (Moscow, 1959), 116.

somewhat confused, since the terms 'symphony' and 'sonata' (musical genres) are not interchangeable with 'sonata form' (a type of musical construction), Fortunatov wrote to Shostakovich asking for clarification, and he quotes from the composer's second letter to him in a footnote to a revised version of his article on Chekhov which he published in 1974.[45] In his letter to Fortunatov in January 1972, Shostakovich declared that he had certainly never said anything about the story being written like a symphony, adding: 'I should have written "like sonata form", not "like a sonata". Most accurate of all would be to put it this way: "The Black Monk" is written in sonata form.'[46]

Whether it was a coincidence, or a result of reading Fortunatov's article, which may have reminded him of earlier plans, it was in the early 1970s that Shostakovich seriously started making plans to write his opera based on 'The Black Monk'. Shostakovich's interest in 'The Black Monk' dates back at least to 1925. On New Year's Eve that year, the 19-year-old composer had a dream which had an obvious parallel with a central event in the story, as he himself was only too well aware. In the letter Shostakovich wrote to Boleslav Yavorsky the following day, he related how he had dreamt that he was walking in a desert, when an old man had suddenly appeared before him and told him that the coming year would be lucky for him. Shostakovich had then woken up feeling extremely happy, and could not get back to sleep again, which made him recall 'The Black Monk', in which the main character Kovrin experiences such great joy after his 'hallucinations' that he does not know what to do with himself.[47]

'The Black Monk' was written in the summer of 1893 at Chekhov's small country estate at Melikhovo (where he avidly cultivated a garden and orchards). It is a brilliant but uncharacteristic example of this writer's literary art. Chekhov never quite left his earlier doctor's training behind, and deliberately set out to write a 'medical' story about a person suffering from 'mania grandiosa'.[48] It begins with a talented young psychology scholar, Andrey Kovrin, travelling to the country estate of his former guardian, a renowned horticulturalist, Yegor Pesotsky. He is in a state of nervous exhaustion and needs a rest. While he is staying with Pesotsky and his daughter Tanya, he experiences hallucinations of a mysterious black monk, who tells Kovrin he is supremely gifted, and destined to serve mankind in some special way. Inspired by the monk with feelings of euphoria, Kovrin proposes to Tanya, and they marry, but their relationship deteriorates after she tries to cure him of his hallucinations. Following a separation from Tanya, Kovrin becomes involved

[45] N. Fortunatov, 'Muzykal'nost' Chekhovskoi prozy', in *Puti iskanii* (Moscow, 1974), 105–34.

[46] See N. Fortunatov, *Puti iskanii*, 108.

[47] Dmitry Shostakovich, letter to Boleslav Yavorsky, 1 Jan. 1926, Glinka Museum of Musical Culture (Moscow), f. 146, ed. khr. 3249. Information supplied by Laurel Fay.

[48] See A. P. Chekhov, *Polnoe sobranie sochinenii i pisem v tridtsati tomakh*, ed. N. F. Belchikov *et al.*, viii (Moscow, 1986), 490.

with someone else and dies of tuberculosis soon thereafter in the Crimea. Seen from a present-day standpoint, the story could also be seen in some respects as a clinical diagnosis of a person suffering from schizophrenia. Schizophrenics, after all, often experience hallucinations and suffer from delusions, and they can be positive or negative. Those with positive symptoms, like Kovrin, are often creative and have imaginative, euphoria-inducing delusions, often to do with the meaning and purpose of life, and man's place in the world. Since the black monk could be construed either as a harbinger of death or new life, the story could be viewed as an exercise in schizophrenia at all levels.

According to an enigmatic comment in *Testimony*, Shostakovich first explored some of his ideas about the story in his Fifteenth Symphony, which was composed between April and July 1971. 'It's not a sketch for "The Black Monk",' we read in *Testimony*, 'but variations on a theme. Much of the Fifteenth is related to "The Black Monk" even though it is a thoroughly independent work.'[49] When the Fifteenth Symphony was first performed in January 1972, the work was pronounced both 'optimistic' and 'pessimistic', and later deemed both banal and profound.[50] Unlike the symphonies directly preceding this one, the Fifteenth is not programmatic in any way, and has continued to remain an enigma. Unfortunately, 'The Black Monk' is also ambiguous and difficult to decipher, inviting diametrically opposed interpretations. The story certainly does not offer a simple key to understanding Shostakovich's Fifteenth Symphony, but one may nevertheless make some conjectures.

A preoccupation with death is naturally what links the two works most strongly, particularly if one remembers that Shostakovich found parallels between 'The Black Monk' and Tchaikovsky's Sixth Symphony, which, roughly speaking, also has death and life as its principal and secondary subjects. Further, it could be argued that Shostakovich's last symphony shares with Chekhov's story a deliberate and consistent juxtaposition of sharply contrasting themes and moods. The seemingly light-hearted 'toy shop' music in the first movement (Shostakovich himself made the comparison, but warned against taking this definition too seriously)[51] is followed by passages altogether more sombre and elegiac in tone. Ebullient music from the cavalcade in Rossini's *William Tell* is thus quoted along with the pessimistic fate motif from Wagner's *Götterdämmerung* for example, and lyricism is partnered by mockery. Such contrasts abound in Chekhov's story, where none of the characters turn out to be what the others think them to be, for example, and where the reader's expectations are confounded at every turn. Towards the end of the story, Kovrin sees unfounded pretensions and delusions of grandeur in thinking that he was a

[49] See Volkov, *Testimony*, 225.

[50] Boris Schwarz, *Music and Musical Life in Soviet Russia* (Bloomington, Ind., 1981), 517–18.

[51] See Grigoriev and Platek, *Shostakovich about Himself and his Times*, 316.

genius, dedicated to the highest ideals, with an important contribution to make to human civilization. A similar process may perhaps be discerned in the caustic penultimate movement of the Fifteenth Symphony, where it is possible that Shostakovich is also mocking his earlier illusions. Finally, as in the concluding chapter of 'The Black Monk', where Kovrin finally accepts death with serenity, the pessimistic evocation of man's loneliness in the final movement of Shostakovich's symphony, where the theme of death looms large, also appears to be balanced by resignation and acceptance. Chekhov's story is about a character who begins to doubt himself as he realizes his perception of reality is mere illusion; he loses faith in himself, stops believing he can achieve great things and contribute to humanity, and becomes cynical. Shostakovich's symphony perhaps echoes that progression.

Although Shostakovich never composed any original music for 'The Black Monk', in September 1972, around the time of his sixty-sixth birthday, he made an arrangement of Gaetano Braga's 'Serenade', a song which plays an important role in 'The Black Monk', for soprano, mezzo-soprano, and violin (as it is performed in Chekhov's story, with the addition of a piano part).[52] At some point he talked about the project to Isaak Glikman, who remembers his friend saying the following:

> I recently wanted to start writing an opera on the subject of 'The Black Monk'. So I asked for the music of that 'Serenade' to be hunted down. Its music, as Chekhov uses it, seemed even disturbing [volnuyushchei] to me. I even thought that I had found the kernel for my future opera. But writing an opera on 'The Black Monk' will be very difficult, since there will be so little action in it.[53]

It is comparatively unusual for Chekhov to include references to specific musical works in his stories, but Braga's 'Serenade' (whose cloying melody was apparently much loved by him, according to his sister)[54] indeed plays a pivotal role in 'The Black Monk', in that its performance (it is first played by Tanya Pesotskaya and her friends) is linked to the two most crucial points in the story—the first and last occasions on which the Black Monk appears to Kovrin, the central character. The song—about a 'girl with a disturbed imagination [who] one night hears some mysterious sounds which are so beautiful and strange that she is forced to acknowledge them as a divine harmony which we mortals cannot understand'[55]—not only directly precedes, but also mirrors Kovrin's experiences with his ghostly visitor.

---

[52] See Hulme, *Dimitri Shostakovich: Catalogue, Bibliography and Discography*, 319. It is curious that the serenade is referred to in *Testimony* (p. 224) as a 'A Maiden's Prayer', which is the name of a popular piece for piano by the 19th-cent. Polish composer Badarzewska (1838–62), and is one of the pieces of music to be heard in *The Three Sisters*, Chekhov's third play, written six years after the composition of 'The Black Monk'.

[53] Glikman, *Pis'ma k drugu*, 293.

[54] See A. P. Chekhov, *Polnoe sobranie sochinenii i pisem*, viii. 490.

[55] Chekhov, 'Cherny monakh', *Polnoe Sobranie Sochinenii*, viii. 232–3.

In March 1975, Shostakovich came to Leningrad to attend the première of *The Madonna and the Soldier*, one of three operas composed by his friend Moisey Vainberg for which Alexander Medvedev had written the librettos. During his stay in Leningrad in 1975, Shostakovich commissioned Medvedev to write the librettos for two one-act operas he now wished to write: 'The Portrait' (based on Gogol's story) and 'The Black Monk'.[56] Both are supernatural stories in which a male hero experiences hallucinations and subsequently dies. Shostakovich stipulated that each opera should be one hour five minutes long, and he met with Medvedev twelve times over the next three months to discuss their composition. Shostakovich quickly approved Medvedev's libretto for 'The Portrait' and began writing the score in May 1975. He also started discussing 'The Black Monk' with Medvedev. It was agreed, for example, that the opera would focus on the four major characters in the story (Kovrin, Pesotsky, Tanya, and the Black Monk) and contain two acts, each with four scenes. This was altogether the more challenging of the two stories, however, and Shostakovich encountered difficulties in conceiving how it would work dramatically, because of its lack of action (as he had mentioned in the letter to Isaak Glikman quoted above). Apart from Kovrin, he also wanted only the audience to see the apparition of the black monk. Shostakovich died in August 1975 before completing either of the two operas.[57]

III

Shostakovich's idea that 'The Black Monk' was written in sonata form clearly influenced his conception of the opera he planned to write. In his conversations with Medvedev in 1975, Shostakovich talked about his understanding of Chekhovian musicality, explaining that all Chekhov's works for him were like brilliant musical compositions that had the potential to become operas, particularly 'The Black Monk', 'The House with the Mezzanine', *The Three Sisters*, and *The Cherry Orchard*. According to Medvedev, Shostakovich was well aware that Chekhov could never have set out consciously to use sonata form, but maintained he was nevertheless instinctively musical in his approach

[56] Medvedev first met Shostakovich when he was a third-year student at the Moscow Conservatoire and working part-time in the editorial offices of *Sovetskaya muzyka*. He got to know Shostakovich better after he graduated, and came into particularly close contact with the composer when he was working at the Bolshoi Theatre in the 1960s. Shostakovich at this time was planning to compose an opera based on Sholokhov's *The Quiet Don* (which had already been used as a subject by Ivan Dzerzhinsky in 1932), and he decided that Medvedev should write the libretto for that work. In 1965 Medvedev began to make a rough plan of each act, and Shostakovich travelled to Rostov-on-Don in order to get something of the atmosphere of the novel. For various reasons, the project was shelved upon his return to Moscow.

[57] Conversation with Alexander Medvedev, Moscow, May 1997. *The Portrait* was later finished by Moisey Vainberg and first performed in Brno in May 1983.

because of the polyphonic construction of his ideas: the numerous 'echoes' in his work which mean that details in his writing never exist in isolation, but tend to echo other details. As has been already mentioned, the Braga Serenade functions precisely in this manner, by mirroring what happens to Kovrin, and Shostakovich wanted to replicate this effect in his opera in other ways. He planned that the projected first act of 'The Black Monk', for example, would end with the wedding of Kovrin and Tanya, when the sound of bells would be heard. He also wanted bells (in this case the warning bells of a lighthouse) to sound at the moment of Kovrin's death in Sebastopol at the end of the opera. According to Medvedev, Shostakovich saw the garden in 'The Black Monk' as a symbol of life, its eventual deterioration echoing Kovrin's death.[58]

Shostakovich's insight into Chekhov's artistic technique offers us a way of seeing more clearly how Chekhov worked, and how infinitely more complex the underlying structure of his stories and plays is than we might have imagined.[59] It also reveals the extent to which the thematic content in Chekhov's writings is intricately linked to the form it is expressed in, and how conscious and deliberate a writer he was, however much he liked to pretend that he dashed off his works casually. Chekhov himself gave several clues to suggest that his approach to form was unconsciously musical (he was very particular about how his stories would sound when read aloud, and declared on one occasion that his early story 'Happiness' was like a symphony).[60] The implications of Shostakovich's observation have yet to be fully explored, however. Only Jonathan Miller independently came to the same conclusion as Shostakovich about the apparent presence of a 'hidden sonata structure' in Chekhov's writing when directing a production of *The Three Sisters*, asserting that 'certain themes are stated, developed, reduplicated, inverted and then returned again to the main theme'.[61]

Sonata form, a kind of musical construction, is not, of course, to be confused with the specific genre of instrumental composition called the sonata. Usually used by composers in the first movements of sonatas and symphonies, it is an inherently dramatic form, consisting of an exposition of contrasting main and secondary themes in different keys, followed by development and recapitulation, and sometimes a coda.[62] It is no coincidence that Shostakovich found in the

---

[58] Conversation with Alexander Medvedev, May 1997.

[59] L. M. Toole has more recently contributed to our understanding of the complexity of the structural principles in 'The Black Monk' in a fascinating article which seems to complement an attempt to interpret the story in terms of sonata form. See his *Structure, Style and Interpretation in the Russian Short Story* (New Haven and London, 1982), 161–79.

[60] See E. Balabanovich, *Chekhov i Chaikovsky* (Moscow, 1978), 154.

[61] Jonathan Miller, 'Subsequent Performances: Chekhov', first published 1986, repr. in *Chekhov on the British Stage*, ed. and trans. Patrick Miles (Cambridge, 1994), 141.

[62] 'The basis for sonata form is the open modulatory plan of binary form, in which an initial modulation from the tonic to a new key (normally the dominant in a movement in major) is answered by a complementary modulation from the new key back to the tonic . . . The first part . . . is known traditionally as the exposition . . . The second part is usually more extended than the first;

works of the nineteenth-century writer Chekhov the prose equivalent of a deeply nineteenth-century type of musical composition, for sonata form is culture-specific. In the context of musical history, sonata form was first used in the eighteenth century, during the 'classical' period of Haydn, Mozart, and Beethoven, and continued to evolve throughout the nineteenth century. In the twentieth century it was notably employed by Shostakovich in his fifteen symphonies, but a type of musical construction predicated on the contrast of two distinct keys has largely become obsolete. With contrast, recapitulation, and yearning for closure as its chief hallmarks, sonata form is the most narratively developed kind of musical writing, yet is still fundamentally different to the more conventional exposition–development–resolution structure.

Shostakovich's *aperçu* about the nature of Chekhov's writing is therefore far from arbitrary. His focus on 'The Black Monk' is equally well considered. This apparently baffling tale about a talented young scholar inspired by hallucinations who dies once he is cured of them is one of Chekhov's most deliberately 'constructed' and uncharacteristic stories. It is regrettable that Shostakovich never gave any detailed explanation of his understanding of sonata form in 'The Black Monk', particularly in view of pertinent statements in *Testimony* which correspond to the views he expressed to Medvedev:

Chekhov was a very musical writer, but not in the sense that he wrote alliteratively: 'chuzhdy charam chernyi chyoln' [*sic*]. That's bad poetry and there's nothing musical in it. Chekhov is musical in a deeper sense. He constructed his works the way musical ones are constructed. Naturally this wasn't conscious, it's just that musical construction reflects more general laws. I am certain that Chekhov constructed 'The Black Monk' in sonata form; that there is an introduction, an exposition with main and secondary themes, development and so on . . .[63]

Nikolay Fortunatov, the critic who *did* try to work out how 'The Black Monk' could be explicated in terms of sonata form argued (unconvincingly) that Kovrin's increasing madness constituted the story's main theme, while the second, contrasting theme was his relationship with Tanya Pesotskaya and the love which developed between them. These themes, according to Fortunatov, are first introduced in the first section or chapter of the story (there are nine in all), and then alternate, following a strict symmetry. Thus the second chapter of the story introduces the theme of the Black Monk (which is linked to the story's main theme), while the fourth develops the 'lyrical' secondary theme of Kovrin and Tanya's love for each other. Similarly, if the third chapter begins and ends

---

it consists of two large sections, each of which may rival the exposition in size and importance: the development and recapitulation . . . The recapitulation . . . is based thematically upon the exposition but now ends as well as begins in the tonic . . . [T]he material formerly heard in the new key now recurs in the tonic, providing a long-range resolution of the tonal tension created by the modulation in the exposition.' See *The New Harvard Dictionary of Music*, ed. Don Michael Randel (Cambridge, Mass., 1986).

[63] Volkov, *Testimony*, 223.

with the main theme, he argues, the fifth, meanwhile, begins and ends with the secondary theme. The sixth chapter, according to Fortunatov, is when the two themes clash (when 'the unhappiness which befalls Kovrin intrudes into other people's lives, the lives of people close to him'), and the culmination of this process occurs in the seventh chapter, when Tanya confronts Kovrin in the middle of one of his hallucinations and decides he must be cured. The eighth chapter provides, according to Fortunatov, 'the last concluding link' of the 'development' section: Kovrin is 'cured', but has now lost all his inspiration and zest for life. Fortunatov argues that the ninth chapter (in which the 'dispassionate tone' of the story's opening returns) performs the function of the 'reprise', in that the structure and the two themes are repeated, not word for word, but in a 'significantly different and transformed way'.[64] Shostakovich was not impressed with this explication, according to *Testimony*.[65] Although a work written in sonata form is traditionally built on the opposition of two contrasting themes, interpreting 'The Black Monk' in such a simplistic way certainly does not do justice to the complexity of the story. Recollecting that the 'basis of sonata form is key relationships',[66] it might in fact be more useful to explore the structure of 'The Black Monk' in another way, for a careful examination reveals that it is perhaps in its constant shifts in tone and deliberate use of contrast on all levels that we may discern a deeper correlation with the language of music.

It is impossible here to undertake that examination in detail (I have done that elsewhere),[67] but it may be summarized briefly. In 'The Black Monk' Chekhov appears to be constantly moving in psychologically unmotivated ways, which may explain why so much prior interpretation of the story has been unsatisfactory and limited chiefly to superficial plot analysis. The reader's expectations are confounded at every turn: by the characters' behaviour and by the narration which sometimes switches abruptly back and forth between images of beauty and images of ugliness, often when least expected. Kovrin's hallucinations make him happy, for example, yet he is judged insane because of them (whereafter his personality really does disintegrate, while the formerly cantankerous Pesotsky becomes milder). Tanya is described in actuality as being neither the person her father thinks she is, nor the person Kovrin thinks she is. Kovrin's declaration of love seems to bring her no happiness. Pesotsky behaves erratically, 'as if there were two people inside him', and there is a discrepancy between Pesotsky's reported reaction his daughter's engagement and his actual physical reaction. The principle of inversion pervades every plane of the story. By presenting characters who begin to live only when they begin to die (the Black Monk is a harbinger of death for Kovrin, despite the fact that the

---

[64] See Fortunatov, *Puti iskanii*, 121–6.
[65] Volkov, *Testimony*, 223.
[66] Michael Kennedy, *Oxford Dictionary of Music* (Oxford, 1985), 679.
[67] For a detailed discussion, see my 'Sonata Form in Chekhov's "The Black Monk"'.

apparition inspires him with new life), who are not what they appear to be, and whose behaviour oscillates between extremes, Chekhov appears to be pointing in 'The Black Monk' to the paradoxes and dualities of human existence, namely, the idea that 'every positive act contains the seeds of its own negation and destruction',[68] that our perceptions of reality are mere illusions, including the meaning we give to our lives, but that perhaps these illusions are vital for our survival and well being. More convincing as main and secondary themes in 'The Black Monk', then, are the antithetical themes at the heart of Chekhov's writing which the critic Pyotr Bitsilli distinguished in Chekhov's earlier story 'The Steppe',[69] namely thirst for life and exclusion from life, expressed symbolically in a myriad of diffuse ways. It is the development of these polarities which forms a subtext to much of Chekhov's writing as a whole. Take, for example, the play *The Three Sisters*, where the collision of these two themes is expressed in terms of the clash between faith and existential nihilism. 'I feel that man should have a faith or be trying to find one, otherwise his life just doesn't make sense,' says Masha in Act II. 'Think of living without knowing why cranes fly, why children are born or why there are stars in the sky. Either you know what you're living for, or else the whole thing's a waste of time and means less than nothing.' This theme is developed through contrast with Chebutykin's humorous yet spine-chilling refrain in Act IV of 'nothing matters'. 'We're not real, neither is anything else in the world,' he says. 'We aren't here at all actually, we only think we are. And who cares anyway?' Examination of 'The Black Monk' through the perspective of sonata form thus also leads the reader to extrapolate ideas lying beneath its surface which are echoed in many of Chekhov's other works. Since sonata form is not self-contained, and is part of a larger whole, one might say this is entirely appropriate, and brings to mind Shostakovich's thoughts on Chekhovian musicality mentioned earlier. Chekhov is a writer particularly noted for his open endings (as demonstrated in his most famous story, 'The Lady with a Little Dog'), which often indicate that the work concluded is really only the prologue to a larger drama.

If chapters 2–7 constitute a kind of 'development section', with the characters of Kovrin and Pesotsky representing the equivalent of tonic and dominant keys, it is the two final chapters of 'The Black Monk' which appear to fulfil the function of the recapitulation and coda requisite to sonata form. In the penultimate chapter the location is once more Pesotsky's estate, exactly a year later and there are frequent references to Kovrin's previous visit a year before, in which the 'exposition' is repeated, although now inverted. Everything has been turned upside down, and we find that the second subject is indeed now in the 'tonic', for it is Kovrin's behaviour which is now ugly, and he is unable to

---

[68] Donald Rayfield, *Chekhov: The Evolution of His Art* (London, 1975), 134.

[69] See P. Bitsilli, *Chekhov's Art: A Stylistic Analysis*, trans. Toby W. Clyman and Edwina J. Cruise (Ann Arbor, 1983), ch. 5.

recreate his previous year's mood. 'If you want to be healthy and normal,' the Black Monk had told him a year before, 'join the herd'; Kovrin has now become one of the 'herd'. Kovrin becomes 'more reasonable and sensible' when he is 'cured', seeing 'strange, utterly unfounded pretensions, superficial passion, impertinence and delusions of grandeur' in his writing, but, as he himself points out, his visions had done no harm to anyone, and he was, paradoxically, a much more attractive person before.[70] The last chapter provides a brief and brilliant 'coda' to conclude the story, in which the narrative pace is considerably quickened. It is another year later, and Kovrin has parted from Tanya. In the last chapter, he receives a professorship, falls ill with tuberculosis, travels from Moscow to the Crimea with his new companion, receives a recriminatory letter from Tanya in which he learns that her father has died and that the beloved garden is also in decline, hears the Braga Serenade a final time, experiences a final hallucination of the Black Monk and dies.

It is probable that many of Chekhov's writings, short stories as well as plays, could be interpreted from the point of view of sonata form, and that such an approach might hold the key to a deeper understanding of Chekhov's works, and of his meticulous craftsmanship in particular. Looking at Chekhov's other main plays, for example, all of which have four acts, we find a similar structure: the principal themes are introduced in the first act, developed in Act II, reach a crisis point in Act III, and are then recapitulated, but in an inverted form in Act IV. And as in Chekhov's stories, each theme is accompanied by an antithetical counter-theme. In *The Three Sisters*, for example, to explore this idea in the most general terms, the most obvious theme of course is the idea of the sisters going to Moscow which is introduced optimistically in, as it were, the tonic key at the very beginning of the play, and is associated with hopes and dreams, and also with beauty. The secondary, contrasting theme in Act I is the ugliness and humdrum reality of the sisters' provincial life, developed particularly through the character of the vulgar Natasha, later to marry their brother. Form indeed matches content, for the language of the sisters' speech is lyrical, that of Natasha coarse. The theme of Moscow is developed in various ways in Acts II and III. In Act II, for example, Andrey's idealistic fantasies about Moscow are grotesquely mirrored by the old servant Ferapont who tells absurd stories about the city, such as the one about the merchant who ate forty pancakes there and died. In Act III, Irina begins to confront the fact that they will never get to Moscow, and we reach the climax of the development section, when Natasha clashes openly with the sisters, and asserts her authority over them. The theme of going to Moscow is recapitulated in Act IV, with the sisters now resigned to the fact that their getting to Moscow is an impossibility, a sentiment now definitely voiced in a minor key. The theme of reality and provincial vulgarity, embodied by Natasha, on the other hand, has developed to

---

[70] Chekhov, *Sobranie sochinenii*, viii. 250, 252.

the point where she has completely usurped the sisters, and ejected them from their home. Whereas this is very much a secondary theme in Act I, by the fourth act it has become the main subject.

By identifying a method of narrative construction akin to sonata form in Chekhov's writings Shostakovich made a contribution of potentially great value to our study of this writer's art. Chekhov, meanwhile, contributed a great deal to Shostakovich's creativity, inspiring him not only with subjects for operas, but with ideas as to how they might be structured. On the personal level Shostakovich's identification with Chekhov clearly provided solace and moral fortitude in difficult times, while the great writer's short stories and plays were, throughout his lifetime, a valued and important source of wisdom, laughter, and aesthetic pleasure.

INDEX